Corporate Environmentalism and

This is the first book to provide a hard-headed economic view of the voluntary approaches to environmental issues, especially toxic chemicals, waste disposal, and global warming, that have become prominent since the mid-1990s. Corporate environmental initiatives are seen as a tool for influencing the behavior of environmental activists, legislators, and regulators, though they may have ancillary benefits such as attracting "green" consumers or reducing costs. Equally, government voluntary programs are seen as a way to achieve modest environmental results when political resistance to mandatory policies is high. Rigorous analysis is illustrated with numerous case studies drawn from the USA, Europe, and Japan, while technical details are relegated to appendices, and each chapter highlights implications for corporate strategy and public policy. Although rooted in economic theory, this book will appeal to business strategists and policy practitioners, as well as scholars and researchers.

THOMAS P. LYON holds the Chair of Sustainable Science, Technology and Commerce of the University of Michigan Business School, Ann Arbor. He is the editor of the forthcoming volume *Regulation* (2004). His primary research interest is the interplay between corporate strategy and public policy and he has served as a consultant to business and to government in these areas.

JOHN W. MAXWELL is Associate Professor at the Kelley School of Business, Indiana University. His primary research focus is the political economy of environmental regulation and the impact of corporate behavior on the development and enforcement of environmental regulations.

Corporate Environmentalism and Public Policy

THOMAS P. LYON AND JOHN W. MAXWELL

CAMBRIDGE
UNIVERSITY PRESS

PUBLISHED BY THE PRESS SYNDICATE OF THE UNIVERSITY OF CAMBRIDGE
The Pitt Building, Trumpington Street, Cambridge, United Kingdom

CAMBRIDGE UNIVERSITY PRESS
The Edinburgh Building, Cambridge CB2 2RU, UK
40 West 20th Street, New York, NY 10011–4211, USA
477 Williamstown Road, Port Melbourne, VIC 3207, Australia
Ruiz de Alarcón 13, 28014 Madrid, Spain
Dock House, The Waterfront, Cape Town 8001, South Africa

http://www.cambridge.org

First published 2004

Printed in the United Kingdom at the University Press, Cambridge

Typeface Minion 10.5/14 pt.   *System* LᴬTEX 2$_\varepsilon$ [TB]

A catalogue record for this book is available from the British Library

ISBN 0 521 81947 4 hardback
ISBN 0 521 60376 5 paperback

We dedicate this book to our families for their love and support.

Contents

Preface

"Corporate environmentalism" – by which we mean environmentally friendly measures that are not required by law – is playing an increasingly visible role in environmental protection. We first encountered this phenomenon in the mid-1990s when we stumbled upon a report that the Council of Great Lakes Industries was offering a prize to the firm that most significantly reduced its emissions of pollutants into the Great Lakes. Immediately our skeptical economists' minds kicked in: "Why would companies voluntarily increase their own costs just to win a plaque they could put on the wall? Would there be any tangible benefits to society?" The conversation that ensued has proven to be much richer and more intellectually fulfilling than we ever imagined.

Investigating these questions with the tools of economic theory has helped us avoid becoming Panglossian optimists or naive cheerleaders for business, unlike the authors of many popular books on the subject. Nevertheless, our research has driven us to the conclusion that corporate environmentalism can indeed produce welfare improvements, though they are by no means guaranteed. Indeed, our ongoing work in this area has made us aware of the many subtle ways corporate environmental strategy intertwines with public policy. Part of our rationale for writing this book is the belief that we have arrived at an overarching framework within which much of the corporate environmental activity we observe can be understood.

While our analysis is rooted in economic theory, we have written this book with both business strategists and policy practitioners, as well as scholars, in mind. We illustrate our analysis with examples drawn from the USA, Europe, and Japan, and we summarize what researchers have learned through empirical study of these issues. We have striven to make sure that each chapter highlights implications for corporate strategy and public policy. Technical details are relegated to appendices, and each chapter includes a non-technical summary for readers who wish to glean the key strategic insights as succinctly as possible.

In parallel with the movement toward corporate environmentalism, governments around the world are turning increasingly to "voluntary" programs rather than traditional command-and-control regulations. We argue that these trends are two sides of a single coin, and reflect growing political resistance to using traditional regulatory tools to cope with emerging environmental issues whose severity is uncertain, whose causes are diffuse, and whose abatement costs may be high. In part III of this volume, we explore the causes and consequences of government involvement in voluntary programs.

Many people and organizations have played a role in helping us develop the ideas presented here. We should begin by acknowledging the contributions of our co-authors Chris Decker, Steve Hackett, and Stefan Lutz to papers that formed the basis for several chapters of this volume. We have learned much from our collaborations with them, and enjoyed their enthusiasm for the ideas that emerged from the process.

Another notable influence on this work has been our participation in Concerted Action on Voluntary Approaches (CAVA), the European research network on voluntary approaches funded by DG XII of the European Commission. We would like to acknowledge the valuable contributions of the project director, François Lévêque, and the organizers of specific workshops, Carlo Carraro, Marc De Clercq, Frank Convery, Birgit Dette, and Anders Larsen. CAVA gave birth to an international research community that has continued to interact beyond the period of the project's funding. Our thinking about voluntary approaches to environmental protection has been shaped in many ways through repeated interactions with other members of this community.

Among the many colleagues with whom we have discussed the ideas in this volume are Seema Arora, Jim Barnes, Allen Blackman, Jim Boyd, Dave Buzzelli, George Carpenter, Carlo Carraro, Martina Chidiak, Bob Charlton, Cary Coglianese, Nicole Darnall, Magali Delmas, Vincenzo Denicolo, Maurizio Franzini, James Frederick, Matthieu Glachant, Lars Hansen, Rich Howarth, Scott Johnson, Madhu Khanna, Skip Laitner, Joe Mayhew, Katrin Millock, Jennifer Nash, Bruce Paton, Frank Popoff, Kate Probst, Francois Salanié, Kathy Segerson, Sam Smolnik, and Alice Tome. In addition, we have benefited greatly from the helpful comments of seminar audiences at numerous universities, research institutes and government agencies in the USA, Canada and Europe. Several of these presentations have appeared as chapters in conference volumes edited by Andrea Baranzini, Chuck Bonser, Philippe Thalmann, and Eric Orts, whom we thank for the opportunity to develop our thinking on various aspects of corporate environmentalism and for providing a broader audience for our work.

This project has been supported by a number of institutions. Indiana University provided an excellent atmosphere for conducting much of this research. We would particularly like to thank our colleagues within the Department of Business Economics and Public Policy, and the Workshop on Political Theory and Policy Analysis, for their helpful feedback and general encouragement. Research support from the Kelley School of Business and sabbatical and travel support from Indiana University are gratefully acknowledged. We also appreciate the support we have received during visits at various other institutions. In particular, Resources for the Future and the Department of Economics at University College, London provided collegial atmospheres for working on this project.

We would like to acknowledge two individuals who were instrumental in bringing forth this book. Our colleague Alan Rugman first suggested to us the idea of a book-length treatment of the topic of corporate environmentalism. Without his encouragement and advice this project would never have been started. Chris Harrison, our editor at Cambridge University Press, has shepherded us through the writing and editing of this manuscript with a friendliness and professionalism that made the process a pleasure.

We are most grateful to our families for the support they provided during this project. Susan and Emily Lyon incurred the costs of moving to Washington, DC, for a year during the writing of this book; their willingness to do so is greatly appreciated.

PART I

The interaction of strategy and policy

1 | A framework for analysis

1 INTRODUCTION

Business-led environmental initiatives have become increasingly prominent in recent years. From McDonald's voluntary replacement of paper
for styrofoam sandwich packaging to the chemical industry's "Responsible
Care"® program, corporate environmentalism has become a familiar phenomenon. At the same time, governments have shown great interest in
"voluntary" programs for environmental protection, which invite pollution abatement rather than demanding it. Neither of these developments
makes sense within conventional paradigms for understanding the environment. Since pollution abatement is costly, firms are expected to avoid it
whenever possible, and governments must impose penalties severe enough
to compel compliance. A sudden shift to a world of cooperation and voluntary environmental protection seems strange, if not downright suspicious.

Several reasons have been suggested for the recent surge of corporate
environmental activity. Perhaps pollution is symptomatic of broader production inefficiencies, and pollution reduction and cost reduction go hand-
in-hand to create "win–win" opportunities in today's economy. Perhaps a
new generation of "green" consumers is willing to pay higher prices for
clean products, and firms are simply responding to this shift. Or perhaps
business has become more savvy about the workings of the political system, taking pro-active steps to avert political conflict rather than reacting
to public pressure after the fact.

Our basic message is simple: political–economic analysis is required to
understand the emergence of corporate environmentalism, by which we
mean environmentally friendly actions not required by law. While cost reduction and green marketing play a role, their impact appears to be modest.
Furthermore, from a research perspective, no new theory of corporate behavior is needed to explain cost control and green marketing: they can be
understood perfectly well in terms of traditional strategies of cost minimization and product differentiation. The political economy of corporate
environmentalism, however, requires new models of the interplay between
corporate strategy and public policy.

The value of our perspective came into sharp relief at the World Resources Institute's Sixth Annual Sustainable Enterprise Summit, held on March 13–14, 2003, in Washington, DC. This event brought together leaders from business, government, academia, and non-governmental organizations (NGOs), all of whom shared a passionate interest in how business can bring about environmental improvement. Yet many participants were puzzled by the challenges facing businesses that aspire to sustainability. Linda Greer, of the Natural Resources Defence Council (NRDC), shared her experience working with Dow Chemical Company to identify opportunities for cost-effective reductions of toxic chemical emissions from Dow's plant in Midland, Michigan. Despite the success of her work with Dow – which cut toxic emissions by 37 percent and saved $5.6 million per year – she was clearly disheartened by the fact that none of the other sixty-five firms that NRDC subsequently contacted accepted the invitation to participate in similar projects. In a session on "Building the Green Power Market Place," speakers lamented the slow growth of renewable electricity sources. For example, David Rappaport, of Northern Power Systems, admitted that, at present, tax credits are still necessary to make most wind power projects economically viable. In contrast to these sobering accounts, Katherine DiMatteo reported on the long but ultimately successful efforts of the Organic Trade Association to legislate federal standards certifying what qualifies as "organic produce." She forecast rapid growth for organic dairy and soy products carrying the US Department of Agriculture's new organic seal. Keynote speaker Randy Overbey, President of Alcoa's Energy Division, enthusiastically described his firm's decision to testify in favor of mandatory climate change legislation. It is of particular importance, he explained, for legislation allocating greenhouse gas emissions permits to take into account past progress, such as Alcoa's 22.5 percent reduction in greenhouse gas emissions relative to a 1990 benchmark. It was not hard to see the link between Alcoa's voluntary emissions reductions and its political strategy. To us, these vignettes confirmed our basic message: while cost reduction and green consumers have a role to play, most of the action in corporate environmentalism is mediated through public policy.

Governments, like many businesses, have embraced corporate environmentalism. Indeed, they have developed a variety of voluntary programs that serve as alternatives to traditional regulatory tools. In Europe and Japan, the voluntary tool of choice is the negotiated agreement, in which industry pledges to meet certain environmental goals developed in consultation with government, often against a background threat of regulation that may be imposed should the pledge not be met. In the USA, the preferred tool is the public voluntary agreement (PVA), in which government provides information, technical assistance, and positive publicity to firms that adopt environmentally desirable practices. Such programs are not driven by government's desire to help reduce industry's production costs or subsidize industry marketing initiatives. Rather, government voluntary programs are best seen as a response to the escalating political and resource costs of creating and enforcing traditional command-and-control regulations. Again, a political–economic analysis is needed to understand the emergence of voluntary programs, in this case as a tool for alleviating problems facing government regulators.

Our goal in this volume is to develop a set of models for understanding the links between corporate environmentalism and public policy. While there has been considerable progress in understanding corporate non-market strategy in recent years, even the leading textbooks fail to reflect the increasingly important role of industry self-regulation as a strategic tool.[1] Nor does most scholarly work on regulation adequately capture the growing government involvement in voluntary programs. We use economic tools from industrial organization and game theory to understand corporate environmentalism within an integrated framework encompassing industry structure, political institutions, and the policy life cycle.

While our analysis is rooted in economic theory, we have written this book with both business strategists and policy practitioners in mind. Thus, in the body of a typical chapter, we present the basic structure of an economic model and its key implications for corporate strategy and public policy. Details are relegated to appendices, and chapters 3–5 and 7–8 include a non-technical summary for readers who wish to glean the key strategic insights as succinctly as possible.

In the remainder of this chapter we present a framework for understanding the myriad ways in which corporate environmental improvement can serve as a strategic tool in the public arena. We focus on the notion of the public policy life cycle as a way to organize our analysis of corporate environmental strategy. We then discuss alternative theories of corporate environmentalism that are based on achieving production efficiencies or appealing to "green" consumers. Of course, neither our theory nor the others we discuss are of much interest to business strategists unless corporate environmental performance has a real influence on the bottom line. We conclude this chapter by reviewing the empirical evidence on the relationship

---

[1] Baron (2003) provides an excellent presentation of corporate non-market strategy, but devotes scant attention to the role of corporate environmentalism, or corporate self-regulation more generally.

between corporate environmentalism and financial performance, which does indeed show a positive relationship between environmental and financial performance. We also survey the limited empirical evidence regarding the drivers of corporate environmental improvement, and find that stakeholder pressure and several firm-specific characteristics such as size and research and development (R&D) intensity appear to be important factors.

2 ELEMENTS OF THE ANALYTICAL FRAMEWORK

In order to understand voluntary initiatives in environmental policy, it is necessary to distinguish:

- The structure of the industry involved
- The institutional structure of the political environment
- The stage of the policy life cycle in which the issue is being addressed.

Let us consider each of these three areas in turn.

2.1   Industry structure

While there are several important dimensions of industry structure, we focus on two: the concentration of the industry, and the heterogeneity of the firms within it. *Concentration* refers to the extent to which a given industry is dominated by a relatively small number of firms. It can be measured through simple indices such as the "four-firm concentration ration" (CR-4) or more sophisticated indices such as the Herfindahl–Hirschman Index (HHI).[2] There has been a vast volume of research in industrial organization on the effects of industry concentration on prices, profits, and anti-competitive activity. Concentrated industries tend to have higher prices, and are more likely to successfully implement price leadership campaigns and to coordinate their activities in the political arena. *Heterogeneity* among firms makes coordinated industry action more difficult, whether this be collusive action to influence market outcomes or political action to influence legislative or

---

[2] The HHI is measured as the sum of the squares of the market shares of all the firms in the industry. It ranges from a low of zero (in a perfectly competitive industry where each firm's market share is approximately zero) to a high of 10,000 (in a monopoly where one firm has market share of 100 percent). For more details, see Baye (2003, pp. 233–234).

regulatory outcomes. At the same time, firm heterogeneity opens up many avenues for market and non-market strategy at the level of the individual firm. Among the familiar market strategies that may be employed are product differentiation (either horizontal or vertical), attempts to raise rivals' costs, cost leadership, and quality leadership. In the environmental arena, two strategies of particular importance are product differentiation to appeal to environmentally sensitive "green" consumers and the use of the regulatory process to raise rivals' costs. There has been little work done on the relationship between concentration, firm heterogeneity, and non-market strategies such as corporate environmentalism. Our work breaks new ground in this regard.

2.2   Policy life cycle

The concept of the public policy life cycle is a very useful framework for corporate "issues management," and is commonly used in textbooks on the relationship between public policy and business strategy. Four stages are typically identified, as illustrated in figure 1.1. First is the *development* stage, in which events occur that lead various segments of the public to become aware that a problem exists. Second is the stage of *politicization*, in which the issue acquires a label, opinion leaders begin to discuss the problem in public, the news media becomes more active in covering the issue, and interest groups begin to mobilize around the issue. This stage is sometimes capped by a dramatizing event that crystallizes the nature of the problem

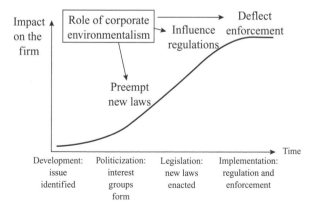

Figure 1.1   Corporate environmentalism and the policy life cycle

in the public's mind. The incident at Three Mile Island, the Thalidomide tragedy, the tampering with Tylenol, and the terrorist destruction of the World Trade Center are examples of such dramatizing events. Third is the *legislative* stage, in which political leaders take action to create new laws responding to the issue. Fourth comes the *implementation* stage, in which administrative agencies flesh out the details of the new legislation and regulators, police and the courts enforce it. The nature of non-market strategy, and the role of corporate environmentalism in particular, differs at different points in the policy life cycle. For example, corporate environmentalism may preempt legislation if conducted early in the life cycle, while later in the cycle it may be useful as a way to influence the stringency of regulations that cannot be preempted. We discuss the policy life cycle in detail in chapter 2.

2.3   Political environment

The institutional structure of the political environment is a complex issue, and a full treatment of all its dimensions is beyond the scope of our project.[3] In this volume, we will be particularly interested in the different approaches to business–government relations in the USA and in Europe and Japan. For example, US regulators tend to employ "public voluntary agreements," (PVAs) which offer information, technical assistance and publicity to firms that take environmentally friendly actions. European and Japanese policymakers are more likely to sign "negotiated agreements" with industry associations or individual firms, under which the industry agrees to meet certain negotiated environmental goals with the expectation that if the goals are met then legislative requirements will not be imposed.

Numerous factors distinguish the US from the European and Japanese political environments. From a structural perspective, American presidential democracy differs from the parliamentary democracies of Europe and Japan in important ways. Perhaps most notably, the American system allows for the legislative and executive branches to be controlled by different political parties, while parliamentary systems by design vest control of both branches in the same party. As a result, executive branch agencies in the USA generally cannot deliver credible threats to impose regulation should voluntary efforts be inadequate. As a result, their ability to sign meaningful

---

[3] For a good introduction to the subject from the perspective of business strategy, see Baron (2003).

negotiated agreements with industry is limited. Project XL, the most prominent program of negotiated agreements in the USA, has met with very limited success, in part because agreements with the Environmental Protection Agency (EPA) could not prevent intervenor groups from challenging aspects of the agreements they did not like.

Another way of distinguishing different political environments is in terms of the extent to which they are adversarial in nature. Robert Kagan argues that "The common ingredient in these low-adversarialism policy areas is that legal authority is centralized and difficult to challenge in court, either legally or practically; that is, governmental legal authority is exercised more hierarchically and with more finality than is the American norm" (Kagan 2000, pp. 386–387). Continental Europe and Japan tend to have more highly centralized political institutions than does the USA, and hence interest groups in Europe and Japan build long-term relationships with a small number of key government representatives. These long-term relationships lead to a sharing of social surplus, more cooperative outcomes, the potential for linkages across different specific issues, and (perhaps) a greater potential for interest group capture of government. The more decentralized American model is more formal, legalistic, adversarial, issue-specific, and (perhaps) less likely to be captured. Because the adversarial US system generates large transaction costs in passing new legislation, there is a strong incentive for firms to preempt such new laws through voluntary environmental improvement. In contrast, the consultative European approach is less costly, and firms there are less likely to engage in preemptive self-regulation. Instead, they typically negotiate a more or less formal "covenant," indicating what actions are required in order to avoid intrusive taxes or regulations.

Another way to characterize the political environment within democratic nations is to distinguish "pluralist" from "corporatist" societies. According to Cawson (1986, p. 104), corporatism differs from pluralism in that:

Whereas in a pluralist system a large number of voluntary interest associations compete with each other for members, resources and access to government in order to influence the direction of public policy, in a corporatist system there is a limited number of non-competitive organizations with compulsory or semi-compulsory membership. These organizations have a privileged status with respect to government in that they co-determine public policy and are responsible for its implementation by disciplining their members to accept bargained agreements.

The privileged organizations in corporatist societies typically "take their identity from the function which they perform in the social division of labour" (Cawson 1986, p. 104). The two key corporatist organizations (aside from the state) are peak associations for capital and for labor, with trade unions and professional groups also quite common. Consumer representation is less frequently observed. In the end, though, "corporatism and pluralism should not be seen as exclusive alternatives, but as end points on a continuum according to the extent to which monopolistic and inter-dependent relationships between interest organizations and the state have become established" (Cawson 1986, p. 104).

We find both the notion of pluralism and that of "adversarial legalism" helpful in understanding the distinctive nature of the US political environment. In the rest of this book, we will use the terms "adversarial" and "pluralist" to characterize the US political environment, and the terms "cooperative" and "corporatist" to characterize the political environments of Europe and Japan.

One of the most striking differences between the two types of political environments is the greater use of negotiated voluntary agreements in corporatist societies. For example, the Netherlands has more than one hundred voluntary agreements, most of them negotiated agreements.[4] In Germany, some seventy voluntary agreements are in use; negotiated agreements that replace regulations are prevalent. France has over twenty voluntary agreements, which typically begin as supplements to regulation but can be transformed into formal regulations as necessary. In the United States, however, the EPA's attempts to create negotiated agreements through Project XL and the Common Sense Initiative have generated disappointing results. The formal nature of the regulatory process in the USA, and the vigor of environmental interest groups in enforcing it, made it difficult for the regulatory agency to pursue flexible regulatory policies.

As an illustration of the different strategies used in corporatist and pluralist societies, consider the use of carbon taxes as a tool for reducing carbon dioxide emissions. In 1995, Germany's overarching industrial trade association, the BDI, under the threat of new carbon taxes aimed at reducing carbon emissions, negotiated voluntary CO_2 emissions reductions for different sectors of the German economy aimed at preempting the proposed tax. The voluntary agreement was successfully negotiated and the tax proposal was withdrawn. It is highly unlikely, given the heterogeneous energy usage of Germany's various industrial sectors, that preemption could have occurred without the existence of the BDI. It is also highly unlikely that such an agreement could be executed in the USA, where peak associations such

---

[4] See Delmas and Terlaak (2002) for a nice overview of how voluntary programs differ with political environment.

as the National Association of Manufacturers (NAM) lack the bargaining power accorded the BDI in Germany.

The German CO_2 agreements illustrate one of the key environmental strategies available to industry: preemption of government mandates. The US experience with carbon taxes illustrates the use of the more traditional strategies of lobbying and campaign contributions. After President Clinton was elected in November 1992, one of his early actions was to announce support for stronger measures to prevent climate change. In the early months of 1993, his administration floated a variety of proposals to tax energy, including a carbon tax and a broader-based "BTU tax" based on the energy content of fuels as measured in British Thermal Units (BTUs). The political response was rapid and powerful:

A cadre of lobbyists began to plot the death of President Clinton's energy tax in December 1992 – a month before Clinton took office and two months before he submitted the tax plan to Congress . . . Jerry Jasinowski, president of NAM [National Association of Manufacturers] . . . helped organize a group of 1400 lobbies, dubbed the American Energy Alliance. The NAM, the US Chamber of Commerce, and the American Petroleum Institute footed most of the bill . . . Behind the scenes, groups lobbied successfully for exemptions . . . By June, what had been a fair, across-the-board tax was riddled with loopholes . . . Lacking any clear popular support for the BTU tax, and facing defeat in the Senate, the White House threw in the towel and withdrew its proposal. (See Winer 1993)

The differences between the German and the US experience are illuminating. As we pointed out earlier, corporatist organizations "co-determine public policy and are responsible for its implementation by disciplining their members to accept bargained agreements." In Germany, the BDI played this role in textbook fashion with respect to the CO_2 agreement. In the USA, the NAM – lacking the disciplinary role of the corporatist BDI – focused instead on coordinating the lobbying activities of the numerous groups that would be affected by an energy tax. By virtue of the NAM's less cozy relationship with government, it was able to take a more confrontational position and ward off the threatened energy tax without the concessions involved in the German CO_2 agreement.

2.4 Summary of the framework

We provide a tabular overview of our organizing framework in table 1.1. Its two key dimensions are the structure of the industry that is involved, and the stage of the policy life cycle in which a particular policy issue exists at

Table 1.1   Corporate environmental strategies, industry structure, and the policy life cycle

Stage of policy life cycle	Political environment	Unconcentrated	Concentrated/ homogeneous firms	Concentrate heterogeneo firms
Pre-legislative (Development/ Politicization)	Adversarial	*Strategic action unlikely*	*Preemption (1)*	
	Cooperative	*Negotiated agreement (2) (Coordination dependent)*	*Negotiated agreement (3)*	*Voluntary ac to induce legislation*
Post-legislative (Regulatory design/ Implementation)		*Promote PVA (if legislation fails) (5) Otherwise comply*	*Promote PVA (if legislation fails) or overcomply to gain regulatory concessions (6)*	*Voluntary ac to influenc future regulation*

Note: (1)–(7) refer to the examples discussed below.

a given point in time; the third dimension, political structure, is captur by subdividing the policy life cycle.

Table 1.1 groups together all unconcentrated industries, since hete geneity of either cost or product attributes is less important in such dustries. The table also groups together the first two stages of the pol life cycle, and treats them separately from the second two stages. We this is sensible because the existence of legislation greatly changes the lo of non-market action, leading firms to focus on tactical activities witl existing regulatory and legal institutions. The remainder of this book l out in detail the nature of the strategy–policy interaction in each of th cases, so we will not attempt to explain them all here. We simply provid flavor of the analysis by presenting concrete examples, drawn from arou the world, for each of the entries in the table. We proceed through the ta from top left, across the top row, and then across the bottom row.

(1)   Preemption: Responsible Care®

This is a global program of voluntary initiatives by the chemicals indus to continuously improve performance on health, safety, and environmen issues. The program, one of the best-known business-led environmen initiatives, was created in 1985 in the wake of the disastrous release toxic chemicals from Union Carbide's plant in Bhopal, India. The four key elements of the Responsible Care® initiative are a formal company commitment to Responsible Care® abiding principles, acceptance of the Codes of Practice, a National Community Advisory Panel, and performance indicators. Countries that have active participation in this program include the UK, Canada, Australia, and the USA. While it had multiple aims, key among them were the goals of regaining society's trust and forestalling excessive government intervention in the industry's activities (see Simmons and Wynne 1993). According to Fred Webber, then president of the industry association, "In my opinion, Responsible Care® is more than a good initiative – it's the industry's franchise to operate" (DeSimone and Popoff 2000, p. 141). The role of preemption is explored in detail in chapter 3.

(2) Negotiated agreement (coordination dependent): German CO$_2$ Emissions Reductions

As described above, in 1995 Germany's overarching industrial trade association, the BDI, under the threat of new carbon taxes aimed at reducing carbon emissions, negotiated voluntary CO$_2$ emissions reductions for different sectors of the German economy aimed at preempting the proposed tax. The voluntary agreement was successfully negotiated and the tax proposal was withdrawn. It is highly unlikely, given the large number of firms in Germany's various industrial sectors, that agreement could have been achieved without the BDI's authority to enforce agreements with its members. Negotiated agreements are explored in detail in chapter 7.

(3) Negotiated agreement: Isogo Thermal Power Station

In Japan, voluntary agreements known as Environmental Pollution Control Agreements (EPCAs) have been in use for over thirty years; as of 1998, there were 31,770 publicly accessible EPCAs. These agreements may be focused not just on a particular concentrated industry, but may actually be firm-specific. In 1964 the first major agreement was made between Yokohama City council and the Isogo thermal power station. The agreement was proposed by the city, since no legal authority existed at that time for making an enterprise take measures against air pollution. The agreement included detailed guidelines for plant design and obligations to control pollution. These measures included the obligation to gather meteorological data and carry out air pollution surveys within the city area, the obligation to control total dust collection efficiency, specification of the height of the chimney and flue gas temperature, and the requirement to use a particular coal with low ash and sulfur contents. The firm was willing to participate because it believed that concluding an agreement would make it easier to obtain administrative approval from local authorities when it wanted to expand its plants.[5] Negotiated agreements are explored in detail in chapter 7.

(4)   Voluntary action to induce regulation: DuPont and CFCs

In September 1987, the Montreal Protocol was signed by a group of countries concerned about the depletion of the Earth's ozone layer caused by emissions of chlorofluorocarbons (CFCs). Signatories to this accord agreed to reduce CFC production 50 percent by the year 1999. DuPont was the world's largest maker of CFCs, and might have been expected to oppose the Protocol. Instead, it announced in March 1988 that it would eliminate production of CFCs altogether by the year 2000. When the Montreal Protocol was renegotiated in June of 1990, the signatories followed DuPont's lead and agreed to a full phaseout of CFC production by the end of the century. While it is unusual for a company to support a ban on its own product, in this case there was a strategic benefit for DuPont. DuPont had invested heavily in developing alternatives to CFCs, and was ahead of its rivals. Thus DuPont saw the ban as a way to shift from a mature market with low profit opportunities (CFCs), to a new and growing market in which it had the competitive edge. DuPont's strategy of a voluntary phaseout demonstrated to policymakers that the costs of a ban would be manageable, and thus encouraged the Montreal signatories to adopt a tougher stance toward CFCs.[6] The use of voluntary environmental improvement to encourage regulation is studied in chapter 4.

(5)   Promote public voluntary agreement: TransAlta Corporation

In 1992, the United Nations Framework Convention on Climate Change was signed at the Rio Earth Summit, and announced a goal of reducing greenhouse gases to 1990 levels by the year 2000. TransAlta, the largest investor-owned electric utility in Canada and heavily dependent on coal, became concerned that future regulations might restrict the use of coal-fired power plants or impose substantial carbon taxes. As part of its overall

---

[5] For more on Japanese voluntary agreements, see Sugiyama (1998).
[6] For more details, see Reinhardt (1989).

environment policy, TransAlta set about lobbying the Canadian government to create a nationwide voluntary initiative program. The company's work was rewarded in 1995 when Canada created the Voluntary Challenge and Registry (VCR), which had attracted over 700 members by 1998. TransAlta believes the VCR program has several benefits. First, it reduces the likelihood that the Canadian government will impose new regulations or taxes. Second, it increases the credibility of the company's environmental policy with external stakeholder groups. Third, it does so while allowing great flexibility in approaches to limiting greenhouse emissions.[7] The possibility that voluntary corporate action can encourage regulators to create public voluntary programs is discussed in chapter 8.

(6) Overcompliance to gain regulatory concessions: Project XL

Short for "eXcellence and Leadership," XL is a nationwide program allowing businesses to work with the EPA to develop innovative strategies that use better or more cost-effective ways of achieving environmental goals. In exchange, the EPA grants regulatory flexibility that reduces corporate regulatory costs. Agreements negotiated under this program are typically focused not just on a particular concentrated industry, but are actually firm-specific. For example, in 1997, Merck and Co.'s pharmaceutical manufacturing plant in Elkton, Virginia, agreed to lower sulfur dioxide and nitrogen oxide (NO_x) emissions in order to protect visibility and reduce acid deposition in the nearby Shenandoah National Park and the neighboring community. To achieve this, Merck invested approximately $10 million to convert its coal-burning power plant to natural gas, a much cleaner-burning fuel. As long as Merck's emissions remain below the negotiated caps, Merck will no longer have to obtain prior approval from EPA or the Virginia Department of Environmental Quality to make changes at the facility that result in emission increases.[8] Outside the context of Project XL, Merck in 2002 applied to the Virginia Department of Environmental Quality to reduce the maximum emissions of hazardous pollutants allowed under its operating permit to 10 tons per year for each individual pollutant, and 25 tons per year for all hazardous pollutants combined. By so doing, Merck would be classified as a "minor source," and not be subject to new federal rules for "major sources" of pollutants in the pharmaceutical

---

[7] The material for this section is drawn from "TransAlta's Sustainable Development Efforts, Successes and Challenges 1988–2000," in International Academy of the Environment (1998).

[8] For more details, see http://www.epa.gov/projectxl/merck/index.htm.

industry.[9] The use of strategic voluntary improvement within a context of regulatory flexibility is studied in chapter 5.

(7)   Voluntary action to influence future regulation: German catalytic converters

In 1984, concerns about acid rain led the Federal Republic of Germany – with the support of the German automotive industry – to adopt a clean-car regulation. Because the regulation applied to all automobiles sold in Germany, it was labeled a barrier to trade and quickly became a European issue. While the EU Commission deliberated, the German government, with the backing of its automakers, adopted fuel emission standards that essentially dictated the use of the three-way catalytic converter technology. The German government's standards allowed German manufacturers to commit to a technology that improved on the emissions of vehicles they currently sold in Europe, and influenced the Commission to raise the standards facing all manufacturers in Europe.[10] The use of corporate voluntarism to influence the stringency of future regulations is explored in chapter 4.

3   NON-POLITICAL THEORIES OF CORPORATE ENVIRONMENTALISM

Corporate environmental initiatives have been attributed to a variety of different motives, including cost-cutting and marketing to "green" consumers willing to pay extra for environmentally friendly products, as well as optimizing regulatory strategy. Understanding what really motivates corporate environmentalism is important for policymakers, since the effectiveness of government environmental policies depends in large part on how corporations will respond to them. It is also important for businesspeople thinking about jumping on the environmental bandwagon, for otherwise they may not obtain the results they hope for. In this section we discuss the two aforementioned non-political "models" of corporate environmental activity, and consider the social welfare implications of corporate actions within each model. In addition, we attempt to identify the empirical implications of each model, setting up a framework within which we will survey the empirical literature on voluntary environmental activity in section 4.

---

[9] For more details, see Pagonis (2002).
[10] See Lévêque and Nadaï (1995).

3.1 Improving corporate productivity

Many writers have argued that companies can cut their costs and improve their environmental performance simultaneously by improving the efficiency of manufacturing processes.[11] Probably the most frequently cited example is 3M Corporation's "Pollution Prevention Pays" program, begun in 1975. For the first time, line workers were involved in identifying opportunities for waste reduction, and between 1975 and 1990, 3M cut its total emissions of pollution by 50 percent (530,000 tons). At the same time, the company claims to have saved over $500 million by cutting the costs of raw material, compliance, disposal, and liability. Results of this sort, if replicable by other firms, provide support for a "win–win" perspective in which environmental performance and corporate profits walk hand-in-hand. From an economic perspective, of course, the puzzle is why there should be any sudden surge in opportunities for making money by cleaning up. Were companies previously sloppy in ignoring internal profitmaking opportunities? Has technological change presented new opportunities for reducing the use of raw materials, thereby lowering costs and environmental effluents simultaneously? Has global competition intensified to the point where formerly marginal projects now look attractive? Have workers' attitudes shifted, so that employee morale now depends heavily on corporate environmental performance? None of these questions, to our knowledge, has been satisfactorily answered. In fact, Walley and Whitehead (1994) argue that the opportunities for painless pollution prevention are rapidly being exhausted. This is consistent with the NRDC's experience, described above, of finding few firms interested in working with them to reduce emissions while cutting costs. Furthermore, Boyd (2001) offers in-depth case studies of three widely discussed "failures" to adopt pollution prevention, and finds that straightforward economic considerations explain all three.

3.2 Responding to "green" consumers and investors

A second common explanation for corporate environmentalism is that there have been shifts on the demand and supply sides of the marketplace that make environmental activity more profitable. Increasing numbers of consumers, at least in the developed nations of the world, have achieved income levels at which they are willing to pay a premium for environmentally

---

[11] For a debate over the merits of this argument, see Palmer, Oates, and Portney (1995) and Porter and van der Linde (1995).

friendly products. Companies want to appeal to these "green" consumers, and to do so are willing to go above and beyond the levels of care required by environmental regulations. Examples of such environmentally friendly products include organic produce, tuna caught with dolphin-safe nets, biodegradable plastic bags, reformulated gasoline, and McDonald's Corporation's substitution of paper wrapping for styrofoam "clamshell" sandwich containers. The basic notion here is that firms can differentiate their products by improving their environmental qualities, and thereby charge a higher price to high-income consumers. There is a small but growing economic literature that studies theoretical models of the "green" consumer phenomenon. These models typically build on the basic model of "vertical" product differentiation developed by Gabszewicz and Thisse (1979) and Shaked and Sutton (1982). In this setup, consumers have identical preferences, but income differences lead to differences in the willingness to pay for product quality. Since greater product differentiation reduces substitutability and price competition, even firms with identical cost functions will offer distinct qualities in the resulting market equilibrium. In fact, a standard characteristic of such models is that the firms – in their attempts to avoid price competition – engage in "too much" differentiation from the perspective of social welfare.[12] Because of this tendency toward excess differentiation, Ronnen (1991) and Arora and Gangopadhyay (1995) show that a minimum quality standard (MQS), if set appropriately, can improve social welfare. An MQS forces up the quality of low-quality firms, making them closer substitutes for the products of high-quality firms, and intensifying price competition. While a high-quality firm responds to an MQS by further raising its quality, this is not enough to offset the effect of the standard, and the quality of the firms' products moves closer together while prices are forced down. Bagnoli and Watts (2003) study several vertical differentiation models where environmental friendliness is only partially internalized by consumers, thereby allowing for a formal analysis of externalities in the context of a "green consumer" model. Their focus is on whether unregulated market forces lead to the socially optimal level of environmental friendliness. They find that only in certain special cases can

---

[12] In the typical version of this model, the consumption of a particular product of a certain quality affects only the utility of the individual consumer. This can be interpreted in two ways. Either individual consumption does not create any externalities, or externalities created by consumption are fully internalized in the utility of the buyer. Some products, such as professional services, generate few externalities. Products involving safety or environmental standards, in contrast, typically create at least some external impacts, and here the assumption of full internalization is less natural, so care must be taken in interpreting the models' results.

unregulated competition for "green" consumers provide the socially optimal level of the environmental public good.[13] There appear to be two main lessons to be learned from these models. First, a clear and coherent theory can indeed be developed around the notion that firms may voluntarily make their products more environmentally friendly in order to attract high-income "green" consumers. Second, voluntary action by corporations is unlikely to provide socially optimal results. Government action, at least in principle, can improve the workings of the market. This suggests that a full understanding of corporate environmentalism requires models that combine firms' strategic choices of environmental quality with regulators' strategic choices of environmental standards. This is the approach we take in part II of this volume. The empirical literature (which we review briefly in section 5) has reached mixed conclusions regarding whether "green consumerism" plays a significant role in influencing corporate environmental decisions. This is consistent with the maxim we have often heard from company managers: If two products are identical in terms of price and product attributes, then some consumers will exercise a preference for the more environmentally friendly one. Otherwise, environmental impact does not appear to make a difference in consumer choices. In surveys, consumers often claim that they are willing to pay more for environmentally friendly products. Nevertheless, when it comes to their actual purchasing decisions, consumers appear to focus on the traditional factors of price and product quality.

4 CORPORATE ENVIRONMENTAL AND FINANCIAL PERFORMANCE

Theories of corporate environmentalism are of limited interest if investors pay no attention to environmental performance. Before proceeding to a detailed presentation of our analytical approach, it is worth reviewing the available evidence on whether investors view corporate environmental improvement favorably. Overall, empirical studies consistently find a positive relationship between environmental and financial performance, although

---

[13] When the firms compete by setting prices ("Bertrand competition"), the public good is always underprovided. If firms compete by choosing quantities ("Cournot competition"), then for some parameter values the efficient level of public good provision can be obtained, but only if the public good involves the elimination of a detrimental activity (rather than the expansion of a beneficial activity) and only if all costs of provision are fixed costs as opposed to variable costs.

the mechanisms linking the two have yet to be fully identified. One set of papers examines the impact of corporate environmental activity on various measures of firms' short- and long-run financial returns. Hart and Ahuja (1996) and Khanna, Quimio, and Bojilova (1998) find evidence that voluntary environmental actions lead to negative short-run, but positive long-run, returns. Hart and Ahuja use several different measures of financial returns (i.e. returns on assets, sales, and investment) to show that reductions in toxic chemical emissions hurt returns in the year the reductions took place, but had a positive effect on returns in subsequent years. Similarly, Khanna, Quimio, and Bojilova show that participation in the EPA's voluntary "33/50" program for reducing toxic chemical emissions lowered chemical firms' current-period return on investment, but increased their market value. In related work, Konar and Cohen (1998) show that poor environmental performance (as measured by releases of toxic chemicals and the number of pending environmental lawsuits filed against the firm) reduces a firm's intangible asset value.

Another set of papers examines investor responses to the release of emissions information to the public. To gauge investor responses, one could ask whether large emitters of toxic chemicals suffer in the stock market when information of their emissions is released to the public. Interestingly, there is ample evidence that the largest emitters of toxic chemicals did *not* suffer most from the release of public information about emissions. Hamilton (1995), Konar and Cohen (1997a) and Khanna, Quimio, and Bojilova (1998) all find that firms suffering the greatest negative abnormal stock returns on the day after Toxic Release Inventory (TRI) information was released were not the largest emitters of toxic chemicals. This is not inconsistent with conventional financial theory, however. As these papers point out, what should matter to investors is not the level of TRI emissions *per se*, but the difference between the actual and the expected levels of emissions. An obvious interpretation of the results is that the largest emitters were expected to be large emitters, so the new data provided investors with little new information. Further support for this interpretation can be found by noting that the largest emitters were consistently part of the chemical industry. Indeed, Khanna, Quimio, and Bojilova (1998) focus on a sample of ninety-one firms, all of which are from the chemical industry. They found no evidence of abnormal returns on the first day toxic emissions information was released to the public, suggesting that investors in this industry were reasonably well informed prior to the release of TRI information. They found, however, that the release of emissions information did appear to cause poorly performing firms (i.e. those firms whose relative performance in terms of toxic releases worsened over time) to experience negative abnormal returns in subsequent years.

The foregoing results suggest that the typical investor views pollution as an economic negative. This may occur for several reasons. Investors could link pollution with inefficient production, they could fear that highly polluting firms will face more intensive regulatory monitoring, or they could fear that large emitters of toxic chemicals face a higher probability of future environmental litigation (even if the releases are legal today). A related question is whether firms take action to counteract environmentally driven stock price drops. Konar and Cohen (1997a) find that the forty firms in their sample suffering the largest negative abnormal returns on the first day of TRI information release (the "Top 40"), subsequently improved their environmental performance (as measured by TRI releases and the amount of chemical spills) more than an industry-weighted counterpart. Khanna, Quimio, and Bojilova (1998) find that the firms in their chemical industry sample that suffered large abnormal negative returns subsequently reduced their releases of toxic chemicals in favour of off-site transfers.

In summary, empirical research shows that superior environmental performance and superior financial performance are positively intertwined. US financial markets reward firms that go beyond legal mandates for the reduction of toxic emissions, and punish firms that have unexpectedly high levels of toxic releases. Furthermore, firms respond to these financial penalties by improving their environmental performance. Quite simply, voluntary environmental protection appears to make good business sense.[14] What remains to be shown, however, are the precise mechanisms that link environmental and financial performance.

5 DRIVERS OF CORPORATE ENVIRONMENTAL IMPROVEMENT

There is a small set of empirical papers that sheds some light on the relative importance of different drivers of corporate environmental improvement. Most of the papers in this area focus on company decisions to participate in various government-sponsored voluntary programs, a topic we discuss in detail in chapter 9. In this section, although we touch upon these results,

---

[14] However, the current literature provides little evidence that small firms undertake voluntary environmental improvements. The studies summarized here have focused almost exclusively on larger firms, and there is some evidence that the smaller of these firms are less likely to undertake voluntary corporate actions.

we emphasize the results of empirical studies that analyze the incentives for firms to undertake unilateral initiatives by joining trade association programs (King and Lenox, 2000), adopting ISO 14001 (Dasgupta, Hettige, and Wheeler, 2000; Delmas, 2001), adopting an environmental management system (EMS) (Khanna and Anton, 2001), or simply reducing emissions (Pargal and Wheeler, 1996; Maxwell, Lyon, and Hackett, 2000). We organize the discussion below in terms of alternative drivers of environmental initiatives.

5.1   Green consumers

The extant empirical literature yields no consensus regarding the economic importance of green consumerism. Several papers find some evidence that is potentially consistent with green consumer pressure. Specifically, Arora and Cason (1996) find that firms operating in industries with higher *industry-average* advertising-to-sales ratios were more likely to join the EPA's "33/50" program. Khanna and Damon (1999) find that, within the chemical industry, consumer good producers were more likely to join the "33/50" program than were their intermediate good producing counterparts. Similarly, Khanna and Anton (2001) find that firms primarily producing finished products, such as pharmaceuticals or cosmetics, were more likely to adopt a comprehensive environmental management system (EMS). However, several other studies find no support for the importance of green consumers. In a study that utilized firm-specific data on advertising-to-sales ratios, Arora and Cason (1995) find no support for the hypothesis that firms with higher *firm-specific* advertising-to-sales ratios were more likely to join the "33/50" program. Furthermore, Konar and Cohen (1997b) find no support for the hypothesis that firms that were heavier advertisers undertook greater emission reductions, after controlling for firm size. Finally, when examining actual releases of toxic chemicals, Khanna and Damon (1999) find no support for the hypothesis that producers of consumer goods in the chemical industry exhibited significantly greater reductions in their emissions than firms not engaged in consumer good production. Note that all but one of the foregoing studies uses data on toxic chemical emissions as their measure of environmental performance. Furthermore, they all measure aspects of the production process, rather than the environmental attributes and the sales levels of products themselves, which makes it impossible to determine whether consumers of the firm's products were shifting their purchases to other firms, or whether consumer products firms are simply more visible and hence more susceptible to threats of consumer boycotts or lawsuits.

5.2 Stakeholder pressure

Substantial evidence indicates that stakeholder pressure is an important factor motivating corporate environmental activity. Pargal and Wheeler (1996) find that Indonesian manufacturing facilities located in neighborhoods with higher average income emitted lower levels of organic waste into local water systems, controlling for output levels and industry categories. Dasgupta, Hettige, and Wheeler (2000) find that perceived pressures from educated employees and management were a significant factor in the adoption of ISO 14001 by Mexican firms. Maxwell, Lyon, and Hackett (2000) find that firms in states with higher numbers of environmental group members *per capita* reduced emissions of toxic chemicals more rapidly. King and Lenox (2000) find that firms that were more visible or concerned about public image were more likely to join the chemical industry's Responsible Care® program. Finally, Khanna and Anton (2001) find that publicly traded firms with a higher ratio of capital-assets-to-sales, and therefore more dependent on the market for capital, were more likely to undertake EMSs, possibly to prevent adverse reactions from stockholders. Taken together, these papers show that corporate environmental performance is sensitive to pressures from many different stakeholder groups, including employees, community members, environmental groups, and investors.

5.3 Competitive pressure

Whether competition encourages better environmental performance remains unclear, from an empirical perspective. Pargal and Wheeler (1996) find that state-owned firms emit greater levels of organic waste than do privately owned firms, suggesting that competitive pressures motivate firms to reduce emissions. However, Khanna and Anton (2001) find that firms operating in less concentrated industries are no more likely to undertake environmental management. Nevertheless, they do find that firms with a larger proportion of their facilities located in foreign countries, which they interpret as being exposed to greater global competition, were more likely to have an environmentally pro-active management system.

5.4   Regulatory and legal pressures

Although it is difficult to measure the extent of regulatory or legal threats, the empirical literature does indicate that such threats play a significant role in motivating corporate environmental activity. Dasgupta, Hettige, and Wheeler (2000) find evidence that regulatory pressures, as perceived by firms, were important in motivating unilateral initiatives. Welch, Mazur, and Bretschneider (2000) find that large electric utilities were more likely to join the EPA's Climate Leaders program if they were located in states with a greater density of environmental group members or they were subject to higher levels of direct federal or state regulation. Khanna and Anton (2001) find that the threat of liabilities, as proxied by the number of Superfund sites for which firms are potentially liable, motivated participation in the EPA's "33/50" and WasteWise programs and led firms to undertake environmental management. They also find that firms belonging to highly regulated industries, as proxied for by the ratio of industrywide pollution abatement costs to sales, were more likely to adopt an EMS.

5.5   Past environmental performance

In general, firms with poor environmental records appear to be more likely to take action to improve. King and Lenox (2000) find that firms with poorer environmental performance, as proxied by high levels of releases or releases per unit of sales/employees, were more likely to participate in Responsible Care®. Maxwell, Lyon, and Hackett (2000) find that toxic emissions were reduced more rapidly by firms in states that had higher initial levels of releases. Welch, Mazur, and Bretschneider (2000) find that higher-polluting electric utilities pledged larger reductions of carbon dioxide releases than did cleaner firms. Khanna and Anton (2001) find that firms that had higher on-site toxic discharges per unit sales but lower off-site transfers per unit sales were more likely to undertake proactive environmental management.

5.6   Government voluntary programs

Several papers have examined whether participation in voluntary programs sponsored by government or by trade associations led firms to measurably improve their environmental performance. Khanna and Damon (1999) find that firms that joined the EPA's "33/50" program reduced their emissions of toxic chemicals to a greater extent than did non-participants. In contrast, Videras and Alberini (2000) find that participation in EPA's WasteWise program made no difference in firms' generation of solid waste. Similarly, King and Lenox (2000) find that participation in the chemical industry's Responsible Care® program had an insignificant effect on corporate environmental improvement.

5.7 Summary

Overall, the empirical studies cited above find a number of significant drivers of corporate environmental improvement. Stakeholder pressure – from shareholders, employees, neighborhood residents, and environmental activists – clearly influences corporate decisions. Regulatory and legal pressures also appear to increase industry incentives for environmental action. These factors will play important roles in the chapters that follow. In addition, firm assets and capabilities surely affect the feasibility and attractiveness of corporate environmentalism, though there has been relatively little empirical research documenting these effects. However, Khanna and Anton (2001) find that firms that spend more on R&D were more likely to adopt a comprehensive EMS. They also find that firms with older equipment were more likely to adopt such systems, possibly because it was less costly for them to replace old equipment with newer less pollution-intensive equipment. Possibly combining these two types of effects, companies with poor environmental records are more likely to improve, which may be due to greater stakeholder pressure, lower marginal cost of improvement due to the age or inefficiency of existing capital equipment, or both.

6 CONCLUSIONS

In this introductory chapter we have presented a broad political–economic framework in which a variety of corporate environmental strategies can be understood. We emphasized the importance of industry structure, political institutions, and the policy life cycle in explaining the emergence of corporate environmentalism. We also discussed alternative, non-political, theories based on the ideas that environmental improvement reduces costs or attracts green consumers. While cost reduction and product differentiation undoubtedly play a role in corporate environmental strategy, they fail to recognize that corporate environmental initiatives tend to arise in the shadow of existing regulatory institutions. In many cases, corporate initiatives aim to preempt emerging regulatory threats, to influence the future course of regulations that cannot be preempted, or to alter regulators' incentives for monitoring and enforcement of existing laws. Our overview of the empirical literature showed that stakeholder pressures, mediated through regulatory and legal institutions, have a significant impact on corporate strategy. In addition, there is considerable evidence that corporate environmental improvement is associated with improved financial performance. In part II of this volume, we present a set of models for better understanding exactly how corporate environmentalism benefits the bottom line. A major category of corporate environmental activity involves partnering with government, and part III of the book addresses these activities in detail. We discuss not only corporate motivations for participating in such programs, but also government incentives to offer them. In addition, we analyze the incentives these programs create for corporate environmental improvement. Our approach highlights the importance of political–economic factors in motivating corporate environmentalism. Thus, before turning to parts II and III, we flesh out our political–economic framework in more detail in chapter 2, and provide an introduction to the types of models we will use to study the interplay of corporate environmentalism and public policy.

2 | Markets, politics, and models

1 INTRODUCTION

One of the most important elements of the framework presented in chapter 1 is the notion of the *policy life cycle*. The strategic effects of corporate environmentalism differ greatly depending on the stage of the cycle in which an issue is at a given time. In this book, we present a series of models that lay out these effects in detail. Since our overall objective is to capture the interplay between corporate strategy and public policy, we devote careful attention to both variations in market structure and stages of the policy life cycle. This chapter provides a context for the chapters to come by surveying the political economy literature on legislative and regulatory behavior. Given the enormous amount of material that has been written on these topics, our review is necessarily highly selective. Our goal in this chapter is to highlight some of the most influential political economic models of legislative and regulatory behavior, and to explain the various models we have chosen to use for the study of corporate environmental strategy. This will prepare the reader for the analytical approach we will take in subsequent chapters.

2 COMPANIES AND MARKETS

Business firms vary widely in size, structure, and success. Nevertheless, economists have made enormous progress in understanding business behavior by using the simplifying assumption that companies maximize profits. Throughout this book, we will take this as a maintained hypothesis. However, we will consider a variety of different market structures within which a firm may operate, ranging from competitive to monopolistic. In general, models with simpler depictions of industry structure allow for more detailed representations of the regulatory process. For example, in chapter 3 we study oligopolies that may have a large number of firms, and use a fairly general and abstract model of the political process. In chapter 4, we include two firms with differing levels of environmental performance, which allows us to capture the essentials of the competitive process while incorporating detailed models of regulatory behavior. Chapter 5 focuses on a single firm, in order to highlight the details of how a firm interacts with regulators in the enforcement process.

Regardless of the market structure we are considering, we will study behavior that represents an *equilibrium*, in the sense that none of the parties within the model could improve his or her situation through any kind of unilateral change of strategy. In other words, we make use of the concept of *Nash equilibrium*, due to Nobel Laureate John Nash, which posits that all parties within the model are doing the best they can, given the behavior of all the other parties. This is a standard notion in game theory and economics, and increasingly within other social sciences as well. The concept has achieved wide currency because any other approach must presume that people persistently fail to take advantage of the opportunities before them. Though we can all think of friends or relatives whose behavior may seem to us anomalous, chess players do not routinely leave their kings exposed, nor do soccer players leave their goals untended. Similarly, few businesspeople are naive enough to expect their rivals to systematically ignore market opportunities.

3   THE POLICY LIFE CYCLE

The use of game theoretic tools has spread rapidly within political science in recent years, allowing for increasingly precise and, we believe, enlightening characterizations of a variety of political institutions. Throughout this book, we highlight the role of interest groups in the political process, and we assume that these groups rationally pursue their own best interests, an assumption that seems consistent with what we read in the newspaper. All industries have trade associations, and these groups typically play important roles in any policy that affects them. For example, the American Chemistry Council (formerly the Chemical Manufacturers Association, CMA) is a well-organized advocate for the chemical industry, the electric industry is represented by the Edison Electric Institute and the Electric Power Research Institute, and the American Petroleum Institute speaks for the oil industry. Few would accuse these groups of failing to recognize what is best for them. Issues that cut across multiple industries may be addressed by the National Association of Manufacturers or the Chamber of Commerce. On the other side of many environmental issues are non-profit groups such as Environmental Defense, Greenpeace, the

Natural Resources Defense Council, Public Citizen, or the Public Interest Research Group. These groups, too, are well organized and knowledgeable about the workings of the policy process.

Mancur Olson's (1971) work on the theory of collective action provides the foundation for most modern analysis of interest group behavior. Olson emphasized that collective action is a public good, the fruits of which cannot readily be refused to individuals who do not contribute to its creation. As a result, the beneficiaries of collective action have strong incentives to "free-ride" on the efforts of others. Olson's interest was primarily in identifying the types of groups that are more likely to overcome (at least partially) the free-riding problem. Groups with relatively small numbers of members, homogeneous interests, and a lot at stake are more likely to be successful engaging in collective action.

As discussed in chapter 1, the stages of the policy life cycle are: development, politicization, legislation, and implementation. We discuss these in more detail below, highlighting the role of interest groups at each stage, and identifying the type of formal models that are appropriate for characterizing the policy process.

3.1 Development and politicization

Chronic environmental problems may go ignored for long periods of time before interest groups form around the issue and begin to take action. A particular issue gradually comes to public recognition as scientists, political activists, and other opinion leaders begin to actively debate its importance, and the various means by which it can be addressed. Often a dramatic event is required before the issue becomes widely acknowledged in public awareness. A good example is the hole in the ozone layer over Antarctica. In 1974, scientists first argued there was a causal link between the use of chlorofluorocarbons (CFCs) and depletion of the ozone layer. While there was some political reaction during the late 1970s, most notably the banning of CFCs in aerosol sprays in 1978, major chemical companies successfully argued there was no justification for more stringent controls. The issue remained dormant until 1988, when the Ozone Trends Panel of the National Research Council provided hard evidence that CFCs were damaging the ozone layer.[1]

---

[1] For a good account of the issue, see Reinhardt (1989).

According to Carol Browner, former EPA Administrator, crises have been the driving force behind many of our existing environmental laws:

When our country began to pass environmental laws in the early 70's, we did it issue by issue, crisis by crisis. I will never forget a photograph of flames, fire, shooting right out of the water in downtown Cleveland. It was the summer of 1969 and the Cuyahoga River was burning. An angry nation was called to action, and the Clean Water Act [CWA] was passed. How can anyone forget the discovery of thousands of leaking barrels of toxic chemicals that had been buried under the community of Love Canal? Again, a shocked country responded. The Superfund law was passed. Our Toxic Substances Control Act passed soon after we watched farmers taking contaminated cows out to the pasture and shooting them to death. And it was the contamination of the New Orleans drinking water supply that spurred passage of the Safe Drinking Water Act.[2]

From the perspective of corporate strategy, public crises are much more difficult to manage than the gradual buildup of public discontent. Crises demand rapid responses, and pose a serious risk that the response will not perfectly match the problem. Chronic discontent, in contrast, offers many opportunities for mitigation before it reaches critical mass. Often, a looming public problem is taken up by one or more activist groups well before it becomes an object of public opinion. If the problem is specific to one or a few companies, activists may target the offenders for a boycott, in what Baron (2001) refers to as "private politics." If the problem is endemic to an entire industry or cuts across multiple industries, then effective collective action may require resort to the political process.

Mobilizing public opinion to make an issue politically salient is no easy feat. Demonstrations, news coverage, editorials, talk shows, all gradually raise public awareness of an issue. It may take years to bring an issue to the top of the public agenda, and once there it can easily be dislodged. Smart companies take advantage of these hurdles to derail threatening issues before they become politically salient.

Numerous techniques are available for corporations to defuse volatile issues. One of the most effective is preemption – taking just enough action that the potential benefits of collective action no longer justify its cost. Another, potentially less costly tactic, is public outreach. For years, Mobil Oil Company (now ExxonMobil) has had a long-standing practice of placing opinion pieces on the op-ed pages of prominent newspapers

---

[2] This quote is taken from a speech Browner gave at the Center For National Policy Newsmaker Luncheon, Washington, DC, July 20, 1994. For the full text of the speech, visit http://gos.sbc.edu/b/browner.html.

such as the *New York Times* and the *Washington Post*, with the goal of influencing the views of opinion leaders. An alternative strategy is Shell Oil Company's practice of making space available in its corporate outreach materials for environmental groups to present their views on topics relevant to the company. While such a move might at first glance seem counter to Shell's interests, it might instead serve to build cooperative relationships with potentially antagonistic groups, and might even serve to reduce the credibility of criticism from groups that are perceived as being "coopted" by industry.

A more aggressive strategy for defusing emerging issues, useful in the politicization stage, is the use of "astroturf lobbying," in which a corporation covertly hires public relations firms to help interest groups with a pro-company stance make their views widely known.[3] Davies Communications is a public relations firm specializing in such activity. Its advertising claims "Traditional lobbying is no longer enough. Today numbers count. To win in the hearing room, you must reach out to create grassroots support. To outnumber your opponents, call the leading grassroots public affairs communications specialists." Davies provides an entertaining explanation of how his firm generates a "grassroots" letter-writing campaign through the use of telephone banks:

We get them on the phone, and while we're on the phone we say "Will you write a letter?" "Sure." "Do you have time to write it?" "Not really." "Could we write the letter for you? I could put you on the phone right now with someone who could help you write a letter. Just hold, we have a writer standing by" . . . If they're close by we hand-deliver it. We hand-write it out on "little kitty cat stationery" if it's a little old lady. If it's a business we take it over to be photocopied on someone's letterhead. [We] use different stamps, different envelopes. Getting a pile of personalized letters that have a different look to them is what you want to strive for. (Stauber and Rampton 1995, pp. 89–91)

Environmental issues are often the target of astroturf lobbying. For example, People for the West! (PFW!) is an organization that bills itself as "a grassroots campaign supporting western communities." In 1992, however, 96 percent of the group's funding came from corporate sponsors such as NERCO Minerals, Cyprus Minerals, Chevron, and Hecla Mining, who have strong interests in maintaining the General Mining Act of 1872 that allows them to acquire and mine public lands at a cost of $5 per acre. In fact,

---

[3] For a rigorous analysis of astroturf lobbying, see Lyon and Maxwell (2004).

the chairman of PFW!, Bob Quick, is the national director of state legislative affairs for Asarco, a large mining company.

Tactics such as astroturf lobbying may seem cynical, and a good case can be made for mandatory public disclosure of corporate funding for such groups. Furthermore, such tactics may backfire on companies if the public becomes aware of them. We are not endorsing them, but simply pointing out that if companies do not defuse public issues during their development and politicization phases – through self-regulation, public outreach, or other means – they may find themselves facing much more costly legislative mandates at a later date.

From a modeling perspective, the key step in the development and politicization of an issue occurs when interest groups organize around the issue. Mobilizing an interest group is a costly process that requires individuals to collect resources, gather information, coordinate on a mutually agreeable political strategy, and reach out to potential members and encourage them to take action.[4] If industry can prevent opposing interest groups from mobilizing, it can greatly reduce the risk that it will face costly new regulations. In chapter 3, we present a model in which consumer groups must decide whether to incur the cost of organizing to press for stronger environmental laws. Industry groups simultaneously decide whether to organize to oppose pressures for new regulations. If the groups do become organized, they compete by allocating resources to influence the political process in the direction they prefer. We emphasize the possibility that corporate self-regulation can achieve enough environmental improvement that consumer groups decide further gains would not justify the cost of organizing.

3.2   Legislation

Once interest groups mobilize around an issue, and public opinion supports its salience, the stage is set for legislative action. The academic understanding of legislative activity advanced rapidly over the 1990s, as theorists used the tools of game theory to analyze voting behavior, bargaining in legislatures, the power of committee jurisdiction, and other aspects of legislative decisionmaking. In addition, empirical work has revealed in increasing detail the links between campaign contributions, lobbying activity, constituent interests, and legislative voting. A thorough survey of this research

---

[4] For further details on the process of creating and organizing interest groups, see Olson (1971) and Peltzman (1976).

is beyond the scope of this chapter.[5] Instead, our goal is the more modest one of laying out some basic principles of legislative behavior, which will underpin the analyses in part II of this volume.

Led by Gordon Tullock and Nobel Laureate James Buchanan, economists associated with the Virginia School developed a body of work that uses economic principles to study collective choice processes. As presented in Buchanan and Tullock (1962), they emphasized the application of competitive market models to understand the supply and demand for policy. Central to their analysis is the idea of "rent-seeking" behavior, through which interest groups attempt to capture the economic rents created by the application of the state's monopoly on the legal use of force. In a seminal paper, Tullock (1967) developed a simple and insightful model of the competition between interest groups for control of the legislative process. He proposed that the probability that a piece of legislation passes is simply equal to the proportion of total interest group resources expended that are devoted to supporting the bill. With this model of the legislative process, it becomes possible to study how interest groups allocate resources to rent-seeking behavior.[6] One of the central insights of the Virginia School is that the welfare cost of government-sanctioned monopolies or tariffs is not just the deadweight loss involved in reduced quantities sold, but must also include the resources wasted in attempts to capture the monopoly rents.

In the 1970s, economists associated with the University of Chicago developed an economic theory of regulation, complementary to that of the Virginia economists, which attempts to provide a general theory of regulatory behavior. In fact, its formulation of political decisionmaking is so general as not really to distinguish between legislative and regulatory behavior, thereby rendering it what might be called an economic theory of politics. In this literature, political action is driven by interest groups that form to advance their own agendas. Stigler (1971) used Olson's (1971) logic of collective action to argue that economic regulation is often imposed at the behest of industry for its own gain. Peltzman (1976) formalized and generalized Stigler's theory, and showed that capture of the regulatory process by a single interest group is unlikely if multiple groups compete for influence. Peltzman postulates a political decisionmaker interested in maximizing political support, who can redistribute wealth across groups of citizens.

---

[5] For more detailed treatments of the recent literature, see Grossman and Helpman (2001) or Persson and Tabellini (2000).

[6] We will use this type of model in chapters 7 and 8, where we study political responses to proposals made by regulatory authorities.

Various interest groups offer support through means such as campaign contributions, promises of future votes, assistance in getting out the vote, etc. The optimizing politician chooses a policy that balances, at the margin, the political support offered by all the different groups. For example, suppose a regulated utility enjoys a reduction in its marginal cost due to innovation. While a market would leave the full benefits of the innovation in the hands of the firm, the regulator divides the benefits between the firm and its customers so as to maximize political support.

Becker (1983) extends Peltzman's analysis to examine the efficiency with which income transfers are effected. Becker argues that groups pressing for transfers that generate little deadweight loss have an inherent advantage in generating political pressure. As a result, equilibrium outcomes are likely to redistribute income in relatively efficient ways.[7] The beauty of the analysis is that it provides an integrative framework in which the economic theory of regulation and the normative ideal of social welfare maximization can be considered jointly. The result is reminiscent of Madison's contention in *The Federalist* that pluralistic competition between "factions" (interest groups) in the political marketplace would result in efficient outcomes, much like the outcome in the economic marketplace. However, Becker does not go so far as to argue that pluralism delivers social efficiency. His theory limits itself to the more modest claim that in a pluralist system there are incentives for income transfers to be delivered in a relatively efficient way.

The Virginia and Chicago approaches to political economy provide interesting insights in part by abstracting from the detailed institutional structure of politics. There is a large and complementary body of work in political science that examines institutions much more closely. One such line of work studies elections explicitly. Downs' (1957) seminal economic theory of democracy focuses on voting behavior rather than interest group pressure, resulting in an emphasis on the preferences of the "median voter." If political preferences can be arrayed along a line, this individual occupies a position such that an equal number of others have preferences to her left and to her right. The median voter is thus "pivotal" to the outcome of a majoritarian vote, and her preferences drive electoral outcomes. Downs' work has been extended in a variety of directions. One recent strand of literature develops models that can be used to assess the efficiency of representative democracy. For example, Besley and Coate (1997) extend the Downsian model by endogenizing the emergence of political candidates from among the electorate. This allows them to assess the efficiency of democracy providing public goods and, in a dynamic extension presented

---

[7] We use a model of this sort in chapter 3.

in Besley and Coate (1998), investing in infrastructure to raise future productivity. (The verdict in both cases is mixed.) Lizzeri and Persico (2001) also study the efficiency of democratic provision of public goods, with an emphasis on the difference between winner-take-all systems and proportional systems.

There is also a literature on the behavior of sitting legislatures. Baron and Ferejohn (1989) present an influential model of the process of bargaining in legislatures, and characterize the equilibria of such processes. Groseclose and Snyder (1996) study the question of how large a legislative coalition must be bribed in order to assure passage of a desired bill at minimum cost. Kroszner and Stratmann (1998) study empirically how interest groups use financial contributions to build relationships with representatives on particular Congressional committees. These papers are positive in nature.

Regardless of whether the focus is on elections or the behavior of sitting legislatures, there is wide agreement that special interest groups wield important influence in the political process. A large literature has developed in recent years that opens up the "black box" of interest group politics to examine interest group strategies in detail. Grossman and Helpman (2001) provide a rigorous approach to these issues, with two main emphases: (1) the role of lobbying in providing information, and (2) the role of campaign contributions in influencing legislative behavior. The analysis of lobbying builds on the model of strategic information transmission due to Crawford and Sobel (1982), Lohmann's (1993) application of the model to mass political action, and Krishna and Morgan's extension to the case of multiple information-transmitting groups (2001). The analysis of campaign contributions builds on the full-information model of common agency due to Bernheim and Whinston (1986), the model of bargaining in legislatures due to Baron and Ferejohn (1989), and Baron's (1994) model of electoral competition with both informed and uninformed voters. Most of this work is positive in nature, intended to describe the nature of political reality rather than assess its performance from a normative perspective. Interestingly, Grossman and Helpman (2001) show that when one models the details of the electoral process, allowing for multiple interest groups that make campaign contributions, the ultimate result is that political parties behave as if they were maximizing a weighted average of campaign contributions and aggregate social welfare. Thus, their analysis provides a rigorous justification for a reduced-form approach that suppresses the structural details of the political process.

As mentioned earlier, a thorough review of the political economy literature is beyond the scope of this chapter. The foregoing quick sketch is meant to accomplish two things. First, it illustrates the critical role played by special interest groups in theories of political process, even in the context of voting models. It may be true that in a democracy, decisions are made on the basis of "one person, one vote." Nevertheless, the information available to voters and the campaign funds available to political candidates derive in large part from special interest groups, which thereby wield enormous power over the political process. This is true across the spectrum of democratic political systems, from the USA to Europe and Japan. Second, our quick literature survey shows the recent evolution from generalized models of political "pressure" to more structured models of particular aspects of political process. While the generalized models present conclusions broadly applicable in a range of political settings, the more structured models may apply more narrowly to particular institutions in particular countries. In general, the movement toward structural models has been more pronounced in the USA than elsewhere, and the formal models have tended to reflect US-style pluralist institutions.

In our view, interest group pressures are critical in both pluralist and corporatist societies, and politicians in both types of societies must seek to trade off the interests of different groups in order to maximize political support. Thus, general theories of political pressure are likely to be applicable to both types of society, even though more structured models may be specialized to a particular set of political institutions.

In this book, we employ a quite general interest group perspective on legislative behavior that we believe has broad applicability. Our basic view is that public policies that impose costs on identifiable groups will be resisted by those groups with increasing vigor as the costs involved rise. This is a perspective that we expect to hold in almost any country around the globe. Thus, in chapter 3 we model legislative behavior as driven by interest group pressures from both consumers (who gain from a cleaner environment but must also pay higher prices for lower pollution) and industry members (who face higher costs as pollution abatement intensifies). In chapters 7 and 8 we model the likelihood that a regulatory proposal receives legislative approval as a decreasing function of the costs the proposal imposes on industry. In chapters 4, 5, 6, and 9, we focus on the behavior of regulators, to which we now turn.

3.3   Implementation

Most legislation, especially concerning the environment, establishes general objectives but leaves the details of implementation to a regulatory agency.

It is important to distinguish between the passing of legislation and its implementation, for the corporate strategies appropriate at each stage are quite different. As the German CO_2 agreement shows, one viable strategy at the legislative stage is the preemption of new legislation. Once a law is passed, however, regulators are required to implement it and preemption is no longer a viable corporate strategy. Instead, strategy must shift toward influencing the regulations that will implement the new law. Furthermore, campaign contributions are usually not viable tools in the regulatory arena, since regulators for the most part are appointed and not elected. Thus the provision of information is the primary tool used by industry to influence the regulatory process. This can be done either directly, through lobbying, or indirectly, by signaling to the regulator. For example, in some cases firms can influence the regulatory process through the technologies they choose, which may provide the regulator with a signal about the costliness of a new technology or convince her that she must accept the newly adopted technology as a *fait accompli* that must be taken into account when designing new regulations.

While much of regulation involves the implementation of legislation passed by others, it is not uncommon for regulators to pursue their own initiatives. For our purposes, there are two important types of regulatory initiatives: (1) negotiated agreements, and (2) public voluntary programs. The former, common in Europe and Japan, involve negotiations between regulators and industry associations which, if successful, may preempt legislative action. The latter, common in the USA, involve provision by government of a package of benefits – including information, technical assistance, and public recognition – designed to facilitate voluntary pollution abatement by corporations. Chapter 6 provides a detailed discussion of why regulators have increasingly turned to public voluntary agreements (PVAs) as a regulatory instrument.

Our purpose in this section is to give a general assessment of what drives regulatory behavior, which will underpin the analysis in part III of this volume. As with our earlier discussion of legislative behavior, we must necessarily skim lightly over the voluminous literature on regulation, and cannot hope to provide a comprehensive survey. Nevertheless, at least a brief overview of the literature on regulatory behavior is necessary in order to explain the approach to the study of regulation that we take in this book.

Freud famously lamented "What do women want?" Many academics have expressed a similar, if perhaps less urgent, confusion over the objectives of regulatory agencies. The matter would be of little consequence if regulatory bodies could be relied upon to faithfully execute the charges delegated to them by legislatures. This is not always the case, however. Indeed, legislatures often give broad, vague, charges to regulators, such as "protect the public health and safety." It is virtually impossible to determine whether a particular regulatory action faithfully executes such a mission. Even if legislative mandates were communicated clearly to regulators, there are good reasons to expect slippage between the wishes of the "principal" (the legislature) and the "agent" (the regulator).[8] For example, Niskanen (1971) argues that a key motivation for bureaucrats, including regulators, is maximizing their budgets, clearly something that is not necessarily the objective of the legislature. Regulators also have future career concerns that may involve obtaining a position within the regulated industry or running for elected office. Neither of these motives can be assumed to align perfectly with the intentions of the legislature.

McCubbins and Schwartz (1984) argue that despite the principal–agent problems that exist between the legislature and regulatory agencies, the legislature may nevertheless retain reasonably close control over agency behavior through the use of "fire alarms," e.g. complaints by constituents who are displeased with agency behavior. Weingast and Moran (1983) provide empirical support for this view in the case of the Federal Trade Commission (FTC). McCubbins, Noll and Weingast (1987) present a theory in which administrative procedures are used as tools to constrain regulatory discretion, though they recognize that these tools will not have complete success.

Given that regulatory discretion appears to be unavoidable, it is important to understand what drives regulatory behavior. Some insight into the US EPA's objective function can be gleaned from its own stated goals. Under the Government Performance and Results Act (GPRA), federal agencies are required by law to develop a five-year plan outlining their strategic goals and a corresponding set of performance measures, and to report to Congress their success in achieving their stated goals. In its strategic plan for 2000–2005, the EPA identifies the following goals: "clean air, clean and safe water, safe food; preventing pollution and reducing risks in communities, homes, workplaces, and ecosystems; better waste management, restoration of contaminated waste sites, and emergency response; reduction of global and cross-border environmental risks; expansion of Americans' right to know about their environment; sound science, improved understanding of environmental risk, and greater innovation to address environmental problems; a credible deterrent to pollution and greater compliance with

---

[8] For an overview of principal–agent models, see Salanié (2002).

the law; and effective management." The agency is considering shortening the list to simply: clean air, clean water, and clean land and ecosystems. It is also considering a five-goal list that would add helping communities and compliance.[9]

Examining the EPA's stated goals suggests that "maximizing environmental benefits" may be a reasonable approximation to the EPA's objective function. Rogerson (1990) presents a (static) model of government agency behavior in which the agency's objective is to maximize the gross benefits of its actions, taking its budget as a constraint. In a dynamic setting, maximizing environmental benefits might tend to maximize the agency's budget as well, a behavioral objective emphasized by Niskanen (1971). However, it is clear that government agencies such as the EPA are not immune from special interest pressures. While activists press for stronger environmental protection, industry groups press for attention to the costs of new regulations. Which group gets the ear of the agency depends in substantial measure on the Administrator appointed by the President. The EPA under Anne Gorsuch, who was appointed by Ronald Reagan, was widely perceived as a handmaiden to industry. Indeed, in 1984 the Senate passed by 74–19 an amendment saying that President Reagan should withdraw Ms. Gorsuch's nomination to serve as Chairperson of the National Advisory Committee on Oceans and Atmosphere (NACOA) in light of her poor performance as EPA Administrator.[10] Conversely, under President Clinton, many important political positions dealing with the environment were filled with individuals who had previously worked for environmental interest groups, and were presumably more likely to be receptive to lobbying from such groups.

In the literature on environmental regulation, a variety of different objective functions are used. Many papers adopt social welfare maximization as the regulatory goal, and solve for optimal regulatory policies. Others adopt the economic theory of regulation and the maximization of political support as the drivers of regulatory behavior. A few papers assume budget maximization. Papers that focus on monitoring and enforcement often assume that regulators aim to maximize compliance with regulations, or seek to maximize the environmental benefits of enforcement. The empirical behavior on regulatory behavior remains quite sparse, although Deily and Gray (1991) and Decker (2000b) find evidence that the economic theory of regulation helps explain regulatory enforcement, e.g. monitoring and

---

[9] *Inside EPA Weekly Report*, January 20, 2003.

[10] See www.adaction.org/voting/html for details on Senate voting records.

penalties are less common at plants that are significant employers in their local area.

Noll (1985) synthesizes the contributions of economics, political science, and sociology to produce an "external signals" theory of regulatory behavior. In this view, which bears some resemblance to Peltzman's (1976) more formal analysis, regulators respond to a diverse set of external pressures. Congressional oversight and budgetary constraints are powerful forces shaping the behavior of regulators. The appointment of top regulatory personnel by governors or the President creates another principal for many regulatory agencies. Lawsuits by various affected parties also must be taken into account, since they consume scarce agency resources. Media coverage also matters, since it may affect the agency's relationship with Congress, or the future job prospects of highly placed regulators.

In light of the above considerations, we take a broad approach to modeling regulatory behavior. To us, it makes sense that environmental regulators would weigh a variety of factors when making decisions, including environmental benefits, costs to industry, budget constraints, and the political preferences of Congress and the White House. However, the importance given to the various factors will vary from issue to issue, from one Administration to the next, and across stages of the policy life cycle. There is little empirical evidence to indicate how regulators in practice balance these diverse concerns. Thus, in chapter 4 we model the regulator's standard-setting decision as maximizing the sum of environmental impacts, consumer surplus, and industry profits; while one could dispute the weights attached to each of these factors, our results do not depend on these weights. In chapter 5, we focus on regulatory enforcement behavior, and there we use a narrower regulatory objective function, i.e. minimizing the sum of environmental damages and the regulator's enforcement costs. We feel this is a reasonable way to represent agency behavior in the circumscribed domain of enforcement practice. Chapters 7 and 8 model the regulator as maximizing the expected sum of environmental benefits, consumer surplus, and industry profits (as in chapter 4) – but subject to the additional constraint that regulatory mandates must be passed by the legislature, and the more stringent the proposed mandate, the more likely it is to be successfully opposed by industry. One important benefit of modeling the regulator as maximizing aggregate social welfare is that it aids us in assessing whether corporate environmentalism raises or lowers social welfare through its effects on public policy.

From the perspective of corporate strategy, there are two main types of regulatory activity, each of which must be approached differently:

(1) implementation of legislation, and (2) regulatory initiatives begun without legislative mandate.

In the case of legislative implementation, the agency is required by law to develop and enforce a policy, and preemption is not a viable option. Corporations can, however, influence the form of the regulations that are ultimately issued. This can be done through the traditional process of lobbying, but can also be done through the technology decisions of the firm, which may signal important information to the regulator. The regulator's enforcement practices can also be influenced. For example, a regulator may shift its monitoring resources away from firms with a good history of compliance with regulations. A regulator may also reward good corporate behavior in one arena with more lenient treatment in another. For example, companies with a good record of compliance may have an easier time siting new manufacturing facilities.

Moving beyond implementation, regulators often create new political initiatives. They can, for example, propose new legislation. Indeed, Landy (1995) points out that EPA officials generated the proposal for Superfund. Another popular form of regulatory initiative in recent years has been the development of public voluntary programs, such as the ENERGY STAR family of programs, sponsored by the Department of Energy and the EPA, which provide information and assistance to firms willing to become partners with government in the pursuit of environmental objectives. We discuss these in detail in chapters 8 and 9.

4 CONCLUSIONS

In the remainder of this book, we present a series of models that examine in detail the most important aspects of the interaction between corporate environmentalism and public policy. All of them share the feature that they combine a representation of industry structure with a representation of a particular aspect of the political process. Throughout the volume, we emphasize the importance of interest group pressure as a determinant of legislative outcomes, and the need for politicians to balance pressures from a variety of groups. When we deal with regulatory behavior, we again recognize the need for regulators to balance a variety of concerns including environmental quality, consumer welfare, and industry profits. While each of the models yields its own unique insights, we view them as complements rather than substitutes. Part II of the volume takes the policy life cycle as its organizing structure, and the chapters move in sequence from the legislative, to the regulatory, to the enforcement phases of the cycle. Throughout this part of the book we emphasize the role of corporate strategy in influencing the policy process. Part III emphasizes the objectives of regulatory agencies, and the options available to them in a context where the emergence of legislative authorization for new programs is uncertain. While corporate behavior remains important, our focus in this part of the book is primarily on government-led programs, rather than programs initiated by industry.

PART II

Corporate strategy and the policy life cycle

3 | Preempting future regulations

1 INTRODUCTION

> While some of the environmental changes now emerging in corporate America are genuine and welcome, a good many are superficial, some are downright diversionary, and a few are being specifically designed to preempt more stringent public policies from emerging. (Brent Blackwelder, President, Friends of the Earth, quoted in Smart 1992)

> In an effort to head off legal restrictions on privately traded derivatives, six of Wall Street's biggest securities firms have agreed to voluntarily tighten their controls on the most hotly contested aspects of their derivatives sales and trading. (*Wall Street Journal*, March 9, 1995, p. C1)

> In today's society any industry as conspicuous as the major home appliance industry is continually faced with the threat of government regulation. In my opinion, the only way to avoid government regulation is to move faster than the government. The alternative to government regulation is judicious self-regulation. (Herbert Phillips, Technical Director, Association of Home Appliance Manufacturers, quoted in Hunt 1975)

To economists, "regulation" means restraints imposed upon firms by government. In many cases, however, firms voluntarily restrain their own conduct; they "self-regulate."[1] While this book is obviously focused on corporate environmental performance, self-regulation is a much broader phenomenon. Examples from other contexts include establishment of financial exchanges, licensing of professionals, setting of safety standards, control of entertainment content, and advertising restrictions. While self-regulation may have a variety of motives,[2] in this chapter we model it as

---

[1] When self-regulation involves restrictions on quantity or sales territory, the terms "cartel" and "collusion" are applied and antitrust investigation may be expected. A large body of economic literature is devoted to identifying when such activities reduce social welfare. For a good overview of this research, see Kaserman and Mayo (1995).

[2] Self-regulation may increase consumer demand by reducing uncertainty about product quality or ensuring interoperability of the products of different firms. It may enhance employee satisfaction by improving the safety or other quality aspects of the workplace. It may also

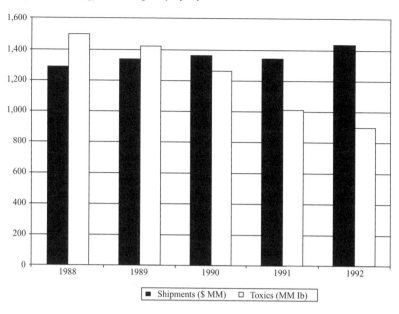

Figure 3.1   Total emissions of seventeen toxic chemicals vs. value of shipments from seven US manufacturing industries, 1988–1992

a way to preempt the passage of new government regulations, examining the conditions under which preemption is possible and, if it occurs, its welfare consequences. Within the framework of chapters 1 and 2, we focus here on the early stages of the policy life cycle. We present our analysis in the context of corporate environmentalism, but it should be clear from the above examples that the basic story has broader applicability. The analysis in this chapter is based on Maxwell, Lyon, and Hackett (2000).

Some intriguing preliminary evidence of self-regulation is presented in figure 3.1, which shows for the USA, over the period 1988–1992, total releases of seventeen selected toxic chemicals against the dollar value of shipments from the seven main industries emitting these chemicals. While shipments rose, toxic emissions dropped off markedly. In fact, the aggregate emissions of these chemicals fell by 40 percent from 1988 to 1992. Changes in government regulation are not driving the reductions, as these emissions are legal. This chapter presents a theory of self-regulation in which this voluntary abatement can be explained by increases in the threat of federal and/or state regulation.

serve more strategic purposes, such as softening competition or preempting stricter government regulations. If self-regulation is more cost-effective than government regulation, firms might self-regulate even if doing so has no impact on the ultimate level of restraint required.

While corporate environmentalism is on the rise, it remains controversial.[3] Critics argue that self-regulation provides less environmental protection than does government regulation. The "Big Three" automakers' Vehicle Recycling Partnership is limited to creating labeling standards for plastic components, and falls well short of the German program of comprehensive automotive disassembly and reuse. Selective cutting in old-growth forests is more environmentally friendly than clear cutting, but many argue that such forests should not be cut at all. The "Responsible Care"® program (see box 3.1) initiated by the Chemical Manufacturers Association (CMA) may be used as a rationale for refusing to adopt more stringent environmental practices; according to Barnard (1990, p. 5), at least one CMA member – Union Carbide – has already done just that. Such considerations raise questions about how social welfare is affected when self-regulation preempts government action. Indeed, these questions are the primary motivation for the model we develop. Welfare concerns are likely to become increasingly important, since as Walley and Whitehead (1994) point out, "win–win" situations – in which pollution prevention raises both corporate profits and consumer well-being – are increasingly difficult to find.[4] One of the striking features of the model in this chapter is the strong welfare analysis that emerges.

Box 3.1 Responsible Care®

In 1984 the worst industrial accident in history killed 2,500 people and injured 200,000 more when methyl isocyanate gas leaked from a Union Carbide storage tank in Bhopal, India. In 1985 the Canadian Chemical Producers Association established a program called "Responsible Care"® designed to improve the industry's environmental and safety performance, and to communicate the industry's improvements to the public. The US Chemical Manufacturers Association (CMA) and the

---

[3] For a survey of corporate environmental programs, see Smart (1992). The idea that "pollution prevention pays" has been widely promoted in the popular and trade press. That firms may engage in the production of "green" products to serve a high-margin market niche and that a reputation for cleanliness may ease the burden of plant location, for example, can be seen in Cairncross (1992).

[4] Many of the opportunities for painless Pareto-improvements have already been implemented. For example, 3M's "Pollution Prevention Pays" program has reduced the company's emissions by over 1 billion pounds since 1975, and has saved 3M roughly $500 million in the process. However, others argue that many recent corporate environmental initiatives have had negative effects on company profits, suggesting that most companies now face sharply rising costs should cleanup standards be further increased.

British Chemical Industries Association followed with similar programs in 1989. According to Frank Whiteley, President of the Chemical Industries Association (CIA), these initiatives were needed to "help regain society's trust" (Simmons and Wynne 1993, p. 201). Another key objective, according to industry observers, was "limiting state intervention to a level that is acceptable to the industry" (Simmons and Wynne 1993, p. 205).

Participants in the CIA's Responsible Care® program agree to adhere to a set of six guiding principles, all of which aim to ensure that the companies "present an acceptably high level of protection for the health and safety of employees, customers, the public and the environment" (Simmons and Wynne 1993, p. 209). The entire CIA membership of roughly 200 companies has signed onto the program, and new firms must accept its principles if they wish to join the association. In the USA, the industry's self-regulatory activities have become easier for the public to monitor since the creation of the Toxic Release Inventory (TRI), mandated under the Emergency Planning and Right-to-Know Act, Title III of the Superfund Amendments and Reauthorization Act (SARA Title III). In the UK, however, "[t]he industry is very cautious about the types of data that it makes available" (Simmons and Wynne 1993, p. 213). According to outside observers, "[a]t best, the CIA's performance index can be seen as a transitional step toward a much fuller form of disclosure" (Simmons and Wynne 1993, p. 213).

Source: Simmons and Wynne (1993).

We model self-regulation and social welfare in a three-stage game where quantity-setting oligopolists face the possibility of stricter pollution abatement regulations. Following Becker (1983), we model these regulations as arising from a political influence game between consumers and firms, with consumers favoring stricter abatement regulations than do firms.[5] Following Stigler (1971) and Peltzman (1976), we assume that it is costly for interested parties to organize themselves to enter the political process and to influence policymakers once involved in the political process. In the

---

[5] One could also devise a somewhat more complex model that subdivides consumers into groups according to their relative disutilities for price increases and for environmental degradation. Because all consumer groups will on balance align with either the firms (lobbying for weaker regulations) or environmentalists (lobbying for stronger regulations), including additional consumer groups would complicate the modeling but seems unlikely to generate substantial new insights.

first stage of our game, symmetric firms choose (possibly zero) levels of voluntary abatement. In the second stage, identical consumers observe the voluntary abatement activity and determine whether to enter the influence game; if they do so, they and the firms exert pressure on government for their desired level of regulations, and an abatement policy is determined. In the third stage, firms play a Cournot production game.

As we discussed in chapter 2, the model of the political influence game we use here is quite abstract and general. It treats the political process as a "black box" whose key characteristic is that it is directly responsive to the influence activities of both firms and consumers. It thus yields results that are robust to variations in the specific structure of the legislative and regulatory process, encompassing both in one parsimonious representation. In later chapters, as we delve into the details of the implementation and enforcement of regulations, we will examine more narrowly specified models of regulatory behavior.

From a methodological viewpoint, this chapter extends the economic theory of regulation in two directions.[6] First, by adding an initial stage of voluntary actions by firms, we allow for the possibility of strategic self-regulation that preempts government action. As a result, we obtain some striking parallels and contrasts with the standard industrial organization literature, which typically takes regulation as either exogenously fixed or as a set of controls to be optimized. Second, by modeling explicitly the dimension of product quality (in this case, pollution abatement), we can address directly issues of regulatory efficiency discussed only informally by Becker.

The key positive implication of this model is that an increased threat of government regulation induces firms to voluntarily reduce pollution emissions. We examine empirically the massive cuts in US toxic chemical releases since 1988 (illustrated in figure 3.1), and the role of potential regulatory entry in stimulating these cuts. We investigate state-level variation in the threat of regulation using a panel data on releases of toxic chemicals over the period from 1988 to 1992. Our most significant finding is that states with higher initial levels of toxic emissions and larger environmental group membership reduced toxic emissions more rapidly. In this situation, firms have relatively low marginal abatement costs, consumers value abatement highly, and consumer organizing costs are low. Since the threat of

---

[6] Although there is a vast literature on the economics of regulation, we take the "economic theory of regulation" to mean the strand of the literature associated with the work of Stigler (1971), Peltzman (1976), and Becker (1983).

mandatory regulation is high while the marginal cost of self-regulation is relatively low, it makes good sense for firms to engage in voluntary emissions reductions.

In addition to the foregoing positive predictions and empirical results, we also derive some striking normative results. We show that interest group rivalry (the influence game) produces weaker pollution regulation than is socially optimal. Nevertheless, we show that when the costs of influencing policy are included, *if* voluntary abatement occurs then both firms and consumers are better off than they would have been under the status quo. More importantly, both firms and consumers are better off than they would have been had they engaged in the influence game, starting from the status quo point (box 3.2).

This chapter has two implications for public policy. First, it lends support to an antitrust policy allowing industries to coordinate on voluntary abatement strategies, since such coordination increases beneficial self-regulation. Second, it raises questions about government financing of consumer intervention into the political process: if consumer involvement becomes *too* easy, firms may eschew voluntary abatement, with the result that both they and consumers are worse off than when consumer involvement was difficult (box 3.2).

Before proceeding, we briefly contrast this chapter with related work in the literature.[7] Despite the ubiquity of self-regulation, the phenomenon has received relatively little attention from economists. There have been several interesting case studies and institutional analyses,[8] and a few papers that apply a vertical product differentiation framework to model the idea that firms voluntarily reduce pollution to attract "green" consumers.[9] A

---

[7] It is important to note that our chapter differs sharply from some earlier work on corporate strategy in the regulatory arena. For example, that firms may benefit from regulation if it raises marginal cost more than average cost, thereby increasing firms' producer surplus, can be seen in Maloney and McCormick (1982). In our model, marginal costs do not change with output, so firms do not have the Maloney–McCormick motive for seeking regulation. Indeed, in our model, firms self-regulate only to avoid government regulation. In addition, because we assume an oligopoly structure with no entry, firms have no incentive to lobby for regulation in order to increase entry barriers.

[8] For example, see Caves and Roberts (1975), Abolafia (1985), Ayres and Braithwaite (1992), and Pirrong (1995).

[9] See Arora and Gangopadhyay (1995), for a presentation of a model where firms voluntarily reduce emissions of pollutants to attract "green" consumers. A similar analysis, which shows that voluntary reductions generally cannot achieve the socially optimal level of abatement, can be seen in Bagnoli and Watts (2003). For a model with minimum quality standards that shows that high-quality firms may have incentives to act strategically to shape future regulations, see chapter 4.

Box 3.2   McDonald's waste reduction action plan

In the late 1980s the McDonald's corporation came under fire for the amount of post-consumer waste its product packaging created each day. In order to keep its pre-made products warm, McDonald's used a Styrofoam packaging system referred to as a "clamshell." This packaging system came under particular attack from environmental critics when information about the damaging effects of CFC on the ozone layer were discovered (CFCs were used in the production of the clamshell packaging system). In 1990, McDonald's USA formed a task force with the Environmental Defense Fund (EDF) to:

- Establish ways to reduce, reuse and recycle materials used and wastes generated by the McDonald's system;
- Provide recommendations consistent with McDonald's business practices and future growth; and
- Create a model approach to waste reduction for other companies to emulate.

In 1991 McDonald's announced a Comprehensive Waste Reduction Action Plan (CWRAP) aimed at reducing the amount of solid waste the company generated. At the same time the company announced its decision to abandon the clamshell system. The system was replaced by light cardboard box packaging and wax paper packaging.

Updated annually the CWRAP now contains "over 100 initiatives, pilot projects and tests to reduce solid waste in all aspects of its business." McDonald's is heavily involved in recycling and reuse of both its packaging and shipping products, and also uses recycled construction and remodeling materials.

Source: McDonald's corporate web site, www.McDonalds.com.

---

number of papers – including Arora and Cason (1995, 1996), Karamanos (1999), Khanna and Damon (1999), and Videras and Alberini (2000) – study empirically which types of firms are most likely to participate in government programs aimed at voluntary abatement. We discuss the results of these studies in more detail in chapter 9.

In a more strategic vein, Braeutigam and Quirk (1984) and Lyon (1991) analyze models where a regulated firm voluntarily reduces its price to avoid a rate review that would cut rates even further. Similarly, Glazer and McMillan (1992) show that the threat of price regulation may induce a monopolist to price below the unregulated monopoly level. Our analysis is related to these earlier strategic analyses, but is richer in several important respects. We consider an oligopolistic industry in which consumers have both price and non-price (e.g. pollution) concerns. We model explicitly the incentives of interest groups (producers and consumers) to expend resources on lobbying for their preferred policies, and allow the stringency of regulations to be determined endogenously. We complement our theoretical analysis with empirical evidence from a unique panel dataset that provides support for our theoretical predictions. Finally, we assess the social welfare implications of regulatory preemption, and address policy questions about appropriate antitrust treatment of self-regulation and about government subsidy of consumer intervention in the political process.

Our results are also related to the literature on entry deterrence.[10] In a sense, our oligopoly invests in pollution control to deter "entry" by consumers to the influence game. Unlike standard entry deterrence models, however, here the "fat cat" strategy – under which investment raises the rival's welfare in the event entry occurs – is effective in preempting entry.[11] The reason is that in ordinary deterrence games staying out yields the potential entrant a fixed reservation level of profits. Here, in contrast, consumers' utility of staying out of the influence game rises as firms invest. Welfare-enhancing preemption is possible because as voluntary abatement increases, consumers' utility of staying out rises faster than the utility of entering.[12]

The remainder of the chapter is organized as follows. Section 2 presents the model, while section 3 develops two key propositions about the conduct of firms and of consumers. Section 4 establishes welfare results and explores policy implications. Section 5 examines our positive hypotheses using cross-sectional data on the fifty US states. Section 6 provides a non-technical summary of the analysis, while section 7 concludes and discusses policy implications. All proofs are presented in the appendix (p. 82).

---

[10] For a good overview, see Tirole (1989).

[11] Tirole (1989), in section 3 of chapter 8, presents a taxonomy of business strategies based upon animal analogies such as the "fat cat effect" and the "puppy dog ploy."

[12] Note also that, unlike Gilbert and Vives (1986) or Donnenfeld and Weber (1995), our oligopolists never have an incentive to engage in excessive entry deterrence, since individual firms do not obtain private benefits from voluntary abatement.

2 THE MODEL

In this section we present a three-stage model of voluntary pollution control. For simplicity, we assume symmetric firms and we do not discount payoffs over time. The sequence of moves in the model is as follows. First, firms choose a level (possibly zero) of voluntary pollution control that is assumed to be binding. For example, it could be built into the production technology, or firms could sell a conservation easement to an environmental group (e.g. the group buys the right to dictate a production technology to the firms, such as selective rather than clear-cut logging), or irrevocably link their image to voluntary abatement through advertising. Second, firms and consumers (who receive utility from the good but disutility from pollution) engage in interest group rivalry for the purpose of influencing pollution control policy. Third, after pollution control policy has been determined, firms produce and sell output in a Cournot oligopoly. We focus on the case in which consumers will successfully lobby for new regulations if the firms take no voluntary action, since there is no other motive for voluntary action in the model. As is standard in multistage games, subgame perfection is achieved by solving the model in reverse chronological order, hence the exposition below is presented from a backward-induction perspective.

2.1 Stage 3: output market equilibrium

In the last stage of the game, N^f identical firms engage in Cournot-style quantity rivalry in an industry featuring pollution externalities.[13] Firm i chooses an output level q_i, and the firms face industry demand curve $P(Q)$, where $Q = \sum_i q_i$; we will also use the notation $Q_{-i} = \sum_{j \neq i} q_j$. Firms install a pollution control input, in the amount Z, which is the sum of a voluntary choice Z^V from stage 1 and mandatory control level Z^M from stage 2 of the game.[14] Firms are then confronted with per-unit output cost $c(Z)$ that is constant with regard to output, and a fixed capital cost $k(Z)$, both of which are increasing and convex in Z. In order to focus on the

---

[13] By assuming homogeneous products, we in effect assume that consumers cannot observe the emissions of an individual firm, though they may be able to observe aggregate environmental damage (e.g. air quality in the Los Angeles basin or water quality in the Great Lakes).

[14] Because the firms are symmetric, the level of Z determined in stages 1 and 2 of the game is the same for all firms and we treat it as a scalar; we avoid vector notation for notational simplicity.

strategic aspects of voluntary abatement, we assume that the costs of self-regulation and government regulation are equal, and are only a function of Z.[15] Given Q_{-i}, firm i's problem is to

$$\max_{q_i} [P(Q_{-i} + q_i) - c(Z)]q_i - k(Z). \tag{3.1}$$

In the symmetric Cournot–Nash equilibrium,[16] firms have equal outputs, defined by

$$q_i^* = -\frac{[P(Q^*) - c(Z)]}{P'(Q^*)}, \tag{3.2}$$

aggregate quantity traded is $Q^* = N^f q_i^*$, and the market clearing price is $P(Q^*)$. Henceforth we shall drop the subscript "i," as in equilibrium all firms are identical. There should thus be no confusion in proceeding to use subscripts to indicate derivatives. Equilibrium earnings per firm, given Q^*, are $\pi^N(Z)$, where the superscript "N" indicates no influence costs are included at this stage. Note that our convexity assumptions on costs imply

$$\pi_Z^N = -c_z q^* - k_z < 0 \text{ and } \pi_{zz}^N = -c_{zz}q^* - k_{zz} < 0.$$

2.2   Stage 2: influence game

Following Becker (1983) we model pollution control policy as the outcome of rival "influence inputs" being transformed through political institutions. In our model there are two interest groups: one is made up of the N^f firms whose costs are increased by additional pollution control restraints, while the other is made up of N^c consumers who purchase the good produced by the firms and who also have disutility over pollution emitted by the firms. All individuals and firms allocate influence inputs non-cooperatively.[17] Firms, if they enter the influence game, always attempt to influence policymakers to reduce mandatory pollution control (the per-firm resources they allocate for this purpose are referred to by the variable l).[18] While consumers care about their consumer surplus from buying the good

---

[15] Obviously self-regulation looks even better if it is cheaper than government regulation.

[16] We assume the existence of a unique pure-strategy equilibrium. For conditions guaranteeing that such an equilibrium exists, and further references on the subject, see Tirole (1989, pp. 224–226).

[17] While environmental groups and trade associations may coordinate the collection of funds from members, we emphasize the fact that the financial contributions of members are made individually and on a non-cooperative basis.

[18] Because firms are symmetric and there is no possibility of entry, it is not profitable to lobby for stricter regulations as a means of raising rivals' costs.

produced by firms, and thus oppose higher prices, they also have disutility over pollution. Thus it is possible for firms to choose a level of voluntary abatement sufficiently high that consumers would actually prefer less than the voluntary level of pollution control. This is never profitable for firms, however, so consumers – if they enter the political process – always allocate resources (in the amount of m per person) to influence policymakers to choose more pollution control.

Following Stigler (1971) and Peltzman, (1976), we assume that consumers wishing to influence the process of policy formation must bear in the aggregate a fixed cost $F(N^c)$; each of the identical consumers then bears a cost $f(N^c) = F(N^c)/N^c$ if the consumer group enters the influence game. In the present context, individuals must inform themselves of the implications of pollution control for their well-being,[19] and of the efficacy of various feasible policy remedies. Individuals of similar interests must then coordinate on a mutual lobbying strategy. We will refer to these various costs collectively as "organizing costs." Firms face similar tasks, but their organizing costs are typically less than those of consumers, since assessing the costs of regulation to the firm is usually much easier than assessing the health and aesthetic benefits to consumers, and the number of firms in an industry is typically very small relative to the number of consumers. Without loss of generality, then, we normalize firms' cost of organizing to zero.

Since the N^f firms are identical, aggregate firm resources allocated to political pressure are $L = N^f l$. Similarly, the N^c consumers devote $M = N^c m$ aggregate resources to pressure activities if they choose to incur the fixed cost of entering the political process. We represent the influence process through a function $Z^M(M, L)$ which gives the mandatory abatement level as a function of influence inputs; when the firm undertakes voluntary abatement, total abatement is then $Z(M, L) = Z^V + Z^M(M, L)$.[20] We assume that $Z_M > 0$, $Z_L < 0$, $Z_{MM} < 0$, and $Z_{LL} > 0$. (We will often suppress the dependence of Z on influence for notational ease.)

Consider a representative firm's optimization problem in the influence game. Firm i, given the influence choices of the other parties (M by

---

[19] These costs are often very high due to the incomplete state of scientific knowledge and its inaccessibility to those who are not experts in the relevant fields.

[20] The additive form of $Z(M, L)$ is consistent with the application of a regulatory design standard requiring all firms to utilize a prescribed abatement process regardless of their existing emissions levels. As will be seen in Proposition 2 (p. 61), this gives oligopolistic firms an incentive to free-ride on industrywide self-regulatory efforts, since they can gain a cost advantage by refusing to take voluntary abatement measures.

consumers, L_{-i} by the other firms), must choose influence input l to maximize:

$$\pi^N(Z^V + Z^M[M, L_{-i} + l]) - l. \tag{3.3}$$

A firm's optimal choice of l is given by the following equation:

$$\pi_Z^N Z_l = 1. \tag{3.4}$$

Consumers are utility maximizers, and choose their per-person lobbying expenditures m independently. Utility falls as the price of the good rises and as the total amount of pollution in the environment increases. Since firms are symmetric, we let $d = f(Z, q)$ be the total environmental degradation caused by an individual firm, and $D = D(N^f, Z, q)$ be the total amount of degradation. Recognizing that q^* is chosen by firms in stage 3 and that the number of firms is fixed, we suppress the dependence of D on q and N^f, and the total welfare of a consumer is then

$$U^N(P(Z), D(Z)) - m. \tag{3.5}$$

A consumer's optimal choice of m is given by the following equation:

$$U_Z^N Z_m = 1, \tag{3.6}$$

where we use the shorthand notation $U^N(Z) \equiv U^N(P(Z), D(Z))$. We assume that $U_{ZZ}^N < 0$; note that U_Z^N is initially positive, but declines and so can become negative.

Equations (3.4) and (3.6) generate reaction functions $l^*(m, Z^V)$ and $m^*(l, Z^V)$ for firms and consumers, respectively, in the influence game. We shall assume that $Z_{ML} \cong 0$, which ensures that the reaction functions are upward sloping, as illustrated in figure 3.2, indicating that lobbying expenditures are strategic complements. We also assume that regulation never mandates an increase in pollution; as a result, firms will curtail their expenditures on influence when $Z^M(M, L)$ reaches zero. This effect is shown in figure 3.2 for the case where firm and consumer pressure is equally effective: firms' reaction curves are the upper envelope of the 45-degree line and the $l^*(m, Z^V)$ function that would apply if regulations could force firms to become dirtier. Equilibrium levels of pressure are $l^e(Z^V) \equiv l^*(m^e, Z^V)$ and $m^e(Z^V) \equiv m^*(l^e, Z^V)$.

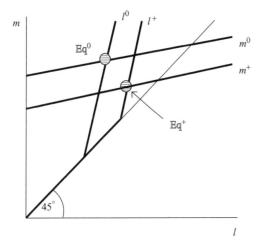

Figure 3.2 Firm (l) and consumer (m) reaction functions in the influence game

2.3 Stage 1: voluntary pollution control

Prior to the interest group rivalry process that generates pollution control policy, firms can choose a level (possibly zero) of voluntary pollution control. Let $Z(Z^V) \equiv Z^V + Z^M(Z^V)$ and assume that $Z(0) > 0$, which avoids the uninteresting case in which the external costs of pollution to consumers are too small to generate any legislative requirements for pollution control. Firms thus choose Z^V to maximize the following equilibrium profit function:

$$\pi^I(Z^V) = \pi^N(Z(Z^V)) - l^e(Z^V), \tag{3.7}$$

where the superscript I indicates that profits are measured net of influence costs. We also denote consumer utility, net of influence costs, by $U^I(Z^V) = U^N(Z(Z^V)) - m^e(Z^V)$.

A crucial effect of voluntary abatement is to change the outcome of the influence game. It is straightforward to establish how the players' reaction curves shift as Z^V rises. Totally differentiating (3.4) and (3.6) and gathering terms shows that $dl^*/dZ^V > 0$ and $dm^*/dZ^V < 0$. Thus, self-regulation makes the firms "tough" in the influence game while also making consumers "soft."[21] Figure 3.2 illustrates the shifts in consumer and

---

[21] For further discussion of the terms "tough" and "soft" in multistage commitment games, see Tirole (1989, p. 327).

firm reaction functions in response to an increase in voluntary abatement. Functions superscripted with a 0 are reaction functions when the level of voluntary abatement is zero, while those superscripted with a + are reaction functions resulting from a positive level of voluntary abatement. With positive voluntary abatement, a consumer's reaction function shifts downward, reflecting a reduced marginal value of further emissions control. At the same time, a firm's reaction function shifts outward, reflecting a higher marginal cost of further control. Note, however, that the lower portion of the firm's reaction curve does not shift. This reflects the constraint that firms are not allowed to become "dirtier," so they just match consumer expenditures on influence once the level of mandatory abatement falls to zero.

3 CONDUCT OF FIRMS AND CONSUMERS

In this section, we analyze the behavior of firms and consumers in the model presented above. We are particularly interested in the question of when preemption via voluntary abatement is profitable. US antitrust law makes illegal all collusive attempts to restrict sales quantity or raise price. To the best of our knowledge, however, these laws do not preclude firms from cooperating to increase their levels of voluntary pollution abatement.[22] In fact, firms often use trade associations to self-regulate via uniform product and production standards; for example, a survey of firms that emit toxic pollutants in the late 1990s found that companies were more likely to participate in pollution programs sponsored by the firm's trade association.[23] Proposition 1 establishes conditions under which firms' profits can be enhanced by cooperative voluntary pollution abatement that preempts mandatory controls.

Proposition 1: *There exists a range of consumer fixed costs of organizing on which a perfectly collusive oligopoly chooses a positive level of voluntary abatement and thereby preempts consumer intervention in the regulatory*

---

[22] See Bittlingmayer (1987) for a discussion of a case in which automobile manufacturers were charged with colluding to reduce R&D expenditures on pollution abatement technologies. We discuss this case further in section 4.

[23] In surveying a group of firms, some of which participated and some of which declined to participate in the EPA's voluntary "33/50" program, Clark (1996) notes that "One of the most significant findings of our study was the identification of a potentially more positive response from some companies for a pollution prevention program sponsored by the company's trade association."

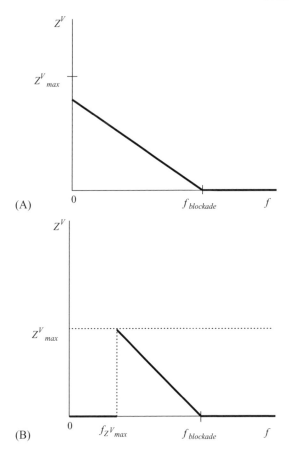

Figure 3.3 Optimal voluntary abatement Z^V
A   If preemption is profitable even when consumer fixed costs f are zero
B   If preemption is unprofitable when consumer fixed costs f are zero

process. Let $[f_{Z^V max}, f_{blockade}]$ be this range. Then $f_{Z^V_{max}} \geq 0$, and for $f_{Z^V_{max}} < f(N^c) < f_{blockade}$ the firm's choice of Z^V is decreasing in $f(N^c)$; for $f(N^c) > f_{blockade}$, consumer intervention is "blockaded," i.e. preempted with $Z^V = 0$.

The basic intuition of the proposition is simple: political costs drive a wedge between the consumer utility of voluntary abatement and mandatory abatement, and firms can take advantage of this wedge to preempt regulation. The relationship between the industry's optimal choice of Z^V and the level of fixed costs faced by consumers is illustrated in figures 3.3A and 3.3B. Z^V_{max} is the maximum voluntary abatement level for which successful preemption is more profitable than choosing $Z^V = 0$ and fighting the influence game. There is a corresponding level of consumer fixed costs such that Z_{max}^V is just sufficient to preempt; we denote this level by $f_{Z_{max}^V}$. For organizing costs above $f_{Z_{max}^V}$, preemption is always profitable, and the requisite level of voluntary abatement declines with f. Of course, if fixed costs are large enough, i.e. $f \geq f_{blockade}$, consumers will decide not to lobby even if $Z^V = 0$; in this case we say that entry is blockaded.

Whether $f_{Z_{max}^V} > 0$ is ambiguous in general. Figure 3.3A and 3.3B represent two possible patterns for low levels of consumer fixed organizing costs.[24] In figure 3.3A, the bold line depicts voluntary abatement for the case when $f_{Z_{max}^V} \leq 0$, in which case the level of voluntary abatement declines monotonically from the level it takes on when $f(N^C) = 0$. In figure 3.3B, $f_{Z_{max}^V} > 0$, so it is unprofitable to preempt when consumer fixed costs are zero; in this case the bold line shows that no voluntary abatement is observed unless $f > f_{Z_{max}^V}$. In this latter case, there is a sharp drop in voluntary abatement if consumer fixed costs fall below $f_{Z_{max}^V}$.

It is important to emphasize that, in general, consumer fixed costs are not necessary for preemption to occur. Whether preemption is profitable at $f(N^c) = 0$ (and hence which of the foregoing cases applies) depends on the magnitude of equilibrium consumer influence costs $m^e(Z^V)$: if these are high enough then preemption can be profitable even if consumers' fixed organizing costs are zero. These influence costs, in turn, depend on the curvature of the profit and utility functions. Consumer expenditures on influence tend to be high when U_Z is large and/or U_{ZZ} is small, since then the marginal consumer benefit of further abatement is high and declines slowly. Consumer lobbying costs also tend to be high when π_z and/or π_{zz} is large, since in this case abatement rapidly becomes very costly to the firms, and they will fight hard to avoid mandatory abatement. In any event, as long as organizing costs are above $f_{Z_{max}^V}$, voluntary abatement declines with f.

While firms may be able to preempt collusively, it is not obvious that preemption is possible when firms must select voluntary abatement levels non-cooperatively. Proposition 2 addresses this issue. While a continuum of asymmetric preemption equilibria exist, we choose to focus on symmetric equilibria for simplicity and clarity.[25]

---

[24] Numerical examples show that either case can easily occur.

[25] Given the multiplicity of Nash equilibria in the model, there is obvious interest in refinements of equilibrium that can yield more precise predictions regarding which equilibria are most likely to emerge in practice. Dawson and Segerson (2002) address this issue by applying the concept of self-enforcing agreement that has been used in the literatures on

Proposition 2: *The threat of regulation can be preempted by a non-cooperative oligopoly for certain levels of consumer-organizing costs. Specifically, there exists a symmetric Nash equilibrium with preemption for* $f(N^c) \in [f_{Z_{NC}^V}, f_{blockade}]$, *where* $f_{Z_{NC}^V} > f_{Z_{max}^V}$.

When the firms cannot coordinate on voluntary abatement, free-riding occurs. At the collusive level of voluntary abatement, any given firm prefers to eschew voluntary abatement and allow the influence game to occur. By so doing, it enjoys at no cost the reduced level of mandatory abatement made possible by its rivals' voluntary abatement activities. In addition, it gains a cost advantage relative to its rivals because it does not undertake the (costly) voluntary action. As a result, the collusive level of voluntary abatement cannot be sustained as a non-cooperative equilibrium. Nevertheless, the threat of mandatory abatement in the second stage of the game will still support an equilibrium with some degree of non-cooperative preemption. The key point is that for small enough voluntary abatement levels, firm i is willing to match or exceed the levels undertaken by the other firms, since its action is pivotal to preempting regulation. Thus preemption will still occur for large consumer fixed costs, but there are some lower levels of $f(N^c)$ for which preemption would have occurred collusively but not non-cooperatively, i.e. $f_{Z_{NC}^V} > f_{Z_{max}^V}$.

Our results in Proposition 2 contrast sharply with those of Gilbert and Vives (1986) and Donnenfeld and Weber (1995), who find that oligopolies have incentives to provide excessive levels of output or quality when engaging in entry deterrence. The key difference is that in those models, firms derive private benefits from contributing to the "public good" of entry deterrence, while in our model contributions carry private costs but not private benefits.

One might think that as the number of firms, N^f, increases, growing free-rider problems would make preemption more difficult. In our model, however, whether preemption occurs depends upon two factors: (1) the firms' ability to coordinate sufficient voluntary abatement ("supply"), and (2) the level of voluntary abatement required to preempt consumer entry into the political process ("demand"). The "supply" of preemption falls

cartel stability and international environmental agreements (see Carraro and Siniscalco 1993 for the latter application). They argue that this "refinement" implies that only a subset of firms will undertake abatement, while the other firms free-ride completely. The firms that take action are strictly worse off than the free-riders, though they are no worse off than if they did nothing and allowed mandatory regulations to be passed. The theory gives no insight into which firms will volunteer to improve the lot of their rivals in the industry. This is an area in which further theoretical work is likely to yield additional valuable insights.

with N^f, since free-rider problems plainly worsen. The "demand" for pre-emption, however, depends on the mandatory abatement level determined in the influence game, which is a function of aggregate lobbying activity, and may either rise or fall with the number of firms. With respect to the firms' pressure activities, for example, Peltzman (1976) shows that firms' aggregate influence rises and eventually falls as the number of firms grows, but one cannot predict in general whether an additional group member strengthens or weakens the group's ability to apply political pressure. Thus, there is no theoretical presumption that voluntary abatement is more likely in industries with only a handful of producers. Interestingly, the empirical work of Arora and Cason (1995) finds that voluntary abatement is actually more likely to occur in unconcentrated industries.

To sum up, the results of this section identify conditions under which firms can profitably preempt, taking advantage of the wedge that lobbying and organization costs drive between voluntary and mandatory abatement. Lobbying costs alone may not be enough to support preemption, and thus a strictly positive level of fixed organizing costs may be required for preemption to be profitable. In either case, once preemption becomes profitable, the equilibrium level of voluntary abatement declines monotonically with consumer organizing costs. The threshold level of consumer organizing costs at which preemption becomes profitable is higher when firms act non-cooperatively than when they coordinate on voluntary abatement (box 3.3).

4   WELFARE IMPLICATIONS

In this section, we assess welfare from two perspectives. First, we establish a benchmark for the socially optimal amount of pollution control and compare it against the outcome of the influence game; we then examine whether self-regulation results in a move toward the social optimum. Second, we examine the more limited, but perhaps more important, question of whether voluntary pollution control Pareto-dominates the outcome of the influence process when there is no voluntary abatement.

A welfare maximizing social regulator would choose Z to maximize

$$N^f \pi^N(Z) + N^c U(Z) \qquad (3.8)$$

yielding

$$\frac{\pi_Z^N}{U_Z} = -\frac{N^c}{N^f}. \qquad (3.9)$$

Box 3.3   Rechargeable Battery Recycling Corporation

"In 1994 the manufacturers of rechargeable batteries and of products that use those batteries established the Rechargeable Battery Recycling Corporation (RBRC) to manage an industry-wide recycling program. This program was established because eight states had already passed laws requiring take-back of Ni-Cd batteries and others were considering doing so. To avoid having to comply with different laws in different states, the industry set up the RBRC, a non-profit corporation to operate the battery take-back and recycling program... The RBRC licenses battery manufacturers to place its seal on the battery cells it produces indicating that the batteries can and should be recycled through the RBRC program at the end of their useful lives. The program charges participating manufacturers a licensing fee based on the weight of the battery cell and the cell type... The RBRC estimates that over 90 percent of the rechargeable Ni-Cd batteries sold in the United States are included in the program. More than 320 companies are paying to apply the RBRC seal to their batteries... Battery returns and recycling have not grown in line with RBRC's expectations. In a 1998 report, RBRC projected that it would recycle over 8 million pounds of Ni-Cd batteries in 2000 and that the rechargeable battery recycling rate for the United States and Canada would increase from 15 percent, its level in the mid-1990s, to 35 percent by 2000. In fact, RBRC reports that it collected approximately 2.4 million pounds of Ni-Cd batteries to be recycled in 2000 and just over 2.5 million pounds in 2001."

Source: Palmer and Walls (2002).

On the other hand, (3.4) and (3.6) imply that the equilibrium of the influence game is characterized by[26]

$$\frac{\pi_Z^N}{U_Z} = -\frac{Z_m}{Z_l}. \tag{3.10}$$

The social optimum, given by (3.9), differs in two ways from the equilibrium of the influence game. First, the welfare maximum weights firms and consumers equally. As a result, (3.9) does not include the relative impact

---

[26] Recall that $Z_l < 0$, so the right-hand side of (3.10) is negative.

of lobbying expenditures, unlike the equilibrium result shown in (3.10). Because the effectiveness of lobbying is subject to diminishing returns, the group that spends more on lobbying will be worse off in the influence game than in the welfare maximum. Second, the welfare maximum reflects the relative number of firms and consumers (as can be seen in the right-hand side of (3.9)), but the equilibrium result does not.[27] The reason for the second difference is that the influence game reflects our assumption that all players make their influence decisions non-cooperatively. Thus, each consumer or firm equates the last dollar of lobbying expenditures to her own individual marginal benefit from a change in the level of abatement. The effects of that marginal expenditure on other parties are ignored, however, so free-rider effects distort the equilibrium away from the welfare maximum. Free-rider problems increase with the number of members in an interest group, so relative to the welfare maximum, the influence game is biased toward the group with the smaller number of members.

It is important to note that both effects – diminishing returns to lobbying and free-rider problems – work against consumer interests. We focus on the case where without voluntary abatement consumer involvement leads to some pollution regulation, i.e. consumers in the aggregate devote more resources to lobbying than do firms. Because of diminishing returns to lobbying, the influence game is worse for consumers than is the welfare maximum. In addition, we assume there are more consumers than firms, so consumers face worse free-rider problems, further reducing consumer welfare in the influence game. We state the foregoing observations as Proposition 3.[28]

Proposition 3: *If an industry has more consumers than firms, and will in equilibrium face some regulatory requirements for pollution control, the political influence game generates less abatement than is socially optimal.*

It is indeterminate in general whether self-regulation moves the level of pollution control closer to the socially optimal level. Proposition 3 guarantees the existence of a preemptive level of abatement if $f(N^c)$ is large enough. As $f(N^c)$ tends toward $f_{blockade}$, this preemptive level goes to zero,

---

[27] Of course, the number of firms and consumers still affects the equilibrium of the influence game through the left-hand side of (3.10), as discussed above.

[28] In a model of multiple interest groups, one might wonder if environmentalists could impose regulations more stringent than socially optimal. This is unlikely in our interest group model, however. Assuming there are more environmentalists than corporations, environmentalists would still suffer greater free-rider problems than firms. Furthermore, consumers who do not care about the environment would side with firms, strengthening firms in the influence game. Thus, the conditions that give rise to Proposition 3 would continue to hold.

and consequently will be *lower* than the total abatement that would result from the influence game alone. Conversely, when $f(N^c)$ is low, firms may self-regulate to a level beyond what would result from the influence game in order to economize on lobbying costs.

A more meaningful question, however, is whether voluntary abatement improves welfare beyond what it would have been with no voluntary abatement. In order to address this question, we first establish a lemma that will provide a sufficient condition for the welfare effects of self-regulation to be positive. The key requirement is that positive or negative "complementaries" between the influence inputs of the two groups (as measured by the magnitude of Z_{ml}) are not too great. As Becker (1983, p. 376) points out, there is no *a priori* rationale for either a positive or negative sign on these complementarities, and we take no position as to their sign, simply considering limits on their magnitude.

Lemma 1: *There exists $\varepsilon > 0$ such that if $|Z_{ml}| < \varepsilon \ \forall(m, l)$, then as Z^V increases, $Z(Z^V)$ rises, $m^e(Z^V)$ falls, and $l^e(Z^V)$ rises.*

As we noted in section 2, voluntary abatement shifts the reaction curves of consumers and firms in the influence game, making consumers "soft" and firms "tough." The lemma provides a simple sufficient condition under which the direct effects of voluntary abatement on each interest group's lobbying expenditures (holding the rival's expenditures constant) are greater than the strategic effects (mediated through a change in the rival's expenditures). When the conditions of the lemma hold, it is straightforward to show that voluntary abatement raises consumer welfare, relative to the case where firms undertake no voluntary abatement (Proposition 4).

Proposition 4: *If preemption occurs, and the conditions of the lemma hold, then both consumer welfare and profits are increased, relative to their levels were government regulation imposed in the absence of voluntary abatement.*

If the industry chooses to preempt, then preemption must be profitable. It is less obvious that consumers are better off; it is not enough simply to show that consumers are better off at $Z = Z^V$ than at $Z = 0$. It is necessary to establish that consumers are better off than they would have been if no voluntary abatement had taken place and they had lobbied for standards $Z(0)$ that might have been stricter than Z^V. The argument proceeds in two steps. First, observe that as long as consumers enter the influence game, they are always better off when firms have engaged in voluntary abatement. This is so because total abatement increases with Z^V and consumers' lobbying expenditures decrease with Z^V, as shown in the lemma. Together the two effects must raise consumer welfare. Second, observe that if the firm preempts, it chooses a voluntary abatement level Z^V such that consumers are just indifferent between entering the influence game to obtain $Z(Z^V)$ and avoiding the influence game altogether. However, the preceding point shows that consumers prefer the influence game with $Z^V > 0$ to the influence game with $Z^V = 0$. Thus, if consumers allow themselves to be preempted by some $Z^V > 0$, they must be better off than they would have been had they fought to impose standards on an industry with no voluntary abatement.

Proposition 4 has two main policy implications. First, it supports allowing industry to coordinate on a choice of pollution limits, as long as the strategic effects of self-regulation on consumers' lobbying effectiveness is not too great. As Proposition 2 indicates, in some situations firms acting non-cooperatively will choose not to engage in voluntary abatement, but will do so if they can coordinate their actions. Proposition 4 shows that welfare will be enhanced by such coordination, as long as Z_{ml} is not too large. In this context, antitrust prosecution of "collusion" will reduce welfare. It is worth noting that as part of the "33/50" program, the EPA has convened several conferences on voluntary abatement that "promoted collaborative action and partnerships among the conference participants" (see Davies and Mazurek 1996).

Previous work suggests that cooperative pollution control activity by industry does not always have a benign effect. For example, Hackett (1995) finds that R&D by industry members to reduce the cost of more stringent pollution abatement technology may be motivated by the opportunity for successful innovating firms to lobby for more stringent industrial regulation and thus raise their rivals' costs. Anticipating this, industry members can organize a pollution control research joint venture to slow the pace of innovation in lower-cost pollution abatement technology. In fact, as discussed in detail by Bittlingmayer (1987), the Department of Justice successfully prosecuted a consent decree with the Automobile Manufacturer's Association for using a research joint venture formed in the 1950s to slow the adoption of more stringent pollution control devices on automobiles. Appropriate antitrust treatment must be sophisticated if it is to distinguish between these different motivations for cooperative pollution control activities by industry.

A second implication of our analysis is that government should not necessarily subsidize consumer involvement in the regulatory process. State regulatory agencies have increasingly taken to funding branches with names like "Division of Ratepayer Advocates" or "Office of Consumer Counsel" to intervene in utility rate cases. These actions appear designed to offset the high costs to consumers of intervening in the regulatory process, and indeed our analysis shows that such subsidies can shift the policy regime from one of no government regulation (because consumer organizing costs are too high) to one of preemption. Our results, however, also indicate that these efforts may unintentionally make consumers worse off by substituting government regulation for less costly industry self-regulation. The fixed cost of organizing implicitly commits consumers to an "acceptable" level of self-regulation beyond which they will not enter the political process. If organizing costs fall too low, this commitment may be eroded and firms may find preemption unprofitable; by Proposition 4 this may make consumers worse off.

Our analysis also identifies a linkage between the effects of antitrust and regulatory policy. Granting industry the right to collude on pollution control lowers the threshold of consumer organizing costs below which self-regulation becomes unprofitable. Thus, for any given $f(N^c)$, antitrust policy allowing such cooperation reduces the danger that regulatory subsidization of consumer political action will undermine self-regulation (box 3.4).

Box 3.4   Forest sustainability and certification

Since the United Nations Conference on Environment and Development (UNCED) was held in Rio de Janeiro in 1992, there has been increasing emphasis on the concept of "sustainable forestry." The World Wildlife Fund (WWF) and the Forest Stewardship Council (FSC) have created certification programs designed to assure concerned consumers that the wood products they buy were harvested in a sustainable manner. The FSC engages independent forest auditing firms to determine whether the on-the-ground forestry practices of a firm are consistent with FSC criteria. Certified wood products are then eligible for eco-labels that may lead to a price premium in the marketplace.

In 1999, the certification movement was given a boost when home improvement retailer Home Depot announced it would give preference to certified wood, and pledged to discontinue the purchase of wood from "endangered regions" by 2002.

The forest industry itself has in turn created its own certification systems, including the Sustainable Forestry Initiative (SFI) created by the American Forest and Paper Association, the Canadian Standards

Association in Canada, and the European Pan Forest Council (EPFC) in much of Europe. By 2002, 74 million acres of US forest, roughly 25 percent of the total, were certified, compared with 53 percent in Europe and 6 percent in developing countries.

With the proliferation of different certification systems has come considerable confusion. The organization Forest Certification Watch has emerged to help navigate the competing claims of these various organizations. In 2002, the non-profit Pinchot Institute for Conservation issued a report comparing the FSC and SFI standards, concluding that both programs "consistently rated high in the fundamental measures of relevance . . . The FSC program was generally regarded as more comprehensive . . . and . . . more relevant to the agencies' forest management objectives." However, the SFI had "clearer guidelines," a better assessment process, and was more "rigorous in requiring continuous improvement over time."

Overall, the industry-sponsored programs appear to have been designed to wrest some degree of control over certification away from non-governmental organizations. One advantage is that industry-led programs may allow for more cost-effective conservation activity. In addition, industry programs may give industry a seat at the table when government proposes new forest regulations. Major changes in forest policy have occurred in most developed countries in recent years, and the opportunity to have influence in the setting of policy could be extremely valuable to the paper and forest products industries.

Sources: Kiedens (2002a, 2002b); Mater, Sample, and Price (2002); Sedjo, Goetzl, and Steverson (1998); Sedjo and Swallow (2002); Sedjo (forthcoming).

5   TOXIC CHEMICAL RELEASES AND THE THREAT OF REGULATION

In the preceding sections, we have presented a theoretical model of self-regulation and used it to assess the welfare consequences of such voluntary corporate actions. In this section, we test empirically the main positive implication of the model, namely that firms engage in more self-regulation when they perceive a greater threat of government regulation. To do so, we use what is to our knowledge the only existing dataset on corporate self-regulation, namely the EPA's Toxic Release Inventory (TRI), which is described in more detail below. We use the TRI data on toxic chemical releases to see if firms engage in more voluntary pollution abatement in states that pose a greater threat of regulation.[29]

Our goal is to explain changes in the rate of toxic emissions over time, controlling for the underlying economic activity that generates these emissions. Toxic chemicals are of special interest because of their potentially important health impacts, recent improvements in the availability of public data on toxic releases, and the threat of both federal and state regulation. Starting in 1987, the EPA stepped up its collection of toxics data as a result of Title III of the Superfund Amendments and Reauthorization Act (SARA) of 1986, also known as the Emergency Planning and Community Right-to-Know Act (EPCRA). This law mandates that companies report releases of over 400 different toxic chemicals, many of which are otherwise unregulated. It applies to all manufacturing facilities that have ten or more employees and that manufacture or process more than 25,000 pounds or use more than 10,000 pounds of any of the reportable chemicals. The EPA makes this information available to the public through the TRI. The first year for which data are available is 1987; this information was released to the public in June 1989.

Our theory, of course, predicts that the release of the TRI would in itself significantly lower the information costs faced by consumer and environmental groups, thereby increasing the threat of regulation faced by firms and increasing the incentives for self-regulation. In fact, there have been massive cuts in emissions since 1987, ranging from 38 percent to 51 percent for different classes of chemicals (Davies and Mazurek 1996, p. 15), although it is impossible to determine the role of the TRI in stimulating these reductions since data were not available before its release. Hamilton (1995) did find that the stock value of firms reporting TRI releases fell by $4.1 million on the day the pollution data were first released. Furthermore,

---

[29] A variety of factors may affect the rate of emissions reductions. For example, it is difficult to distinguish the potential role of technological change in making abatement less costly. There is no reason to believe that states differ in their access to new technology, however, so this factor is unlikely to explain cross-sectional variation in abatement. Another potential factor is the role of "green" consumers who are willing to pay a premium for environmentally friendly products. As is discussed below, however, most of the industries releasing toxic chemicals produce intermediate products such as chemicals, plastics, or metals, which are not directly purchased by consumers, and are unlikely to be greatly affected by "green" consumer demand. Furthermore, products produced in a given state need not be sold there, so green consumers are unlikely to have a significant effect on voluntary abatement in their home state.

Konar and Cohen (1997a) found that firms that faced the largest stock price decline upon the initial release of the TRI to the public subsequently reduced their emissions more than their industry peers. These findings are consistent with the notion that the TRI reduced information costs and increased the threat of regulation, although the authors of these papers do not attempt to establish the chain of causation that links stock value to environmental performance.

Our empirical analysis focuses on reductions over the period 1988–1992 in total toxicity-weighted releases of seventeen key toxic chemicals per producer price index (PPI)-deflated dollar value of shipments.[30] Emissions of the toxic chemicals we study are currently legal, but these chemicals have been identified by the EPA as "high priority" chemicals. These chemicals are listed in table 3.1, along with information on their relative toxicities. Some but not all of the chemicals have been identified as potential carcinogens, so in order to standardize our risk measure across chemicals we have focused on non-cancer risks from inhalation and ingestion.[31]

To control for the important link between production and pollution we collected data on the value of shipments for the seven two-digit manufacturing industries responsible for over 70 percent of the releases of our seventeen toxic chemicals. These industries are Chemicals (SIC Code 28), Petroleum Refining (29), Rubber and Plastics (30), Primary Metals (33), Fabricated Metals (34), Electrical Equipment (36), and Transportation Equipment (37). We deflated the dollar value of shipments for each industry by the industry-specific producer price index generated by the Bureau of Labor Statistics (BLS). The shipments data and other data we use are summarized in table 3.2.

---

[30] In February 1991, the EPA announced the "33/50 program," a voluntary scheme designed to induce firms to cut their emissions of seventeen key toxic chemicals 33 percent by 1992 and 50 percent by 1995, relative to a 1988 baseline, by providing some favorable publicity and some limited technical assistance. The EPA has been criticized for the program's weak incentives (there are no penalties for failure to participate or failure to achieve the stated goals), and for overstating its results. Nevertheless, the existence of the program may have signaled an increased threat of federal regulation for these chemicals: emissions of the "33/50" chemicals fell 42 percent from 1991 to 1994, while emissions of all other TRI chemicals fell only 22 percent. For an overview of the performance of the "33/50" Program, see Davies and Mazurek (1996).

[31] Risk assessment data are taken from www.scorecard.org, a website on toxic chemical emissions maintained by the Environmental Defense Fund (EDF). To create our toxicity weighting, we divided each chemical's risk value by the average risk value for all seventeen toxic chemicals for both inhalation and ingestion risks. We then averaged these two normalized values across inhalation and ingestion risk. A few chemicals had a risk value only for either inhalation or ingestion, but not both, in which cases we simply used the one measure available.

Table 3.1 Seventeen key toxic chemicals

	Inhalation non-cancer risk value[a] (ug/m^3)	Ingestion non-cancer risk value[a] (mg/kg-day)
1,1,1-Trichloroethane	1,000	0.5
Benzene	60	n/a
Cadmium	0.01	0.0005
Carbon Tetrachloride	40	0.0007
Chloroform	300	0.01
Chromium	n/a	0.005
Cyanide	n/a	0.02
Dichloromethane	300	0.06
Lead	0.15	0.0000785
Mercury	0.3	0.0003
Methyl Ethyl Ketone	1,000	0.6
Methyl Isobutyl Ketone	80	0.08
Nickel	0.05	0.02
Tetrachloroethylene	40	0.01
Toluene	400	0.2
Trichloroethylene	600	n/a
Xylene (mixed isomers)	200	2

Notes: [a]These measures provide a standardized estimate of the amount of a given substance that must be inhaled or ingested in order to produce a given risk of harmful health effects.

n/a = not applicable.

We include a number of variables expected to shift the marginal benefits and costs of abatement, and to affect consumer information and organizing costs. Our independent variables can be broken into six major categories: (1) geographic/climatic data, (2) socioeconomic data, (3) industry characteristics, (4) general business climate, (5) legal climate, and (6) state attitudes toward the environment.

We include three control variables that characterize the geographic and climatic situation in each state: water area, mean elevation, and average July temperature; we also include land area indirectly through a variable measuring population density per square mile. We have no strong prior hypotheses regarding the effects of the first three variables, but include them because they may cause states to vary in their vulnerability to emissions of pollutants.[32] For example, states with large surface water areas may face

---

[32] Henderson (1994), finds that states with large land areas and low mean elevations incur greater expenditures on pollution abatement.

Table 3.2   Summary statistics

Variable	Definition	Mean	Std Dev.	Min.	Max.
Tox/Value 1988	Toxicity-weighted pounds of seventeen toxic chemicals released per $000 of shipments (deflated) from seven key manufacturing industries in 1988	151.647	485.827	0.786	3031.
Tox/Value 1992–88	Change in Tox/Value from 1988 to 1992	−43.697	258.093	−1425.69	933.9
Population density	Population per square mile average for 1988 to 1992	0.166	0.233	0.001	1.04
Water area	Surface water area of state (square miles)	5039	13027	145	8605
Mean elevation	Mean elevation of state (feet)	543.1	552	18	207
Temperature	July daily maximum temperature	86.154	6.164	62.7	105.
Greens/capita	Members of NRDC and Sierra Club per 000 state residents, averaged over 1988–1992	2.233	1.318	0.494	7.1
Income	State income *per capita* in $1987 averaged over 1988–92	13,947	2,244.5	9,972	2,0158
Education	Percentage of state population with a bachelor's degree or higher in 1990	19.754	3.71	12.3	27.2
LCV 1985–90	League of Conservation Voters' rating of state's Congressional delegation over 1985–90	50.718	18.301	9.9	90.4
Policy initiatives	Institute for Southern Studies' index of state performance on sixty-seven policies	44.76	14.4	23.1	77.4
Spending on air quality	*Per capita* spending in fiscal 1988 for state programs to administer clean air laws	1.113	0.741	0.26	3.87
Strict	= 1 if state imposed strict liability for toxic waste cleanup in 1991 or before	0.72	0.45	0	1
Lawyers *per capita*	Number of lawyers per 000 population in 1990	2.646	0.874	0	1
Right-to-work	= 1 if state has a right-to-work law	0.42	0.496	0	1
Plants	Number of plants emitting our seventeen selected toxic chemicals in 1988	261.35	263.461	5	1049
Shipments	Real value of shipments from seven key manufacturing industries ($MM)	26.5	33.9	0.156	147

greater health threats from water-borne toxic emissions, but alternatively they might also be able to absorb greater levels of toxic emissions without health dangers; hence we simply include the variable as a control. With regard to population density, however, we do have a clear hypothesis: we expect that the pressure to reduce toxic emissions is greater in densely populated states, since the potential harm from toxic emissions is higher there.

We include a number of socioeconomic variables in addition to population density. We use *per capita* income and educational attainment (percentage of residents with college degrees or higher), expecting both of these variables to increase the demand for pollution abatement. In addition, we collected data on the number of members in the Sierra Club and the Natural Resources Defense Council (NRDC) *per capita* in each state. Higher levels of this variable are expected to increase the pressure for pollution abatement, since environmental group members presumably place high marginal values on abatement, in addition to having an existing organizational structure that lowers the fixed costs of organizing to press for toxics regulation. We also construct an interaction term equal to the product of the state's initial emissions/shipment level in 1988 and its environmental group membership *per capita*. Our expectation is that initially dirty states with high environmental group membership will face strong political pressures to reduce emissions.

Several variables capturing industry characteristics in each state are included. We include the real value of manufacturing shipments from our seven key industries as a control variable, but without a clear sign prediction. On one hand, high shipments indicate an industry that may have considerable political power that it can use to resist regulatory threats. On the other hand, high shipments may mean that industry is viewed as having "deep pockets" that can be tapped through additional regulatory requirements or through lawsuits, or just that industry can better afford investments in voluntary pollution abatement. Another included variable is the number of plants emitting our seventeen key toxic chemicals, as a measure of the coordination problem facing industry in a given state. While we also gathered data on the number of firms emitting these chemicals, the two measures have a correlation coefficient of 98.4 percent, so we decided not to include both measures. Since coordination issues within a firm presumably increase with the number of plants the firm operates, we chose to use the former measure. We also include as an independent variable the toxicity-weighted emissions in each state in 1988. Assuming that the marginal cost of abatement is increasing, currently dirty states should have relatively low marginal costs of abatement, so these states should find emissions reduction easier than do other states.

The variables described thus far provide a set of "shifters" that strengthen or weaken the latent political pressure for corporations to self-regulate. Each of these variables affects either the marginal benefits of abatement to state residents, the marginal costs of abatement to firms, or the information and organization costs faced by state residents who wish to pressure corporations to reduce their toxic emissions. If these variables prove significant, this supports our thesis that the threat of interest group action can drive firms to self-regulate. It is also of interest, however, to understand exactly *how* these interest group pressures are transmitted to firms. States differ substantially in terms of their overall business climate, the legal precedents they operate under, and their propensity to pass environmental regulations. The next three sets of variables we introduce attempt to capture these three types of state characteristics, so as to gain insight into the mechanisms through which latent political pressure is transmitted. For example, environmentalists may impose new state regulations on toxic emissions, or they may sue a company for liability under the federal Comprehensive Environmental Response, Compensation, and Liability Act ("CERCLA"), under state versions of CERCLA, or under common law.[33]

To characterize a state's overall business climate, we follow Holmes (1998) and use the presence or absence of a "right-to-work" law as indicative of how favorable a state is as a business location.[34] We expect pro-business states (those with a right-to-work law) to pose less of a threat of government regulation and hence to observe less corporate self-regulation.

A state's legal climate is characterized here by two variables. First, we use 1990 Census data on the number of lawyers *per capita* as a measure of the overall threat of litigation in a given state. Second, we include a dummy variable indicating whether a state has a law imposing strict liability in toxic waste cleanup cases.[35] By creating legal precedents requiring polluters to bear pollution damages, such laws encourage legal action against polluters and should encourage firms to handle toxic substances with greater care. If either of these variables is significant in the regressions to follow, this

---

[33] According to Boston and Madden (1994), the most frequently used theories of legal liability in environmental and toxic torts cases are nuisance, trespass, negligence, strict liability for abnormally dangerous activities, and statutory strict liability.

[34] These laws ensure non-union employees the right to work at companies within the state, thus reducing the bargaining power of unions.

[35] For a presentation of an interesting empirical analysis of states' hazardous waste liability regimes, see Alberini and Austin (1999).

supports the hypothesis that at least a portion of interest group pressure is transmitted through the threat of litigation, not just through the threat of direct regulation.

We also include four measures of a state's political climate with specific reference to environmental issues: (1) the League of Conservation Voters (LCV) rating for the state's Congressional delegation over the period 1985–1990, (2) a composite index of state policy initiatives compiled by the Institute for Southern Studies, (3) a measure of state and local funds spent on air quality management in fiscal 1988, and (4) a variable indicating whether a state had a law as of 1991 promoting cuts in toxic chemical production at its source (even though these laws do not require facility plans or detailed reporting).[36] Each of these variables provides additional insight into a given state's propensity to support measures protecting the environment.

Inspection of the data reveals Montana to be a clear outlier, with far higher emissions per unit of shipments in 1988 than any other state. Even more strikingly, Montana shows a sharp increase in emissions per unit shipments over time that is unique among the fifty states. Recall that our theoretical analysis shows consumers may effectively be blockaded from the political process when their costs of producing political pressure are too high. The data suggest that Montana is such a state, apparently immune from the pressures present in the rest of the US. Given these concerns, we include a dummy variable for Montana to account for its unique status.

Our regression analyses of toxic releases per value of shipments are presented in table 3.3. The first estimation includes all the variables discussed above. It explains 98 percent of the variation in toxic reductions across states. Heteroskedasticity is controlled for by using White-corrected standard errors. Although many of the variables in the regression are not statistically significant, several provide insight into the forces behind voluntary abatement of toxic emissions. Two of the geographic/climatic variables prove significant. States with greater water areas reduced toxic emissions less rapidly over time, as did states with higher average July temperatures.

Turning to the socioeconomic variables, we find that higher population density is associated with greater voluntary abatement, although the relationship is not statistically significant. Similarly, high-income states saw greater abatement, but again the relationship was statistically insignificant. In fact, only one of the socioeconomic variables proved significant, namely the interaction between initial emissions level and environmental group

---

[36] Measures (1)–(4) are from Hall and Kerr (1991).

Table 3.3   Reductions in toxic emissions/value of shipments, 1988–1992

Variable	(1)	(2)
MT dummy	2941.751***	2917.615***
	(21.415)	(47.493)
Water area	0.00129*	0.00102
	(1.824)	(1.643)
Mean elevation	0.00127	
	(0.114)	
Temperature	5.4107*	4.9466*
	(1.827)	(1.679)
Population density	0.7561	
	(−0.039)	
Income	−0.0029	
	(−0.657)	
Greens/capita	11.4223	12.0738**
	(1.504)	(2.334)
Education	0.0447	
	(0.018)	
Greens*(Tox/Value 1988)	−0.2783***	−0.2847***
	(−6.974)	(−31.983)
Number of plants	0.0577*	0.05669*
	(1.782)	(1.711)
Shipments	−0.634**	−0.613**
	(−2.255)	(−2.062)
Tox/Value 1988	−0.0224	
	(−0.171)	
Right-to-work	9.8227	5.7535
	(0.938)	(0.550)
Strict	7.9086	9.600
	(0.937)	(1.104)
Lawyers *per capita*	1.5183	
	(0.234)	
LCV 1985–90	0.2647	
	(0.717)	
Policy initiatives	0.3332	
	(0.898)	
Spending on air quality	8.9101	6.3541
	(1.362)	(1.110)
Toxic cuts dummy	−2.5369	
	(−0.317)	
Constant	−504.7815*	−470.1004*
	(−1.868)	(−1.745)
Observations	50	50
Adjusted R^2	0.9791	0.9834

Note: *** = Significant at the 1 percent level; ** = Significant at the 5 percent level; * = Significant at the 10 percent level.

membership. Its coefficient is negative and significant at the 0.005 percent level. As expected, initially dirty states with large environmental memberships experience substantial pressure to reduce emissions. This provides strong evidence that the political salience of initial emissions levels depends critically on the strength of state environmental group membership.

Two variables indicating industry characteristics produced interesting results. States with a greater number of plants in our seven selected industries engaged in significantly less abatement, consistent with the hypothesis that coordination and free-rider problems become worse as the number of facilities to be coordinated rises. In addition, states with a higher level of manufacturing shipments – controlling for the number of plants – reduced emissions faster. This suggests that states where firms have "deep pockets" face a greater threat of more stringent policies toward toxic emissions, or are simply better able to afford abatement.

To a substantial extent, the structural variables that shift the costs and benefits of self-regulation enter the regression as expected, supporting our basic model of preemptive self-regulation. Our attempt to determine the precise pathways through which political pressure is exerted fared less well. Our measure of overall business climate has a positive coefficient, indicating that states with pro-business attitudes (as proxied by the presence of a right-to-work law) saw less voluntary pollution abatement. The result was not statistically significant, however. Neither of our measures of legal climate were significant, nor were the measures of state policies toward the environment.

We have a small sample, and some of our explanatory variables are highly correlated with one another. It is thus possible that some economically significant variables are imprecisely estimated in regression (1) in table 3.3 and appear statistically insignificant. Hence, we present in regression (2) the results of sequentially eliminating the least significant independent variables in each category of explanatory variables. The results are largely unchanged from those in estimation (1). One difference is that the number of environmental group members *per capita* becomes significant. Note that two steps are needed to interpret the effect of environmental group membership when both this term and the interaction term are taken into account, since the marginal effect of more environmental group members enters the regression through both terms. Using estimation (2), we see that the marginal impact on abatement of an increase in membership is now equal to (12.0738 − 0.2847*Tox/Value 1988). The sample mean of toxic releases/value in 1988 was 151.647 pounds of toxicity-weighted chemicals per 1,000 dollars of shipments. Evaluated at this level, an increase in state environmental group membership of one member per 1,000 state residents reduced the level of toxic emissions by 31.1 toxicity-weighted pounds per 1,000 dollars of shipments.[37]

Overall, then, we identify three main factors that explain toxic reductions over time. First, and most important, is the presence of strong environmental group membership in a state with high emissions levels. In this situation, firms have relatively low marginal abatement costs, consumers value abatement highly, and consumer organizing costs are low. The threat of mandatory regulation is high while the cost of self-regulation is low, so it makes good political–economic sense for firms to engage in voluntary emissions reductions. Second, states with a smaller number of plants enjoy greater levels of voluntary emissions reduction; in these states, firms are better able to overcome free-rider problems. Third, states with higher values of manufacturing shipments enjoy greater voluntary abatement.

Our results indicate that latent political pressure does indeed encourage firms to undertake voluntary self-regulating actions, and that firms are more responsive to such pressures when the costs of coordination are low. We are unable to shed much light on the precise mechanisms by which pressure is transmitted, however. All of the measures of state political climate – including measures of overall business climate, legal climate, and the state's propensity for environmental regulation – were statistically insignificant. Given the complex nature of the political environment, and the limited power of a pure cross-sectional analysis of the fifty states, this is perhaps not surprising. Future research exploring exactly how environmental groups create political threats would be a valuable contribution.

6   NON-TECHNICAL SUMMARY

In this chapter, we have presented a game theoretic model of self-regulation conducted in the face of political pressure from consumers opposed to pollution. In order to generate political pressure, consumers must incur a variety of costs. Individuals must inform themselves of the implications of

---

[37] We also performed a regression, not presented here, that included a variable interacting the presence of a right-to-work law with the initial level of toxicity-weighted emissions per value of shipments; this variable was intended to parallel our other interaction variable. The results confirm that states with pro-business attitudes engage in less voluntary pollution abatement and that states with larger environmental group membership show more voluntary abatement.

pollution control for their well-being, and of the efficacy of various feasible policy remedies. Consumers of similar interests must then coordinate on a mutual strategy for gaining political influence. These various costs are collectively referred to as "organizing costs." Even after consumers are organized, they must incur expenses to wield political influence, which might be attained through a variety of means, including lobbying activities, election campaign contributions, and tolerated forms of bribery such as revolving-door arrangements, junkets, and honoraria. Costs that are required after consumers are organized are referred to as "influence costs" or "lobbying costs."

The formal sequence of moves in the game is as follows. First, firms choose a level of voluntary pollution control. Second, firms and consumers (who receive utility from the good but disutility from pollution) engage in (costly) interest group rivalry for the purpose of influencing pollution control policy. Third, after pollution control policy has been determined, firms produce and sell identical products in a Cournot oligopoly. Because the products are homogeneous, absent any threat of regulation firms would have no incentive to engage in voluntary abatement.

The key to the analysis is the political influence game, and how it is affected by the firms' voluntary environmental efforts. In the influence game, firms whose costs are increased by additional pollution control restraints will press for a lower level of abatement regulation. Consumers purchase the good produced by the firms and could support weaker regulations if they view regulatory costs as raising prices too much. Consumers, however, also suffer adverse effects from the pollution emitted by the firms, and thus are likely to favor and lobby for tighter abatement regulations than those supported by firms. On either side of the influence game, the aggregate resources marshaled by either set of interests are transformed into political influence through a process that features diminishing marginal returns.

The crucial effect of voluntary abatement is to change the outcome of the influence game. This effect depends on how the firms and consumers react to increases in voluntary abatement. Because abatement reduces firm profits at an increasing rate, voluntary abatement (self-regulation) makes the firms fight harder in the influence game. At the same time self-regulation makes consumers less motivated to fight, because consumers obtain diminishing returns from further environmental improvement. On balance, voluntary abatement works to strengthen the hand of the firms in the political process (if it is not preempted), and reduces the additional abatement requirements that would emerge from the political battle.

The political costs faced by consumers drive a wedge between the consumer benefits of *voluntary* abatement and the benefits of *mandatory* abatement that is obtained only through political pressure. Firms can take advantage of this wedge to preempt regulation. Naturally, if consumers' costs of political action are too high then consumers are effectively "blockaded" from the political process, so self-regulation becomes an unnecessary expenditure and will not be observed. As consumer costs of gaining political influence fall, however, the model predicts that corporate self-regulation will intensify. In other words, an increasing threat of government regulation induces firms to voluntarily reduce pollution emissions. The theory predicts that government actions which significantly lower the information costs faced by consumer and environmental groups would thereby increase the threat of regulation faced by firms and increase the incentives for self-regulation.

Does this type of voluntary abatement raise social welfare? When consumer-organizing costs are high, firms may be able to preempt regulation with a very modest amount of voluntary abatement, which might be much less than would have been imposed by government. Poorer environmental performance, however, must be weighed against the reductions in regulatory and legislative costs when abatement is voluntary rather than mandatory. In fact, it can be shown that the regulatory savings more than outweigh any reduced environmental performance. The basic idea is that giving consumers some abatement for "free" strengthens consumers' position in the influence game – if it is actually played: they obtain a higher level of *total* abatement (voluntary plus mandatory) at a lower political cost. Hence, if consumers allow themselves to be preempted, they must be even better off than they would have been had they fought the influence game. Thus, if preemption occurs, one can presume that both firms and consumers are better off than if consumers had fought to impose standards on an industry that undertook no voluntary abatement.

7   CONCLUSIONS AND POLICY IMPLICATIONS

We have developed a model in which firms can use self-regulation to preempt government-imposed regulations. When it is costly for consumers to organize and to influence the political process, firms can match the net utility consumers expect from regulatory controls with a *lower* level of voluntary controls, and can thereby deter consumer groups from mobilizing to enter the political process. As the threat of regulation grows, e.g. because of reductions in consumers' informational and organizational costs, self-regulation becomes more stringent. Furthermore, our theory shows that firms cannot use self-regulation to undermine consumers' threat of imposing mandatory regulations; as a result, when self-regulation preempts government action, both firms and consumers are better off.

Evidence on recent reductions in toxic chemical emissions is consistent with the positive predictions of our thesis. When Congress reauthorized Superfund in 1986, Title III of the legislation required companies to report their emissions of over 300 toxic chemicals, thereby dramatically lowering consumer information costs. In our framework, after this data began to be collected total releases of toxic chemicals should have dropped significantly. This hypothesis cannot be tested directly, since the data were not collected prior to the passage of the law, but the massive cuts in emissions since 1987 (ranging from 38 percent to 51 percent for different classes of chemicals) are certainly consistent with our model's predictions. Furthermore, the EPA's voluntary "33/50" program, initiated in 1991, may have signaled a greater threat of federal regulation for the seventeen chemicals it encompasses (which are also the ones we examine here); emissions of these seventeen chemicals fell 42 percent from 1991 to 1994, while emissions of the other TRI chemicals fell by 22 percent, further suggesting that the threat of regulation matters. Finally, we use the new data on toxic releases to examine how state-level variation in the threat of regulation affects incentives for voluntary abatement. Our most striking finding is that states with high initial emissions levels along with strong environmental group membership generate more voluntary pollution abatement. In these states, firms have relatively low marginal abatement costs, and face consumers who highly value marginal improvements in environmental quality and are already well organized to apply political pressure. The cost of self-regulation is low while the threat of government regulation is high, so voluntary abatement is a sound business decision.

Two main policy implications follow from the analysis in this chapter. First, it may be socially desirable to allow industry to coordinate on a choice of pollution limits. This view runs counter to historical antitrust precedent, most notably the case against the Automobile Manufacturers' Association, which was accused of using a research joint venture to slow the adoption of more stringent pollution control devices. We show that in some situations, firms acting non-cooperatively will choose not to engage in voluntary abatement, but would do so if they could coordinate their actions. Furthermore, we show that welfare would be enhanced by such coordination. In this context, antitrust prosecution of "collusion" will reduce welfare. Antitrust officials need to be cognizant of both the potential benefits of abatement coordination as well as its potential anticompetitive effects. One factor that may make this job easier is assessing regulatory threats facing cooperating firms. In the absence of such threats, our analysis does not apply, and antitrust officials should be especially vigilant for possible anticompetitive effects of coordinated pollution control.

A second implication of our analysis is that government should not necessarily subsidize consumer involvement in the regulatory process. State regulatory agencies have increasingly taken to funding branches with names like "Division of Ratepayer Advocates" or "Office of Consumer Counsel" to intervene in utility rate cases. These actions appear designed to offset the high costs to consumers of intervening in the regulatory process, and indeed our analysis shows that such subsidies can shift the policy regime from one of no government regulation (because consumer-organizing costs are too high) to one of preemption. Our results, however, also indicate that these efforts may unintentionally make consumers worse off by substituting government regulation for less costly industry self-regulation. The fixed cost of organizing implicitly commits consumers to an "acceptable" level of self-regulation beyond which they will not enter the political process. If organizing costs fall too low, this commitment may be eroded and firms may find preemption unprofitable, which would make consumers worse off.

Our analysis in this chapter reached some strong conclusions regarding the effects of self-regulation. However, it is important to keep in mind that this analysis was designed to apply to a particular stage of the policy life cycle. Specifically, we focused in this chapter on the development and politicization stages of the cycle, and on the possibility that corporate environmentalism can preempt legislative and regulatory threats. Chapter 4 examines the role of corporate environmentalism in influencing, rather than simply preempting, regulation.

APPENDIX

Proposition 1: *There exists a range of consumer fixed costs of organizing on which a perfectly collusive oligopoly chooses a positive level of voluntary abatement and thereby preempts consumer intervention in the regulatory process. Let* $[f_{Z^v_{max}}, f_{blockade}]$ *be this range. Then* $f_{Z^v_{max}} \geq 0$, *and for* $f_{Z^v_{max}} < f(N^c) < f_{blockade}$ *the firm's choice of* Z^V *is decreasing in* $f(N^c)$; *for* $f(N^c) > f_{blockade}$, *consumer intervention is "blockaded," i.e. preempted with* $Z^V = 0$.

Proof: We first establish that feasible preemption exists. The firms can always preempt consumers by choosing a level of voluntary abatement that will yield consumers the same utility they would receive from engaging in the influence game, *i.e.* Z^V such that $U^N(Z^V) = U^I(Z^V) - f(N^c)$. (Note that in what follows we drop the functional dependence of f on N^c to avoid excessive notation.) To show that such Z^V exists as a feasible choice, we need to show that $\pi^N(Z^V) > \pi^N(Z(0)) - l(0) = \pi^I(0)$. That is, it must be more profitable to engage in preemption than not to engage in preemption and enter the influence game. It is clear that for sufficiently large f such a Z^V exists since for sufficiently large f, $U^I(0) - f = U^N(0)$ and $\pi^N(0) > \pi^I(0)$. Call this level of fixed cost $f_{blockade}$, since at this level consumers will not enter the influence game even if the firms undertake no abatement.

Note that there is a maximum level of voluntary abatement, $Z^V_{blockade}$, that the firms will be willing to undertake, where $\pi^N(Z^V_{max}) = \pi^I(0)$. The relevant comparison point on the right-hand side of the equality is zero abatement because $d\pi^I/dZ^V < 0$. Since π^N is also declining in Z^V, any level of voluntary cleanup beyond Z^V_{max} will not be profitable. Next we define the minimum level of Z^V required to preempt consumers. For any given f this level is given by $U^N(Z^V_{min}) = U^I(Z^V_{min}) - f$. Consequently we write Z^V_{min} as a function of the level of consumer fixed costs. It remains to be shown that $Z^V_{min}(f)$ is decreasing in f. This result follows from two observations. First, $U^N(Z^V)$ is independent of f and, second, $U^I(Z^V) - f$ is strictly decreasing in f. Now consider two levels of f, with $f(A) < f(B) < f_{blockade}$. Then $U^I(0) - f_B > U^N(0)$, because consumers cannot be preempted by a zero level of voluntary abatement. Now define $\theta_B(Z^V) = U^I(Z^V) - f_B - U^N(Z^V)$, a continuous function. Then $\theta_B(0) > 0$. Recall that $Z^V_{min}(f)$ is defined such that $U^I(Z^V_{min}(f_A) - f_A = U^N(Z^V_{min}(f_A)))$. Thus, since $f_B > f_A$, $\theta_B(Z^V_{min}(f_A)) < 0$. By Bolzano's Theorem, there exists a $\widehat{Z} \in (0, Z^V_{min}(f_A))$ such that $\theta_B(\widehat{Z})$. By the definition of $\theta_B(Z^V)$, we see that $\widehat{Z} = Z^V_{min}(f_B)$. Therefore, $Z^V_{min}(f_B) < Z^V_{min}(f_A)$. ∎

Proposition 2: *The threat of regulation can be preempted by a non-cooperative oligopoly for certain levels of consumer-organizing costs. Specifically, there exists a symmetric Nash equilibrium with preemption for $f(N^c) \in [f_{Z^V_{NC}} > f_{blockade}]$, where $f_{Z^V_{NC}} > f_{Z^V_{max}}$.*

Proof: $\pi^N(Z^V_{-i}; Z^V_i)$ is firm i's profit when the influence game is preempted, all firms but i abate to (scalar) level Z^V_{-i} and firm i abates to level Z^V_i. Similarly let $\pi^I(Z^V_{-i}; Z^V_i)$ and $l^e(Z^V_{-i}; Z^V_i)$ be firm i's profit when the influence game is played and its optimal lobbying expenditure, given the aforementioned voluntary abatement levels. The maximum symmetric collusive level of voluntary abatement, denoted $Z_{max}^{V/C}$, is defined by $\pi^N(Z_{max}^{V/C}; Z_{max}^{V/C}) = \pi^I(0;0)$. On the other hand, the maximum non-cooperative level of voluntary abatement, denoted $Z_{max}^{V/NC}$, is defined by $\pi^N(Z_{max}^{V/NC}; Z_{max}^{V/NC}) = \pi^I(Z_{max}^{V/NC};0)$. Two things must be shown. First, non-cooperative voluntary abatement is possible. Note that there exists Z_i such that $\pi^N(0; Z_i) \geq \pi^I(0;0) \equiv \pi^N(0;0) - l^*(0;0)$. This is easy to see, assuming that $l^e(0;0) > 0$: there must exist some small Z_i that is profitable *if* it successfully preempts, since the firm is thereby spared the lobbying cost $l^e(0;0)$. From the continuity of $\pi^N(Z_{-i}^V; Z_i^V)$, similar results hold for small Z_{-i}^V. Thus, some non-cooperative preemption is possible for sufficiently high levels of consumer fixed costs. Second, it must be shown that $Z_{max}^{V/NC} < Z_{max}^{V/C}$. Consider firm i's best response when all other firms play $Z_{max}^{V/NC}$, which is determined by $\pi^N(Z_{max}^{V/C}; Z_i^V) = \pi^I(Z_{max}^{V/C};0)$. Note that $\pi^N(Z_{-i}^V; Z_i^V)$ passes through $\pi^N(Z_i^V)$ but is rotated clockwise. Note also that $\pi^I(Z_{max}^{V/C};0) > \pi^I(0;0)$, so it cannot be a best response for firm i to select $Z_i = Z_{max}^{V/C}$. Instead, since $d\pi^N(Z_{-i}^V; Z_i^V)/dZ_i < 0$, firm i's best response requires $Z_{max}^{V/NC} < Z_{max}^{V/C}$. Thus, the maximum level of non-cooperative voluntary abatement is lower than the maximum collusive level. As a result, there are some values of the consumer fixed cost f for which collusive preemption is possible but non-cooperative preemption is impossible. ∎

Lemma 1: *There exists $\varepsilon > 0$ such that if $|Z_{ml}| < \varepsilon$ $\forall(m, l)$, then as Z^V increases, $Z(Z^V)$ rises, $m^e(Z^V)$ falls, and $l^e(Z^V)$ rises.*

Proof: Note first that the reaction curves in the influence game shift when the level of Z^V changes, as expressed in the equations

$$\frac{dm^*}{dZ^V} = \frac{-U_{ZZ}Z_m}{U_{ZZ}Z_m^2 + U_Z Z_{mm}} < 0$$

and

$$\frac{dl^*}{dZ^V} = \frac{-\pi_{ZZ}Z_L}{\pi_{ZZ}Z_L^2 + \pi_Z Z_{LI}} > 0.$$

Then we write out the expressions for changes in the equilibrium levels of resources devoted to influence seeking as Z^V changes:

$$\frac{dm^e}{dZ^V} = \frac{\frac{\partial m^*}{\partial l}\frac{\partial l^*}{\partial Z^V} + \frac{\partial m^*}{\partial Z^V}}{1 - \frac{\partial m^*}{\partial l}\frac{\partial l^*}{\partial m}}$$

and similarly,

$$\frac{dl^e}{dZ^V} = \frac{\frac{\partial l^*}{\partial m}\frac{\partial m^*}{\partial Z^V} + \frac{\partial l^*}{\partial Z^V}}{1 - \frac{\partial m^*}{\partial l}\frac{\partial l^*}{\partial m}}.$$

These expressions show that the *equilibrium* change in lobbying levels as a function of Z^V depends on both the shift in the player's own reaction curve as well as the movement along his reaction curve caused by the shift in the rival's reaction curve. Letting $\lambda \equiv 1 - (\partial m^*/\partial l)(\partial l^*/\partial m)$, we note that $\lambda > 0$ because the reaction curves are assumed to be stable. We can now write $dm^e/dZ^V \equiv (\theta/\lambda)(dZ/dZ^V)$ and $dl^e/dZ^V \equiv (\theta/\lambda)(dZ/dZ^V)$, and some expansion of terms yields

$$\theta = \frac{U_{ml}^I}{U_{mm}^I}\frac{\pi_{zz}Z_l}{\pi_{ll}^I} - \frac{U_{ZZ}Z_m}{U_{mm}^I}$$

and

$$\Phi = \frac{\pi_{lm}^I}{\pi_{ll}^I}\frac{U_{zz}^I Z_m}{U_{mm}^I} - \frac{\pi_{ZZ}^I Z_l}{\pi_{ll}^I}.$$

Now we can write $dZ/dZ^V = 1 + dZ^M/dZ^V = 1 + Z_m(dm^e/dZ^V) + Z_l(dl^e/dZ^V) = 1 + Z_m(\theta/\lambda)dZ/dZ^V + Z_l(\theta/\lambda)dZ/dZ^V$. Rearranging terms yields $dZ/dZ^V = 1/(1 - Z_m\theta/\lambda - Z_l\Phi/\lambda)$. Thus, sufficient conditions for $dZ/dZ^V > 0$ are $\theta < 0$ and $\Phi > 0$.

Next, note that $U_{ml}^I = U_{ZZ}^I Z_m Z_l + U_Z Z_{ml}$, and if $Z_{ml} = 0$ then $U_{ml}^I = U_{ZZ}^I Z_m Z_l$. Substituting this into the expression for θ, and noting that $\pi_{ll}^I = \pi_{ZZ}^I(Z_l)^2 + \pi_Z^I Z_{ll}$, we obtain:

$$\theta = \frac{-U_{ZZ}^I Z_m}{U_{mm}^I}\frac{\pi_z Z_{ll}}{\pi_{ll}^I} < 0.$$

Similar reasoning yields

$$\Phi = \frac{-\pi_{ZZ}^I Z_l}{\pi_{ll}^I}\frac{U_{zz}^I Z_{mm}}{U_{mm}^I} > 0.$$

Hence $dZ/dZ^V > 0$. Furthermore, $dm^e/dZ^V \equiv (\theta/\lambda)(dZ/dZ^V) < 0$ and $dl^e/dZ^V \equiv (\theta/\lambda)(dZ/dZ^V) > 0$. All of the above arguments will still go through for Z_{ml} of sufficiently small absolute value. ∎

Proposition 4: *If preemption occurs, and the conditions of the lemma hold, then both consumer welfare and profits are increased, relative to their levels were government regulation imposed in the absence of voluntary abatement.*

Proof: If the firms preempt, they choose Z^V so that

$$U^N(Z^V) = U^N(Z(Z^V)) - m^e(Z^V) - f(N^c).$$

Note that the lemma shows that $m^e(Z^V) < m^*(0)$ and that $Z(Z^V) > Z(0)$, so $U^N(Z(Z^V)) > U^N(Z(0))$.

Therefore

$$U^N(Z^V) = U^N(Z(Z^V)) - m^e(Z^V) - f(N^c)$$
$$> U^N(Z(0)) - m^e(0) - f(N^c). \qquad \blacksquare$$

4 | Influencing future regulations

1 INTRODUCTION

Chapter 3 showed how corporate environmentalism can preempt new legislation and regulation. Preemption is by no means the only function for corporate environmentalism, however. Often legislation is passed, and the policy process moves on to the implementation phase. In such cases, corporate environmentalism takes on a different strategic role, that of influencing the formulation of new environmental laws. Examples of such influence on environmental, health, and safety regulation are legion.[1] In the USA, interest group influence is virtually guaranteed by the Administrative Procedures Act of 1946, which requires regulators to give notice to all interested parties before promulgating new regulations, and requires that parties be allowed to provide commentary to regulatory authorities on proposed rules. Furthermore, it is often the case that Congress mandates the imposition of new health, safety, or environmental regulations, but delegates the technical details – which are determined only after considerable delay – to a regulatory agency such as the Environmental Protection Agency (EPA) or the Department of Energy (DOE). While previous work has focused on the use of traditional tools of influence, such as lobbying and campaign contributions, we emphasize the ways in which corporate environmental actions can influence policy.

In this chapter, we examine how corporate environmentalism shapes future regulations by using two distinct models, which we label *quality leadership* and *signaling*. The following paragraphs illustrate the settings in which each of these strategies is used, and sketch out the basic ideas behind the two models. Because the effect of corporate environmentalism on social welfare differs in the two models, it is important for policymakers to be able to distinguish the underlying structure of the two settings from one another.

---

[1] See Stigler (1988) for a collection of political economic studies, many of which focus on the causes and consequences of government regulations.

1.1   Quality leadership

The Clean Water Act of 1972 and its 1977 amendments mandated, among other things, that the EPA establish standards for emissions of organic chemicals. The EPA finally issued proposed effluent guidelines in March 1983, which "were established by averaging the effluent quality achieved by existing plants that were selected as being well controlled."[2] Obviously standards would have been weaker if industry quality leaders had installed poorer control techniques. The deliberation process explicitly weighed economic considerations, including effects on firm profitability and potential employment losses from plant closures. In fact, due to economic considerations, neither the "Best Practicable Technology" (BPT) standards nor the more stringent "Best Available Technology" (BAT) standards actually required the use of the most effective abatement technologies on the market.[3] Nevertheless, the fact that the standards were based on the observed quality achieved by existing plants provided these plants the opportunity for strategic action to influence regulations.

In our quality leadership model, we allow a high-quality firm to make a sunk investment in a technology that exceeds both current and anticipated government quality standards. This action is followed by the setting of a new minimum quality standard by government, which aims to maximize social welfare.[4] After the standard is set, firms not presently meeting the standard comply with it, and all firms compete in the product market. Our key result is that by strategically exceeding anticipated standards by a limited amount, the high-quality firm can influence the government to set lower standards, thereby leading to a *lower* level of social welfare than would be achieved under the "government as leader" scenario. Our analysis thus calls into question the benefits of corporate environmentalism within the implementation phase of the policy life cycle.

1.2   Signaling

In the mid-1980s, the Puerto Rican government was considering adopting US regulatory standards and procedures for its dairy industry, which

---

[2] See Caulkins and Sessions (1997) for further details. A careful reading of Caulkins and Sessions indicates that approximately eleven out of 300 plants were deemed to be well controlled; (see 1997, pp. 95–105).

[3] The discussion in this paragraph is drawn from Caulkins and Sessions (1997).

[4] Note that the qualitative nature of our results does not depend on the regulator maximizing social welfare, but merely that the regulator takes into account the various components of welfare, including firms' profits, consumer surplus, and environmental damages.

would allow the Puerto Rican dairy industry to sell its products to the USA.[5] Harmonization of Puerto Rican with US regulations would mean that products from the Canadian firm Lactel Inc., which had a sizable share of the market, would be effectively banned from entering Puerto Rico.[6] Puerto Rican consumers might suffer from the resulting reduction of competition, and the government was unsure whether the economic benefits accruing to the Puerto Rican industry dominated these costs. Aware of the government's hesitance, domestic dairy producers voluntarily made the investments required to come into compliance with US regulations. This sent a powerful signal that the benefits of harmonization to the industry were large, and in 1987 legislation mandating the adoption of US standards was passed (box 4.1).

Box 4.1   The Puerto Rican dairy market

The market of concern is the Puerto Rican dairy market. In 1987 the Puerto Rican government adopted US regulatory standards and procedures, ostensibly to allow the Puerto Rican dairy industry to sell its products to the United States. US laws prohibit the sale of foreign dairy products from countries or regions that do not have identical regulatory standards and procedures.

The implementation of US standards and procedures required not only changes from the Puerto Rican government but also capital investments on the part of Puerto Rican firms. In order for the Puerto Rican government to pass legislation dictating harmonization with US standards, the government had to be certain that the benefits outweighed the costs. While access to the US market was cited as the reason for the change in the Puerto Rican regulations, a possible second and not unsubstantial benefit to the domestic industry existed.

The harmonization of Puerto Rican with US regulations meant that products from the Canadian firm Lactel, Inc. would be banned from entering Puerto Rico. Lactel had a fourteen-year trouble-free history of exporting to the Puerto Rican market, and held a substantial market share in the UHT milk market. Lactel's products were banned because Canadian regulations differ from those of the USA. While the Puerto Rican market was important for Lactel, it represented a small market for

---

[5] For a detailed discussion of this case see Rugman, Kirton, and Soloway (1999).
[6] US laws prohibit the sale of foreign dairy products from countries or regions that do not have identical regulatory standards and procedures.

the Canadian dairy industry as a whole. Consequently, it was not eco-
nomical for the Canadian government to alter its regulatory procedures,
which constituted a sophisticated and effective federal–provincial legal
framework governing milk production.

In 1992, following failures to gain access for Lactel on the diplomatic
front, the Canadian government initiated actions against the USA under
provisions of the Canada–US Free Trade Act of 1989, claiming the new
Puerto Rican Health and Safety standard was a restriction of trade and
an outright violation of the Free Act. The arbitration panel sided with
the US government, finding that it had a right to set laws governing
the sales of products within its own jurisdiction. It did, however, find
that the Puerto Rican government was at fault for not seriously pursuing the awarding of a certificate of equivalency from the US Food
and Drug Administration attesting that the milk standards in Lactel's
home province of Quebec provided the same degree of protection as the
Puerto Rican standards, as the government was required to do under
the FTA.

Two years after the ruling Lactel obtained the certificate of equivalency allowing it to resume its exports to Puerto Rico. However, after
an absence of seven years Lactel has found it difficult to regain market
share. As of 1999 Lactel holds a very small share of the Puerto Rican
UHT milk market.

In this case the environmental or health benefits of the new Puerto
Rican legislation were probably minimal. We know that the products
of Lactel were produced according to procedures that already provided
equivalent health and safety benefits as would products produced under the new standards. It may be true that the new standards raised the
health and safety benefits arising from Puerto Rican produced products, but there is no evidence that the Puerto Rican dairy industry had
a history of problems in this area. The decision appears to have been
driven by economic factors. Puerto Rican consumers might have suffered from the restriction of a firm holding substantial market share.
The local government had, therefore, to be convinced that the economic
benefits accruing to the Puerto Rican industry dominated these costs.
The fact that the domestic industry made the investments required to
allow them to be in compliance with US regulations provided a powerful signal of these benefits, and probably helped push the legislation
through.

The ban on Lactel's UHT milk products due to the passage of new
legislation provides an extreme example of raising rivals' costs. While the

domestic industry incurred costs to comply with the new Puerto Rican legislation, the costs of compliance for Lactel were effectively infinite. We were unable to determine whether Puerto Rican firms gained profitable access to the US market. What is clear, however, is that they were the main beneficiaries of the ban on Lactel products. If this were not the case, it would be highly unlikely that the Puerto Rican government would have dragged its feet in certifying the equivalency of the Health and Safety benefits of Lactel's products.

Source: Rugman, Kirton, and Soloway (1999).

In our signaling model we examine how the adoption of a high-quality environmental technology can be used to induce the government to mandate the use of that technology throughout the industry. In this case the firm's voluntary adoption of the high-quality technology serves as a costly signal to the regulator that the technology's adoption costs are low. Consequently the regulator, in balancing corporate profits, consumer welfare, and environmental externalities, is convinced that mandating the adoption of the high level of quality will be socially desirable. The motivation for the firm's voluntary adoption in this model is to raise its rivals' costs by inducing the regulator to mandate the high-quality technology across the industry.[7] The model makes two main points. First, signaling alone, without accompanying lobbying activities, can be enough to influence regulatory decisions in a powerful way. Second, signaling increases the information available to the regulator, and allows it to make better-informed decisions. Thus, unlike traditional methods of raising rivals' costs, such as campaign contributions aimed at changing voting behavior, raising rivals' costs through signaling should not be presumed to make society worse off.

2 QUALITY LEADERSHIP

Several authors have shown how minimum quality standards (MQSs) can raise welfare when products are vertically differentiated and buyers fully internalize the benefits of quality.[8] The basic notion is that by forcing up

---

[7] The antitrust literature on raising rivals' costs, initiated by Salop and Scheffman (1983), generally considers such activities to be a form of socially undesirable non-price predation.

[8] This section is based on Lutz, Lyon, and Maxwell (2000). For papers on the benefits of MQSs, see, for example, Ronnen (1991), Arora and Gangopadhyay (1995), Boom (1995), and

the lowest-quality level on offer in the market, the regulator can intensify price competition to the benefit of consumers. The best response of the high-quality firm is to raise its own quality level in an attempt to reduce price competition. It is not optimal, however, for the high-quality firm to fully offset the rise in the MQS. Thus, prices fall and qualities rise as a result of the MQS.[9]

When the benefits of quality are not fully internalized by consumers, concerns about externalities must also be taken into account.[10] If one considers health, safety, and a clean environment as aspects of product quality, then minimum quality standards can be thought of as a way to mitigate externalities. The model includes both externalities and insufficient price competition as motivations for government to promulgate minimum quality standards.

The key structural difference between our quality leadership model and earlier models of MQSs (see, e.g., Ronnen 1991 and Arora and Gangopadhyay 1995) is the timing of firm and government actions. Previous work has examined how both high- and low-quality firms *react* to the imposition of MQSs; in these models, the government is the first mover, and the firms are followers. Our model, in contrast, grants the leadership role to a high-quality firm (box 4.2). An important assumption in our analysis is that the high-quality firm can commit to a given level of quality.[11] For this commitment to be credible, the firm must face a fixed cost of changing quality levels large enough to outweigh any additional benefits from adjusting quality after standards are imposed. We thus have in mind a "putty/clay" technology, where the firm has a continuum of quality choices *ex ante*, but is effectively locked into a single quality *ex post*.[12] This is particularly plausible when improving quality requires the firm to retool its production process, as is

Crampes and Hollander (1995). See Maxwell (1998), however, which shows that the presence of a welfare maximizing regulator that sets a minimum quality standard may discourage innovation and reduce social welfare.

[9] Linneman's (1980) study of the 1973 mattress flammability standard found that the price of the highest-quality mattresses did indeed fall after the imposition of the standard. He notes (p. 454) that the standard had greatest impact on small producers, as "most large producers had adopted the requisite production technology" already. Linneman did not examine formally changes in the vector of qualities on offer before and after the standard, but he does note (n. 24, p. 459) that even after the imposition of the standard, it was not true that "all passing mattresses are of the same quality with respect to flammability."

[10] For an excellent textbook treatment of externalities from a regulatory perspective, see Viscusi, Vernon, and Harrington (1995, section III).

[11] This is a standard assumption in multi-stage models of product differentiation; see, e.g., Lehmann-Grube (1997).

[12] In some cases, regulation may force all firms to change their production processes, e.g., by imposing "technology-forcing" standards that require development of innovative new

---

Box 4.2   ARCO's reformulated gasolines

In response to growing public concerns about air pollution from auto-mobiles, ARCO introduced a line of reformulated, cleaner, gasolines under the names "EC-1" (introduced September 1, 1989), "EC-Premium" (September 6, 1990), and "EC-X" (July 1991). The new fuels have garnered ARCO very favorable treatment in the press, and were dubbed the "Product of the Year" by *Fortune* magazine. They have also been made the subject of a Stanford University case study for use in business management classes. Furthermore, according to the *Los Angeles Times*, the firm's "return on stockholder equity in 1991 was 29.3 percent, making ARCO the best performer in the oil industry. Its success is due to an unprecedented new-product development strategy, an environmental strategy. ARCO anticipates environmental regulations to gain significant market advantages."

Lodwrick Cook, ARCO's CEO, clearly believes his own claim that, for firms in the 1990s, "the greatest opportunity for competitive advantage will be in leveraging environmentally improved products and services to differentiate themselves from competitors." However, by "breaking ranks with the majors" and introducing EC-X, Cook not only differentiated his product, he also launched a "frontal assault on those advocating the more expensive vehicles that use methanol fuel." ARCO's action thus appears to be very much driven by a desire to stave off government regulations that would have imposed costly requirements that ran counter to the firm's interests.

Sources: Piasecki (1992); Schaefer (1993).

---

often the case when firms undertake a "pollution prevention" approach to abatement.[13] For reasons of both theory and practice, we assume that the low-quality firm cannot precommit to a quality level. From a modeling perspective, if all firms can make a *binding* commitment before the regulator steps in, then the regulator is rendered powerless, making impossible any analysis of the interaction between regulation and corporate strategy.[14]

---

    technologies. Such cases are interesting, and voluntary actions in these cases may involve a different set of incentives; however such a model is beyond the scope of the present chapter.

[13] In future work, it may be of interest to explore in depth the leader's choice between technologies that offer different levels of sunk costs, as in Williamson (1985, chapter 7).

[14] Interesting issues arise if all firms can precommit to a MQS, but regulators can later require additional improvement. Maxwell, Lyon, and Hackett (2000) examine this possibility for the case of homogeneous firms, and characterize the conditions under which the emergence of

From a practical perspective, casual empiricism strongly suggests that regulations typically do not simply ratify the lowest quality currently offered by any firm; instead they have demonstrable effects on low-quality firms, forcing them to improve their products.[15]

Often there is a substantial lag between the passage of legislation and the implementation of regulation. When this happens, there is ample time for firms to take actions that will influence the outcome of regulatory deliberations. Consider, for example, the National Appliance Energy Conservation Act of 1987 (NAECA), which required that minimum energy efficiency standards be met by January 1, 1990, for room air conditioners and gas water heaters. The specifics of the standards were delegated to the DoE, and determined only after consultations with industry members. The manufacturers did not wait until the deadline to meet the standards, but instead began positioning themselves in advance. Newell, Jaffe, and Stavins (1998) provide a detailed empirical analysis of the changes in energy efficiency for these appliances over the period 1958–1993. For example, in 1958 the average room air conditioner produced 5.9 BTU/hour/watt and the standard deviation across units was 1.0; by 1993 the average had risen to 9.0 with a standard deviation of only 0.6. As the authors discuss, there is a menu of products that varies in quality, with the upper end exceeding the minimum standard by a significant amount. They estimate that for room air conditioners 24 percent of the improvement in energy efficiency since 1973 can be attributed to the standards, while for gas water heaters 69 percent of the improvement was due to standards. Interestingly, the technological frontier did not appear to shift outward in the wake of the standards; instead "the primary effect was the elimination of the distribution's lower tail" (Newell, Jaffe, and Stavins 1998, n. 35). Apparently high-quality firms committed in advance to certain technologies and did not readjust their products after the government set its standards.

An even more striking example of the delay between the passage of laws and the promulgation of standards involves the Clean Air Act (CAA)

mandatory government regulations may be preempted altogether. An interesting topic for further research may be a model that combines our model with that of Maxwell, Lyon, and Hackett (2000), allowing for the possibility of preemption, but also for the sorts of regulatory manipulation we describe here.

[15] This was the case for the Clean Water Act (CWA), as discussed above, which set a standard based on "well-controlled" plants, not on the basis of the most poorly controlled plants. Similarly, appliance standards for air conditioners and gas water heaters had significant effects on the low-quality end of the market, as discussed above. In like manner, Linneman (1980) reports that flammability standards for mattresses forced low-quality manufacturers to eliminate the use of untreated cotton and to include a layer of polyurethane in their products, requiring a significant retooling of their production processes.

Amendments of 1990. This Act identified a group of 189 toxic chemicals to be subjected to National Emission Standards for Hazardous Air Pollutants (NESHAP) by the year 2000. The decade between the announcement of the new standards and their actual implementation gave firms ample opportunity to position themselves in a way that would favorably influence the standards. In fact, many firms have already made investments that have substantially reduced their emissions of various toxics identified in the CAA Amendments.[16] Whether these actions were specifically motivated by a desire to influence the ultimate standards, or were purely anticipatory, is an interesting empirical question which would probably be best tackled through a case study of the development of the ultimate standards.

In the global arena, high-quality firms may work with their domestic governments to require the use of particular technologies, with the goal of influencing international standards. An interesting example is provided by the European Union (EU) Commission's 1985 decision regarding the stringency of automobile emissions standards. In 1984, concerns about acid rain led the Federal Republic of Germany – with the support of the German automotive industry – to adopt a clean-car regulation. Because the regulation applied to all automobiles sold in Germany, it was labeled a barrier to trade and quickly became a European issue. When the EU Commission proposed NOx standards later in 1984, producers and governments quickly fell into two groups. The German-led group pressed for standards that dictated best available control technologies (which effectively meant the use of three-way catalytic converters), while the second group, led by France and French producers, argued for further study of potentially better "clean-engine" technologies. While the EU Commission deliberated, the German government, with the backing of its automakers, adopted fuel emission standards that essentially dictated the use of the three-way catalytic converter technology.[17] Two months later the EU Commission enacted standards that led to the adoption of catalytic technology for the EU. The German government's standards allowed German manufacturers to commit to a technology that improved on the emissions of vehicles they currently sold in Europe, and influenced the Commission to raise the standards facing all manufacturers in Europe. However, the German move may have also resulted in emissions standards that were lower than those that might have been set had all technological options been studied. Lévêque and Nadaï (1995) note that

---

[16] See Khanna and Damon (1999) for further discussion of the Clean Air Act's NESHAP and some empirical evidence indicating that firms had been reducing their emissions of toxic pollutants prior to the imposition of forthcoming standards.

[17] Of course, differences in fuel efficiency and other design features meant that some cars remained cleaner than others despite the new MQS.

there was potential for better technologies, including the coupling of clean engines and catalytic converters. The emission standards set by the EU Commission were not strict enough to force this technology, however, and French producers abandoned (at least temporarily) active research on the clean engine to focus on equipping their existing engines with the German catalytic converter technology.

The foregoing examples show that firms may have an extended period of advance warning before the imposition of new standards, and that the products and production processes firms choose affect the standards chosen by regulators. Our analysis, by allowing quality leaders to influence future standards, leads to interesting results which call into question the universal applause for pro-active corporate quality leadership. Specifically, we find that the leader's quality choice will be *lower* than it would have been had the government set an MQS first. By strategically sinking the costs of a technology that exceeds anticipated government standards by a limited amount, the leader influences the government to set a lower MQS. This lower MQS means that the leader's action leads to a *lower* level of social welfare than would be achieved under the "government as leader" scenario.

2.1   A general model

In this section, we present our argument in general form. Two firms compete on the basis of both (vertical) quality and price. Since product differentiation relaxes price competition, even firms with identical cost functions will offer distinct qualities in equilibrium. We refer to the high-quality firm as firm H and the low-quality firm as firm L. The regulator may set an MQS either to increase price competition or to reduce the external impacts of production. As a benchmark, we analyze the case where the regulator and the high-quality firm choose qualities simultaneously in the first stage of the game. This benchmark provides a convenient point from which to approach the timing of quality standards, with either the high-quality firm or the regulator acting as the first mover. First, we characterize the equilibrium when the regulator leads, setting a binding minimum quality level for firm L, with firm H making its quality choice after the regulation is set. To this equilibrium we compare the equilibrium in which the high-quality firm H commits to its quality level *before* the regulator promulgates a standard.[18]

[18] We have not modeled explicitly solvency constraints for the firms; these constraints will not be binding if welfare is sufficiently concave in quality. Positive profits can be assured through a number of means. For example, the regulator might weight profits more heavily than other

Throughout the chapter we use the following notation. Quality levels are denoted by s_i $i = \{H, L\}$, where H denotes the high-quality firm and L denotes the low-quality firm. Similarly, profits are denoted by $\pi_i(s_H, s_L)$ $i = \{H, L\}$. External costs, e.g. environmental damages due to pollution, are represented by $D(s_H, s_L)$, and consumer surplus from the purchase of the firms' products is given by $CS(s_H, s_L)$. Choice variables without subscripts denote 1×2 vectors, and are in bold type. Inequalities written in vector form apply to all arguments of the vector.

For simplicity, we assume the regulator's objective is to maximize social welfare, given by $W(s_H, s_L) = \pi_H(s_H, s_L) + \pi_L(s_H, s_L) + CS(s_H, s_L) - D(s_H, s_L)$. We define the 1×2 vector of qualities $\mathbf{s}^* = argmax\ W(s_H, s_L)$ to be the unconstrained welfare maximum. It is important to note that our results are not driven by the precise specification of the regulator's objective function, however. For example, we could place weights on the different components of the objective function, and the qualitative nature of our results would be unchanged. Similarly, the same type of results would emerge in a model where the regulator is driven by interest group pressures rather than welfare maximization. Indeed, even if the regulator cared nothing about the firms' profits, it would still attempt to avoid driving the low-quality firm bankrupt, in order to ensure competition in the product market for the benefit of consumers.

We begin our formal analysis by presenting a set of assumptions sufficient to generate our results:

(1) Profit functions $\pi_i(s_H, s_L)$ $i = \{H, L\}$ and social welfare $W(s_H, s_L)$ are globally concave. In addition, $\partial^2 \pi_i / \partial s_i s_j > 0$ $i = \{H, L\}$, $\partial^2 W / \partial s_H \partial s_L > 0$, and $\partial \pi_H / \partial s_L < 0$.

(2) The regulator sets an MQS. The high-quality firm chooses to exceed it, but the low-quality firm does not. In the simultaneous-move game between the standard-setting regulator and the high-quality firm, there exists a unique Nash equilibrium in qualities, $\mathbf{s}^N = (s_L^N, s_H^N)$.

(3) $\mathbf{s}^* > \mathbf{s}^N$.

Let $k_H(s_L)$ be firm H's reaction curve, that is, its best response to any possible quality choice s_L made by firm L. Similarly, $k_L(s_H)$ is firm L's

---

factors in its objective function, the firms might start the game with large positive quality levels, the firms might operate in multiple markets with economies of scope and/or scale, or the regulator might, if necessary, intervene to ensure that firms remain solvent after standards are imposed. Even if solvency constraints were modeled explicitly, the qualitative nature of our results would remain: the high-quality firm would prefer to commit to a lower level of quality than it would choose if the regulator moved first.

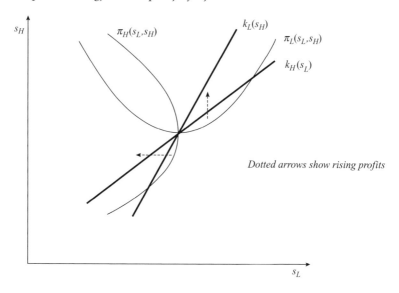

Figure 4.1   Quality strategic complements

reaction curve. Note that assumptions 1 and 2 together ensure that quality choices are strategic complements, so reaction curves $k_L(s_H)$ and $k_H(s_L)$ are upward sloping.[19] Thus, each firm will increase its own quality if the other firm does so. This is illustrated for the two firms in figure 4.1, which also shows iso-profit curves for each firm at the Nash equilibrium of the simultaneous-move game (the point where the reaction curves cross). These iso-profit curves show the set of points, for each firm, that are equally as profitable as the Nash equilibrium. The arrows in the figure show that profits for firm L increase as firm H's quality, s_H, increases, but that profits for firm H increase as firm L's quality, s_L, falls. Thus, each firm's profits grow as the difference in their quality levels increases. As a result, firm L will set the lowest quality level it can, subject to the MQS set by the regulator. Note that although figure 4.1 does not depict the regulator's reaction curve, $v(s_H)$, it also slopes upward, as shown in figure 4.2. Assumption 3 states that the regulator prefers a higher level of quality than is provided in the Nash equilibrium.[20]

---

[19] For an explanation of the notion of strategic complements, and the technical assumptions that underpin them, see Tirole (1989, pp. 207–208). For an excellent, and relatively non-technical, discussion of strategic complements and substitutes, see Besanko, Dranove, and Shanley (1996, chapter 9).

[20] Note that an MQS is useless if the regulator desires a lower quality level than is provided at the Nash equilibrium.

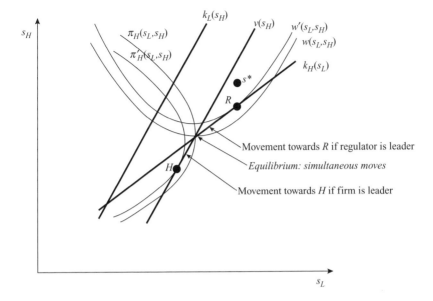

Figure 4.2 Equilibria for different first movers

2.2 Results in the general case

In this section, we show that the effectiveness of MQSs depends in subtle but important ways on the timing of moves in the quality choice game. In particular, we show that if the high-quality firm is able to move first and to commit to its quality choice, it can induce the regulator to set a weaker MQS than the regulator would set if it moved first. Furthermore, we show that overall social welfare is reduced as a result.

Our overall argument can be seen geometrically, as illustrated in figure 4.2. This figure is similar to figure 4.1, but there are two important differences. First, although we continue to show the low-quality firm's best response function, $k_L(s_H)$, its iso-profit curves are not shown in figure 4.2, since firm L simply operates at the lowest quality level allowed by the regulator. Thus, firm L is not really an active player in the game. Second, we focus instead on the regulator, who is very much an active player. This allows us to treat the game as essentially a two-player game between the regulator and the high-quality firm. We show the regulator's iso-welfare curves and its best response function $v(s_H)$. Note that the regulator's best response function $v(s_H)$ lies to the right of firm L's best response $k_L(s_H)$, indicating that social welfare maximization calls for higher quality than does firm L's profit maximizing calculation. (This follows because firm

L ignores externalities and also prefers excessively low quality as a way to mitigate price competition.)

When one player gets to move first in such a game, she takes as a given that the other player will play her best response to the leader's move, that is, she will operate on her reaction curve. Thus, the first mover chooses her most preferred point from among all the points that are on the second player's reaction curve. This most preferred point can be identified using the first mover's iso-payoff curves. She chooses the point that allows her to achieve her highest iso-payoff curve, subject to the constraint that the point must also be on the other player's reaction curve. In fact, this highest feasible iso-payoff curve will be just tangent to the rival's reaction curve; any higher iso-payoff curves would fail to touch the reaction curve at all.

If the regulator promulgates standards *before* firm *H* sets its quality level, the regulator will pick the point on firm *H*'s best response function that offers the highest level of social welfare, i.e. that is on the highest possible iso-welfare curve. This means that the regulator chooses the point *R* at which firm *H*'s best response is just tangent to the best feasible iso-welfare curve, which is labeled $w'(s_L, s_H)$.[21] Point *R* involves higher quality on the part of both firms than would the simultaneous-move equilibrium where the regulator and the high-quality firm choose quality levels simultaneously but independently.

Conversely, if the high-quality firm moves first, it chooses the point *H* where the regulator's best response function is tangent to the highest feasible iso-profit curve for firm *H*, which is labeled $\pi'_H(s_L, s_H)$. This involves lower qualities for both firms than the simultaneous-move outcome, and thus necessarily lower qualities than if the regulator had moved first.[22]

We now formalize the main points from the preceding discussion in a series of propositions, the proofs of which are presented in the appendix (p. 117). In Proposition 5, we compare the benchmark simultaneous-move equilibrium between the regulator and the high-quality firm to the equilibrium of the game in which the regulator sets the MQS before firm *H* chooses its quality level.

Proposition 5: *Compared to the benchmark equilibrium in the simultaneous-move game between the regulator and the high-quality firm, the*

---

[21] The regulator's most preferred point **s*** is not attainable, given firm *H*'s reaction curve.

[22] Note the possibility that the regulator's ideal point may occur where the high-quality firm's profits are driven negative. In this case the regulator may set an MQS that is below its desired outcome, but still above the Nash, or lump sum transfers may be used to implement the desired MQS.

equilibrium in which the MQS is determined prior to the quality choice of the high-quality firm features higher quality levels for both firms, lower profits for the high-quality firm, and a higher level of social welfare.

Proposition 5 shows that the regulator benefits from being able to move first, since it can thereby set a higher MQS, but the high-quality firm is worse off. The high-quality firm thus has incentives to try and prevent the regulator from exercising a first mover advantage. In particular, we would like to know the optimal strategy for firm H to adopt if it anticipates an MQS will be imposed by the regulator. The following proposition characterizes the equilibrium if firm H chooses its quality level prior to the regulator's choice of the MQS.

Proposition 6: *Compared to the benchmark case, if the high-quality firm can precommit to a quality level before minimum quality standards are promulgated, it will induce the regulator to set a weaker standard, and both firms will produce lower quality. While the high-quality firm's profits increase, welfare falls.*

Proposition 6 shows that the high-quality firm benefits from having a first mover position, and uses its position to induce lower qualities. In particular, it commits to a lower quality level than would emerge if the regulator moved first. If the regulator imposed the same standard anyway, both firms' profits would fall due to the increased price competition. Because the regulator cares about profits, however, it weakens the MQS in response to the high-quality firm's positioning, although the reduction in the MQS is less than one for one. While the restricted range of qualities that results intensifies price competition, the cost savings from reduced quality more than make up for any revenue lost from lower prices, and the firms enjoy increased profits relative to the benchmark case. The reduction in prices is not sufficient to compensate consumers for the loss in quality, however, and total welfare falls relative to the simultaneous-move case.

Given the results of the two preceding propositions we can compare directly the two sequential-move equilibria discussed above.

Proposition 7: *The equilibrium in the sequential game in which the high-quality firm chooses its quality level prior to the regulator's choice of the MQS features lower levels of quality, higher profits for the high-quality firm, and a lower level of social welfare than the equilibrium of the sequential game in which the MQS is set first.*

Propositions 5–7 illustrate that by clever strategic positioning, the high-quality leader can lower the quality "ceiling" below which the regulator must operate, thereby mitigating the impacts of the regulation on corporate profits. As mentioned earlier, such positioning requires that the high-quality firm commit to a quality level and not readjust the "quality frontier" of products on offer after the imposition of a standard. Interestingly, this appears to have been the case for appliance efficiency standards, as the technological frontier did not shift outward in the wake of the imposition of the standards. Of course, the overall effect on welfare of the reduced quality levels must be balanced against the sharper price competition that results when product differentiation is diminished. In our model, however, the net effects of the high-quality firm's strategic move are negative for both consumers and for social welfare in general.

It is important to note that our results are not driven by the precise specification of the regulator's objective function. The same type of results would emerge, for example, in a model where the regulator is driven by interest group pressures rather than pure welfare maximization. Indeed, even if the regulator cared nothing about the firms' profits, it would still attempt to avoid driving the low-quality firm bankrupt, in order to ensure competition in the product market for the benefit of consumers. After the quality leader sinks its initial investment, the bankruptcy constraint for firm L would occur at a lower level of s_L, and hence the regulator would still respond to the quality leader's action by setting a lower standard than it would choose if acting first.

2.3   Quality leadership in a vertical product differentiation model with pollution externalities

In this section, we study a specific model of duopolistic competition with endogenous (vertical) product qualities, and show that it satisfies the sufficient conditions identified in subsection 2.2.[23] (For details on the calculations in this section, see the appendix, p. 117.) Consumers have identical preferences, but income differences lead to differences in the willingness to pay for a particular product quality. Two firms offer products of different qualities in one market. The firms bear convex quality-dependent fixed costs and compete in qualities and prices in a two-stage industry

---

[23] Key papers in this line of research include Gabszewicz and Thisse (1979), Shaked and Sutton (1982), and Ronnen (1991).

game. Since greater product differentiation reduces substitutability and price competition, even firms with identical cost functions will offer distinct qualities in the resulting market equilibrium.

In the standard version of this model, the consumption of a particular product of a certain quality affects only the utility of the individual consumer. Products involving safety, efficiency, or environmental standards, however, typically create at least some external impacts. Accordingly, we build a model in which an individual consumer internalizes some but not all of the benefits of higher quality, and we explicitly model the external effects of firms' quality choices.[24] It is worth noting that while the model of this section is a special case of the model presented in subsection 2.2, the explicit inclusion of externalities makes it more general than much of the existing literature on vertical product differentiation, e.g. Ronnen (1991) or Arora and Gangopadhyay (1995) (box 4.2).

2.3.1 The model

There are two firms, the high-quality firm H and the low-quality firm L. If both firms remain in the market, then they produce distinct goods, sold at prices p_H and p_L, respectively. The two products carry a single quality attribute denoted by s_H and s_L, respectively. Sales quantities are given by q_H and q_L. Each firm faces a fixed cost $F_i = b_i s_i^2$, $i = \{H, L\}$. We assume that $b_L \geq b_H$, that is, the firm which chooses to produce the higher-quality product faces per-unit quality costs that are no greater than those faced by its rival.[25] Marginal production costs are equal to zero for both firms.

There is a continuum of consumers (indexed by t) distributed uniformly over the interval $[0, T]$ with unit density.[26] Each consumer purchases at most one unit of either firm H's product or firm L's product. The higher a

---

[24] For a pure public good, consumers derive no private benefit from purchasing a high-quality product and individual firms derive no private benefit from quality leadership. Firms' only rationale for self-regulation in this setting is the complete preemption of future regulations; this case is studied in Maxwell, Lyon, and Hackett (2000).

[25] One way to interpret our assumption that the high-quality firm can commit to a quality level is to assume the firm must incur cost F_i for any change of quality s_i. This corresponds to the case in Williamson (1985, chapter 7), in which all advance costs are non-salvageable.

[26] The parameter t represents willingness to pay and increases with income. Let $U[0, T]$ be the uniform probability distribution. Then this distribution of consumers corresponds to $T^*U[0, T]$ with density $T^*1/(T - 0) = 1$ for all t, regardless of the upper bound T. The total mass of consumers representing population size is equal to T, while the average income parameter $T/2$ represents *per capita* income. The assumption of a uniform distribution of consumers is a common simplification used in product differentiation models. Other distributional assumptions (such as distributions with mass points of consumers at zero) are

consumer's income parameter t, the higher is her reservation price. Consumer t's utility is given by $u_t = s_i t - p_i$ if good i is purchased.

The two firms play a two-stage game. In the first stage, firms determine qualities to be produced and incur costs F_i, $i = \{H, L\}$; these choices may be constrained by an MQS imposed by the regulator. In the second stage, firms choose prices simultaneously (Bertrand competition).[27] While we begin our exposition in this section with the unregulated equilibrium, it should be clear that our main interest is in quality choices when the regulator enforces an MQS, as discussed in subsection 2.2. As we will show, the MQS will be binding for the low-quality firm, so the game is effectively between the regulator and the high-quality firm. The interpretation of quality as the inverse of an index of environmental pollution is simple. Let pollution per unit of good i be $1/s_i$. Pollution per total quantity consumed of good i is then $D_i = q_i/s_i$, and total pollution is given by $D = D_H + D_L$.

2.3.2   The unregulated equilibrium

Despite the introduction of externalities, the equilibrium of the unregulated model is identical to that of Ronnen (1991) and Lehmann-Grube (1997), so in this section we simply record some of its key properties. It is straightforward to solve for the second-stage pricing equilibrium. Given this price equilibrium, demands and thus profits can be expressed in reduced form as functions of qualities. For positive qualities s_i ($i = H, L$), these profit functions are:

$$\Pi_H = \frac{4T^2 s_H^2(s_H - s_L)}{(4s_H - s_L)^2} - b_H s_H^2 \quad \Pi_L = \frac{T^2 s_H s_L(s_H - s_L)}{(4s_H - s_L)^2} - b_L s_L^2.$$
(4.1)

Similarly, consumer surplus, and environmental degradation costs can be expressed in the following way:

$$CS = \frac{T^2 s_H^2(4s_H + 5s_L)}{2(4s_H - s_L)^2} \quad D = \frac{T(2s_L + s_H)}{s_L(4s_H - s_L)}.$$
(4.2)

Total welfare, W, is the sum of profits and consumer surplus, less environmental degradation costs.

---

equally legitimate and may yield different results. However our intention here is simply to illustrate that voluntary actions can be welfare reducing.

[27] To derive solutions, we use the concept of subgame-perfect equilibrium, computing the solutions for each stage in reverse order. Both firms choose their respective product quality from the same interval $[0, \infty)$. The resulting market equilibria will include some consumers in the lower segment of the interval $[0, T]$ not valuing quality enough to buy any product. This guarantees an interior solution of the price game.

From the properties of the profit functions, it can be shown that the two firms' qualities are strategic complements, as pictured in figure 4.1. This is easy to understand for high-quality firm H: when firm L's quality improves, H has incentives to raise its quality further in order to maintain product differentiation and the relaxed price competition it provides. The upward slope of firm L's reaction curve has a slightly different explanation. One might expect that when firm H increases quality, firm L would not respond at all, enjoying the increased product differentiation. This is incorrect, however; the marginal revenue to L of a quality increase is rising with s_H. When H raises its quality, this relaxes price competition and allows L's price to rise. The higher margin, in turn, makes it worthwhile to raise quality in order to expand demand. Hence firm L follows an increase in quality by firm H, although at a rate less than one for one.

The regulator, of course, takes a broader view than do the firms, and includes consumer surplus and external costs in its objective function, as well as the firms' profits. Since the low-quality firm is interested only in profit maximization, the assumed distribution of consumers implies that the low-quality firm will always want to choose a lower quality level than the MQS. Hence, the regulator's reaction curve lies to the right of the low-quality firm's reaction curve, and the MQS chosen by the regulator will always be binding on the low quality firm. In the appendix (p. 118), we show that the assumptions made in subsection 2.2 of the chapter are satisfied in the particular case of a vertical product quality model with externalities and minimum quality regulation. Hence the results derived there apply here. While the model analyzed in this section is in a sense a "special case," it is of interest for two significant reasons. First, it demonstrates by example that the assumptions made in subsection 2.2 are general enough to encompass economically meaningful models. Second, it extends the existing literature on vertical product differentiation by explicitly incorporating external costs.

3   SIGNALING

Our signaling model follows very much in the spirit of the "raising rivals' costs" literature that was initiated by Salop and Scheffman (1983). Unlike our quality leadership model, this model casts corporate voluntary actions in a positive light. Since the regulatory authority's decision regarding whether to mandate the high-quality technology follows the firm's adoption decision, and that decision signals the true adoption costs, the regulator will mandate the high-quality technology only if by doing so it improves social welfare.[28] Unlike our preemption model of chapter 3, however, the firm's voluntary actions here do not lead to a Pareto-improvement. In fact the firm's action is motivated by the desire to put its rivals at a cost disadvantage, making them worse off. The mandated technology may also lower consumer surplus. These losses, however, may be outweighed by the gains to the firm undertaking the voluntary adoption and the environmental improvements from the mandated technology.

3.1   Du Pont corporation and Freon Products

The idea that regulations can benefit some firms to the detriment of others is not new; the twist here is that corporate voluntary actions can be used to induce the regulatory mandate. The international ban on the production of chlorofluorocarbons (CFCs) is a classic example of corporate voluntary actions, in this case by Du Pont, being used to gain a competitive advantage over rival firms.[29] CFCs were first linked to reductions in stratospheric ozone in 1974 in a scientific study by Mario Molina and Sherry Rowland, two chemists at the University of California at Irvine. At that time, Du Pont was the world leader in the production of various forms of CFCs, which were used in refrigeration, air conditioning, foam blowing, and consumer aerosol sprays, among other products. Du Pont first developed CFCs in the 1930s, and held patents over various forms of the product until the late 1940s. Around this time, the use of CFCs exploded. While its patents had expired by the 1970s, Du Pont maintained its position as the world's leading producer, maintaining market leadership in America, Europe, and Japan.

The Molina and Rowland article prompted many stories in the popular press, especially in the USA and Canada, focusing on the link between ozone depletion and health risks, including skin cancer. The articles prompted a widespread decline in the use of CFCs in consumer products in America, notably aerosol sprays, but the same was not true in Europe and Japan. Du Pont's initial reaction to the 1974 report was that the issue needed further study, and it supported a business-as-usual approach until more evidence was produced. In the early 1980s, new scientific models cast doubt on the 1974 findings, suggesting that the reductions in stratospheric ozone were much smaller than early studies had indicated. During this period, Du Pont

---

[28] For the signal to credibly convey information, it must be the case that it is cheaper for a firm with low abatement costs to undertake environmental improvement than it would be for a firm with high abatement costs, an eminently reasonable situation.

[29] For a detailed account of the story, see Reinhardt (1989).

established and led the industry association "Alliance for Responsible CFC Policy," made up of CFC producers and consumers. The Alliance lobbied congress and the EPA for a measured response to the ozone issue. In 1985, however, a group of British researchers working in Antarctica reported a dramatic decrease in spring-time stratospheric ozone over the continent. This discovery suggested not only that initial studies were more accurate than the one that followed them, but also that the early studies were too optimistic.

The 1985 finding regarding the ozone "hole" was widely reported in the popular press and further reductions in consumer-related CFC use continued in Europe and Japan. The CFC industry began to experience widespread excess capacity, and the industry found itself being transformed from a profitable oligopolistic industry into a bulk chemical industry with the resulting decline in profitability. By mid-1986, sophisticated computer models of ozone depletion showed that sustained use of CFCs at current levels would lead to considerable damage to the ozone layer for years to come.[30] Following the release of this information, Du Pont changed its position.

Du Pont, departing from other member firms in the Alliance that were pushing for reductions in the rate of growth in CFC production, called for production caps and reductions in CFC production. Du Pont broadly supported the 1987 Montreal Protocol, which called on developed countries to cap CFC production at the 1986 level by 1989, and reduce CFC production to 50 percent of 1986 levels by 1999. A prime concern for Du Pont, and eventually other members of the Alliance, was that any caps or reductions in CFC production should be made on an international basis and not done unilaterally by the USA. American producers of CFCs felt that the EPA's earlier actions had harmed their competitiveness in relation to European and Japanese producers. The Montreal Protocol was signed by almost all industrialized nations and was to become law once two-thirds of signatories had ratified it.

In 1988, the intergovernmental Ozone Trends Panel, led by the National Aeronautics and Space Administration (NASA), released an influential report providing strong evidence linking ozone depletion to the presence of CFCs in the atmosphere. In response, Du Pont took a bold step and announced its intention to halt production of CFCs altogether by 1999. Since the early 1970s, Du Pont had invested heavily in developing CFC substitutes. Though its commitment waxed and waned in the late 1970s,

---

[30] The nature of CFCs means that it takes several years before CFCs released into the atmosphere reach, and break down, stratospheric ozone.

by the early 1980s it was investing heavily in substitutes development. Du Pont's actions following the discovery and development of CFC substitutes illustrate the importance of political–economic considerations in the development of the CFC substitute markets. While CFC substitutes could be produced, they were much more expensive than CFCs and generally did not perform as well in industrial applications. Even with the Protocol in place, the substitute market would be small because of the costs.

In order for the CFC substitute market to be economically attractive, the production of CFCs would need to be cut back further. In order for such cutbacks to be put in place by governments, however, the existence of economically viable substitutes would have to be a certainty. Du Pont's commitment to abandon CFC production signaled its commitment to the large-scale production of CFC substitutes. Du Pont lobbied for a strengthening of the Montreal Protocol to call for the eventual elimination of the production of CFCs.

The amendments to the Montreal Protocol not only helped eliminate the supply of CFCs, they also eliminated competitor producers. While Du Pont's patents on CFCs had lapsed by the early 1940s, the company held patents on CFC substitutes. Thus, Du Pont was able to transform its position as the dominant firm in a low-margin commodity market into a near-monopoly on the production of CFC substitutes.[31] While Du Pont's rivals in the CFC industry suffered losses from the Protocol, and CFC substitute prices were much higher than prevailing CFC prices, politicians were convinced that the environmental benefits of the phaseout outweighed these losses. The existence of known and proven CFC substitutes was crucial in the signatories' ultimate decision to support the total ban on the production of CFCs.

3.2   The signaling model

We now present a simple model developed by Denicolo (2000) in which the voluntary adoption of an environmental technology signals (conveys credible information to) a regulator about the firm's adoption costs. For simplicity's sake we assume that the industry of concern consists of two firms, A and B. Further, we assume that there are only two production technologies, a high-quality clean technology, C, and a lower-quality dirty

---

[31] ICI of the UK was the only other firm to hold patents on the production of some CFC substitutes.

technology, D. The regulator faces a choice of whether to mandate the use of the clean technology. In doing so, its objective is to maximize social welfare, defined by

$$W = \pi_A + \pi_B + CS - E, \qquad (4.3)$$

where π_x, $x \in \{A, B\}$ denotes firm profits, CS denotes consumer surplus, and E denotes environmental damages. The clean technology might be mandated because it reduces the level of environmental damage.

The timing of the game is as follows. In period 1, firm A decides whether to adopt the clean technology or the dirty technology.[32] In period 2, the regulator, having observed firm A's decision, decides whether or not to mandate the use of the clean technology. If the clean technology is mandated, both firms must produce using the clean technology. If the clean technology is not mandated, then firm B will produce using the dirty technology, while firm A will use the clean technology.[33]

The clean technology produces less pollution, but it is also a more expensive production technology. Although, this is known to the regulator, what is unknown is the exact cost of the technology. We assume that the true cost of the clean technology is the realization of the random variable $\theta \in \{\underline{\theta}, \bar{\theta}\}, \underline{\theta} < \bar{\theta}$. The realization of θ is known to firm A prior to its adoption decision. The regulator believes there is probability p that $\theta = \underline{\theta}$ (and therefore probability $1 - p$ that $\theta = \bar{\theta}$.) The regulator's prior belief regarding p is assumed to be common knowledge.

In order to simplify the analysis, we assume that all abatement costs are fixed costs, rather than variable costs. In this case, the adoption decision affects neither the output nor the pricing decisions of firms, so the regulator cannot use these decisions to infer anything about the firms' adoption decisions. We are interested in determining the conditions under which the adoption of the clean technology by firm A in period 1 will induce the regulator to mandate the clean technology.

Let us denote by $\pi_i \left(T_i, T_j, \theta \right)$ the profits of firm i, $j \in \{A, B\}$, $i \neq j$ given the technology T_i with clean-technology production costs θ. We make the following assumptions

$$\begin{aligned} \pi_i \left(C, D, \theta \right) < \pi_i \left(D, D, \theta \right) \text{ and} \\ \pi_i \left(C, C, \theta \right) < \pi_i \left(D, C, \theta \right), \end{aligned} \qquad (4.4)$$

---

[32] We shall assume that firm A holds an adoption cost advantage over firm B. Thus, it is not rational for firm B to voluntarily adopt the technology.

[33] We assume it is too costly for firm A to reverse its production technology.

that is, profits are lower for either firm when using the clean-production technology, for any technology used by the rival firm. Total firm profits are given by $\pi_i = \pi_i^1 + \delta \pi_i^2$, where superscripts denote time periods and δ is the discount factor.

Letting W^{NR}, $\underline{W}^R$, and $\overline{W}^R$ denote welfare under no regulation, welfare under regulation when clean-technology production costs are low, and welfare under regulation when clean-technology production costs are high, respectively, we make the following assumptions

$$\pi_A\left(C, C, \underline{\theta}\right) > \pi_A\left(D, D\right) \tag{4.5}$$

and

$$\underline{W}^R > W^{NR} > \overline{W}^R. \tag{4.6}$$

Assumption (4.5) implies that when clean-technology production costs are low, firm A would prefer that the regulator mandate the clean-production technology, rather than face a regime of no regulation. Under no regulation, the costs of the clean-production technology are irrelevant because no matter their level, both firms will find it more profitable to produce using the dirty technology. Assumption (4.6) implies that the regulator will want to mandate the adoption of the clean technology only when production costs are low.

3.3   The separating equilibrium

The model admits three type of equilibria, depending on the government's interpretation of firm A's actions. In one type, called a "separating equilibrium," firm A makes a different adoption decision when its cost is high than it would make if its cost were low. In the second type of equilibrium, called a "pooling equilibrium," firm A makes the same adoption decision regardless of the adoption cost, while the third type of equilibrium, called a "hybrid equilibrium," combines the characteristics of the first two. For our purposes, the relevant equilibrium type is the separating equilibrium. In the separating equilibrium, firm A adopts the clean-production technology in period 1 if the clean-production technology is low-cost, while firm A will not adopt if the clean-production technology is high-cost; the regulator mandates the clean-production technology only if firm A adopts it in period 1.

To construct this equilibrium, we denote by q the regulator's second-period posterior beliefs regarding the cost of operating the clean technology, that is, q is the new probability with which the regulator expects the technology to have a low cost. Then the expected welfare from regulating the clean technology is

$$W^R(q) = q\underline{W}^R + (1-q)\overline{W}^R. \tag{4.7}$$

From assumption (4.7) there exists a $\tilde{q} \in (0, 1)$ that results in $W^R(\tilde{q}) = W^{NR}$. If $q > \tilde{q}$ the regulation will be mandated and not otherwise.

We now examine firm A's incentive to signal low cost through the adoption of the clean technology in the first period. Recall that $\pi_A(C, D, \theta) < \pi_A(D, D)$ so adoption in period 1 requires firm A to sacrifice profits. Let z be the probability that the regulator mandates the clean technology, and $\phi(z, \theta)$ be firm A's expected net benefit from signaling by adopting technology C. Then we can write

$$\phi(z, \theta) = [\pi_A(C, D, \theta) - \pi_A(D, D)] + z\delta[\pi_A(C, C, \theta) - \pi_A(D, D)]. \tag{4.8}$$

Thus, the net benefits from signaling are the sum of the (certain) sacrifice of profits in the first period, and the (uncertain) expected discounted profits in the second period if the regulation is actually imposed; assumption (4.5) assures that if the regulation is imposed, then the firm benefits. Clearly firm A will want to adopt in period 1 if and only if $\phi(z, \theta) > 0$. From assumption (4.5), it is clear that $\phi(z, \theta)$ is increasing in z. Further, because θ is the cost of adopting the clean technology, we know that $\phi(z, \theta)$ is decreasing in θ. Taken together, these two observations imply that firm A has a greater incentive to send the signal when the cost of the clean technology is low, i.e. $\theta = \underline{\theta}$. We are now ready to characterize the separating equilibrium.[34]

Proposition 8: *If $p < \tilde{q}$ and $\phi(1, \underline{\theta}) > 0 > \phi(1, \overline{\theta})$, then there exists a unique separating equilibrium in which the low-cost type of firm A adopts the clean technology in period 1, while the high-cost type does not, and the regulator mandates the clean technology in period 2 if and only if firm A adopts it in period 1.*

Under the conditions of Proposition 8 we see that voluntary overcompliance in the form of unmandated clean-technology adoption serves to induce the regulator to mandate the clean technology. The first condition of Proposition 8 states that $p < \tilde{q}$, which implies that absent the technology adoption by firm A the regulator would not mandate the technology.

---

[34] For a proof of the proposition, see Denicolo (2000).

The second condition, $\phi\left(1, \underline{\theta}\right) > 0 > \phi\left(1, \bar{\theta}\right)$ states that if the regulator, upon seeing the adoption, mandates it with certainty, then firm A would adopt only if the clean technology were low-cost. Firm A would not find it profitable to adopt if the clean technology was high-cost, even if it was then mandated on firm B. Knowing this, the regulator will wish to mandate the technology after seeing firm A adopt, because it knows that social welfare under a low-cost clean technology exceeds the social welfare that would arise under no regulation.

We can gain considerable insight into the economics of the separating equilibrium from further consideration of the conditions used to derive it.[35] Note first that firm A's profits are greater under the regulated equilibrium than under the unregulated equilibrium. We know also that the level of environmental damage must be lower under the regulated equilibrium. In order for the regulator to mandate the clean technology, these two gains must outweigh any losses in consumer surplus and any loss in profits incurred by firm B. We know from (4.4) that forced adoption of the clean technology does lead to a profit reduction for firm B. Similarly, under all common models of duopoly we know that consumer surplus will be lower under the mandate since both firms will face higher production costs. When clean-production technology costs are low, however, the benefits resulting from regulation outweigh the costs.

In an extension to his model, Denicolo (2000) develops an example in which firm B is a potential entrant, facing a fixed cost of entry. He assumes that the fixed cost is such that if firm B is forced to adopt the clean technology, entry will be unprofitable. A separating equilibrium of the type just discussed is again generated. In this separating equilibrium, however, firm A maintains its monopoly in period 2. While consumer surplus is clearly lower under regulation, and firm B's profits are by definition zero, the regulator nonetheless mandates adoption of the clean technology because the combination of environmental benefits and firm A's enhanced profits outweigh the costs.

Our analysis in this section has assumed that the regulator maximizes overall social welfare. In this case, society always benefits if the regulator is informed about the costs of pollution control before making its decision. This conclusion might not hold if the regulator were biased, e.g. if it were captured by firm A. Suppose society were made worse off by

---

[35] Denicolo (2000) provides examples of the separating equilibrium using specific functional forms. The separating equilibrium is found to exist under both Cournot and Bertrand duopoly competition.

mandating the clean technology, even if its costs were relatively low. This might occur if the environmental benefits of the technology were modest, but prices would rise significantly, thereby reducing consumer surplus. As long as the mandate raised firm *A*'s profits, perhaps by forcing firm *B* to exit the market, the regulator would respond to *A*'s signal by imposing the technology mandate. Indeed, this may have been the case in the UHT milk example mentioned at the beginning of the chapter. The environmental benefits of the US milk standards were non-existent, and the primary effect of the Puerto Rican regulation was to allow Puerto Rican firms to sell into the US market. The regulation reduced domestic competition, harming domestic consumers. It is possible, however, that if domestic producers greatly increased their sales in the USA, the total effect of the regulation on Puerto Rico could have been positive. Nevertheless, this is not assured if the regulator is captured by the domestic firms, in which case it might impose the regulation even if overall social welfare were reduced.

4 NON-TECHNICAL SUMMARY

In this chapter, we have studied models in which firms can raise their profits by the voluntary adoption of high-quality technologies. In our quality leadership model we saw that some firms in an industry have incentives to engage in pro-active environmental quality improvements in order to differentiate themselves from other firms in the industry. By doing so, they soften price competition, and raise their profits. We extended this basic model by incorporating the possibility of MQSs set by the regulator. The regulator uses the MQS to induce both firms to increase the quality of their products, thereby making consumers better off.

In the model, the sequence of moves is as follows. First, the high-quality firm sinks an investment in choosing a particular quality level. The reason he does this is to influence the standard that will be set by the regulator in the future. Second, the regulator observes the firm's investment and sets an MQS. Because the high-quality firm's choice is already sunk, the regulator is loth to set a higher MQS, which could severely reduce the firm's profits. Third, the low-quality firm increases its quality level up to the minimum level required, and consumers make their choices between products. The low-quality firm is thus a fundamentally passive player in the model, and it does not engage in strategic behavior. This allows us to focus on the interaction between the high-quality firm and the regulator.

The game involves what are often called "strategic complements," that is, both the high-quality firm and the regulator have incentives to increase their quality choice if the other strategic player does so; in a strategic sense, quality increases are complementary to one another. From the high-quality firm's perspective, it wants to raise its quality when the regulator sets a higher MQS, in order to differentiate itself from the low-quality firm and thereby reduce the price competition between them. From the regulator's perspective, when the high-quality firm increases its quality choice, this relaxes price competition somewhat and allows the MQS to be raised a bit without driving the low-quality firm into bankruptcy.

Our key results emerge by contrasting the outcomes of two cases, one in which the regulator moves first, and the other in which the high-quality firm moves first. The key point is that the high-quality firm prefers a low MQS to a high one. When the regulator increases the standard, the high-quality firm also raises its quality, in an attempt to maintain some product differentiation. However, the higher the standard, the lower is the ultimate gap between the low-quality and high-quality firms. (In other words, we show that it is not profitable for the high-quality firm to match increases in the MQS one for one.) Thus, price competition becomes more intense as the MQS is raised, and profits for both firms fall. As a result, if the high-quality firm gets to move first, it will commit to a lower level of quality than would be preferred by the regulator, in an attempt to reduce price competition as much as possible. From society's perspective, consumers are harmed by the loss of competition that results. Our analysis thus implies that corporate environmentalism can have negative social consequences when it occurs during the interval between the passage of legislation and the implementation of regulations that enact the legislation.

The signaling model involves quite a different type of model. A key feature in this model is that the regulator does not know the cost to firms of implementing a new regulatory policy; this cost may be high or it may be low. We focused on a case where implementing the regulation would be worthwhile, from the regulator's perspective, only if the adoption cost were low.

In the signaling model, there are two firms, one of which (firm A) has a lower cost of adopting a clean technology than does the other (firm B). This might occur, for example, if firm A is better able to deal with production process changes because of its superior technical or managerial skills. Firm A moves first, having a choice of either voluntarily adopting the clean technology or not. The regulator then has the option of requiring both firms to adopt the clean technology. We investigate the possibility that firm

A's voluntary adoption can induce the regulator to mandate the use of the clean technology. This can occur if the regulator correctly infers the cost of adoption from observing A's behavior, i.e. it knows the cost is low if firm A adopts voluntarily. For such an inference to be valid, it must be the case that firm A *would not* find it profitable to adopt when the cost is high, even if its adoption results in the regulator forcing firm B to adopt the clean technology as well, while firm A *would* find it profitable to adopt if the cost were low. In addition, signaling is worthwhile only if the regulator would not otherwise mandate the use of the clean technology, e.g. because it has a strong prior belief that the environmental benefits of the technology would be outweighed by the costs of adoption. If the foregoing conditions are met, then we can show that firm A's voluntary adoption of the clean technology can serve as a credible signal that induces the regulator to require firm B to adopt the technology, too.

Although firm B is placed at a disadvantage by the regulator's mandate, we found that the decision to mandate the technology is not a mistake on the regulator's part. Because the signal correctly indicates that the adoption costs of the quality improvements are low, the regulator correctly calculates that her objectives will be served by mandating the clean technology. If the regulator is concerned to maximize social welfare, this means the social benefits arising from the environmental improvements of the clean technology outweigh firm B's lost profits and any reduction in consumer surplus. Thus, the regulatory mandate raises social welfare. If the regulator were simply captured by firm A, however, then it might mandate the technology even though its overall social effects were negative, as long as firm A gained from the requirement.

5 CONCLUSIONS AND POLICY IMPLICATIONS

Our analysis of the two models in this chapter indicates that when corporate environmentalism influences future regulations, rather than preempting them, its effects on social welfare may be quite subtle. In fact, corporate environmentalism has negative social effects in the quality leadership model, but can have positive effects in the signaling model.

The quality leadership model implies that the sometimes substantial delays in standard-setting which follow Congressional directives can be damaging to welfare. As discussed above, the delays in setting minimum efficiency standards for air conditioners and water heaters came to almost three years, while delays for new NESHAP requirements under the CAA

Amendments stretched to a decade, and delays for effluent guidelines required by the Clean Water Act were even longer. Delays of these magnitudes allow industry leaders ample time to reposition their product lines and influence the regulator's MQS. By making a sunk investment that precommits the firm, a quality leader can constrain the regulator's subsequent choices in a way that increases the firm's profits but makes society worse off. While some delays are unavoidable, our results imply that better outcomes may be expected when regulatory agencies have ample staff and funding to allow them to implement new laws rapidly and without undue resource constraints. In addition, our analysis suggests that consumer and environmental groups may want to take a cautious view of seemingly beneficent corporate quality leadership when it occurs during the gap between passage and implementation of new laws, and may benefit from working to expedite the timely implementation of new standards.

The signaling model reminds us that the precommitment associated with corporate environmentalism does not necessarily have negative effects on regulatory outcomes. It can play a useful role by providing credible information to regulators, e.g. demonstrating by example that the costs of pollution control are not too onerous. When regulators are unsure of the costs of reducing pollution, corporate leadership by example can speak louder than words, conveying information that traditional lobbying cannot. This information provision function can enhance overall social welfare, in contrast to the harmful effects of precommitment in the quality leadership model. Nevertheless, it is important to recognize that having a well-informed regulator is only guaranteed to benefit society if the regulator's goal is aligned with overall social welfare. If the regulator is captured by a portion of the regulated industry, then signaling via corporate environmentalism may make society worse off.

In future research, it would be interesting to incorporate asymmetric information in a model of quality leadership. In the quality leadership model, a tougher standard reduces the profits of both firms, so the high-quality firm wants to avoid conveying information that would trigger a tougher standard. This fear weakens the high-quality firm's incentive to undertake voluntary environmental improvement, working against the motives we examined in subsection 2.2 of this chapter. In a similar vein, it would be interesting to explore the effects of allowing asymmetric information in a preemption model. In such a setting, industry's incentives to use voluntary action to preempt regulatory threats would be in tension with the possibility that voluntary action signals low costs and thus prompts new regulations. The objective of such research would be to identify the conditions under which the signaling incentives outweigh preemption incentives, and vice versa.

APPENDIX

A.1 Proofs for the general quality leadership model

Proposition 5: *Compared to the benchmark equilibrium in the simultaneous-move game between the regulator and the high-quality firm, the equilibrium in which the MQS is determined prior to the quality choice of the high-quality firm features higher quality levels for both firms, lower profits for the high-quality firm, and a higher level of social welfare.*

Proof: Let $k_H(s_L)$ be firm H's reaction curve. Assumptions 1 and 2 imply that the high-quality firm's reaction function is upward sloping, i.e. $dk_H/ds_L > 0$. At the Nash equilibrium, the regulator is on an indifference curve in (s_L, s_H)-space defined by the equation $W(s_H, s_L) = W^N$. The regulator – if granted commitment power – can improve welfare by moving away from the Nash equilibrium if the following expression is positive:

$$\frac{dW(k_H(s_L), s_L)}{ds_L}\bigg|_{S^N} = \frac{\partial W}{\partial s_H}\frac{dk_H}{ds_L}\bigg|_{S^N} + \frac{\partial W}{\partial s_L}\bigg|_{S^N}. \tag{4.9}$$

Note that the last term is equal to zero at the Nash equilibrium, and recall that $dk_H/ds_L > 0$. Hence the sign of the expression as a whole is equal to the sign of $\partial W/\partial s_H$. To sign this term, we totally differentiate the implicit function defining the regulator's indifference curve, $W(s_H s_L) = W^N$, yielding

$$\frac{ds_H}{ds_L}\bigg|_{W=W^N} = \frac{-\partial W/\partial s_L}{-\partial W/\partial s_H}. \tag{4.10}$$

Because W is globally concave, level sets are convex. Assumption 3 ensures that in the neighborhood of the Nash equilibrium, the regulator's indifference curves are convex toward the origin. Hence, $ds_H/ds_L < (>)0$ for points on W^N just to the left (right) of s^N. Furthermore, s_L^N is a best response and welfare is concave, so in the neighborhood of s^N, $\partial W/\partial s_L > (<)0$ for $s_L < (>)s_L^N$. Together, these observations imply that in the neighborhood of s^N, $\partial W/\partial s_H > 0$. Hence, the sign of $dW(k_H(s_L), s_L)/ds_L$ is positive and the regulator can improve welfare by increasing the MQS above the Nash equilibrium level and thereby inducing the high-quality firm to increase its quality as well.

Because the high-quality firm's indifference curves are convex toward the origin, it is immediate that movement outward along its reaction curve reduces the high-quality firm's profits. Thus we have established that the equilibrium in which the MQS is determined prior to the quality choice of the high-quality firm features higher quality levels for both firms, lower profits for the high-quality firm, and a higher level of social welfare.   ∎

Proposition 6: *Compared to the benchmark case, if the high-quality firm can precommit to a quality level before minimum quality standards are promulgated, it will induce the regulator to set a weaker standard, and both firms will produce lower quality. While the high-quality firm's profits increase, welfare falls.*

Proof: An argument similar to that used in the proof of Proposition 5 establishes that there exists a point $s^H = (s_L^H, s_H^H)$ on the regulator's reaction curve such that $s^H < s^N$ with $\pi^H > \pi^N$. Assumption 3 ensures that social welfare increases, moving outward along the regulator's reaction curve until the point s^* is reached; since $s^H < s^N < s^*$, social welfare at s^H is strictly lower than at s^*.   ∎

A.2   Sufficient conditions for the vertical differentiation model

In this section we show that the sufficient conditions identified in subsection 2.2 hold in the specific case of our model of vertical product differentiation with externalities. It is straightforward to show that the high-quality firm's profits are globally concave in qualities. In addition, this firm's revenues are declining in s_L, and the cross-partial derivative of the high-quality firm's revenue function is positive. Global concavity of the social welfare function requires that the corresponding Hessian matrix of second derivatives of the welfare function be negative definite. This condition is straightforward, if somewhat tedious, to establish. The slope of the reaction functions, and the existence of an equilibrium when the regulator and firm H move simultaneously, are established in the following lemma, the proof of which follows closely that of Lemma 1 in Lehmann-Grube (1997), and is omitted here.

Lemma 2: *The regulator has an MQS best response function $v(s_H)$ with $v'(s_H) > 0$. An equilibrium exists in the simultaneous-move game in which the regulator sets an MQS that is binding on the low-quality firm and firm H chooses its own quality.*

Lemma 2 establishes the existence of the simultaneous-move equilibrium and the sign of the regulator's reaction function; as in subsection 2.2, we denote this equilibrium by $\mathbf{s}^N = (s_L^N, s_H^N)$. We turn now to a comparison of the welfare maximum $\mathbf{s}^*$ and the Nash equilibrium $\mathbf{s}^N$, as presented in the following lemma.

Lemma 3: *Relative to the Nash equilibrium, $\mathbf{s}^N$, the welfare maximum is attained at a point $\mathbf{s}^* > \mathbf{s}^N$.*

The logic behind Lemma 3 follows a series of steps. Note first that the regulator cares about consumer surplus, environmental damages, and the low-quality firm's profits, in addition to the high-quality firm's profits. When we focus on just the first three of these, it can be shown (after some laborious calculations) that their sum is increasing in s_H. As a result, if the regulator were setting firm H's quality level, it would choose a higher quality level than would firm H operating on its own, i.e. $s_H^* > s_H^N$, since the firm ignores the effects of its actions on consumers, the environment, and the low-quality firm. Lemma 2 shows that $v'(s_H) > 0$. Thus, the MQS set by the regulator (and hence s_L) also increases when firm H's quality rises. Hence $s_L^* > s_L^N$, and we have $\mathbf{s}^* > \mathbf{s}^N$.

5 | Deflecting enforcement of existing regulations

1 INTRODUCTION

Our analysis in this part of the book has treated various stages of the policy life cycle. We began in chapter 3 with an analysis of how corporate environmentalism can preempt the emergence of legislation. Preemption does not always occur, of course, so chapter 4 explored how corporate environmental strategy can influence legislative and regulatory requirements. Even after regulations are finalized, corporate environmentalism can still have important effects. All regulations must be enforced, through monitoring of corporate behavior and the imposition of penalties in the event that non-compliance is detected. In this chapter, we examine how voluntary environmental investments can alter the monitoring and enforcement activities of regulators.

In examining firm motivations for the adoption of environmental plans, which are natural precursors to environmental investments, Henriques and Sadorsky (1996) found that the overwhelming motivation was compliance with existing and future regulations. Some government programs, such as the EPA's StarTrack, provide incentives for firms to voluntarily increase compliance activities with respect to existing environmental regulations. Under the StarTrack program, participating firms are required to establish a self-auditing compliance program, conduct periodic audits, and institute plans for correcting any discovered violations. Initial findings and progress reports are to be submitted to the EPA and made available to the public. In addition to public recognition, participating firms benefit from being considered *"a lower inspection priority"* by the regulatory agency.[1] We shall refer to this shift in inspection behavior as "regulatory responsiveness."

The StarTrack program is very much in the spirit of the EPA's changes in its audit practices contained in the publication *Audit Policy: Incentives for Self-Policing* (US EPA 1998b). The policy encourages regulated entities to voluntarily discover, disclose, and correct violations of existing environmental statutes. In exchange for these increased compliance efforts, the

---

[1] See US EPA (1998a, p. 2); emphasis added.

EPA will eliminate gravity-based penalties (that is, penalties based on the severity of environmental damage), abstain from pursuing criminal prosecution, and refrain from additional audit requests. For example, in 1997, the EPA's Region 5 office in Chicago encouraged a number of mini-mills (i.e. small steel mills) in the Midwest to conduct self-audits. According to the EPA's *Audit Policy Update* (1998c):

Approximately half of the mini-mills conducted self-audits and several disclosed violations. EPA now has inspected most of the facilities that *did not conduct* a self-audit. (1998, emphasis added)

Examples of regulatory responsiveness are not limited to the federal level. Cothran (1993) and Hemphill (1993–1994) cite examples of regulatory responsiveness by state and local regulators. International examples also exist. Corporate motivations for the promotion of the Environmental Management Audit System (EMAS) certification (a certification similar to, but more stringent than, ISO 14001) in Germany include the expected relaxation of regulatory enforcement for participating firms.[2]

We investigate the phenomenon of voluntary environmental investments (such as investments in self-audit programs or direct investments in cleaner technologies) by focusing particular attention on the monitoring and enforcement behavior of the regulator.[3] We first establish that, faced with a credible offer of regulatory responsiveness (i.e. a credible commitment to reduce the probability of monitoring and enforcement for firms that take observable environmental actions), a firm will undertake additional environmental investments. We show that the extent to which the firm is willing to invest voluntarily depends on the investment's impact on the probability of compliance. We then turn our attention to the regulator, and examine how differences in the efficiency of regulatory resources might influence the regulator's responsiveness. Finally, we examine the question of whether regulatory responsiveness is necessarily welfare improving.

The remainder of this chapter proceeds as follows. In section 2 we first provide an overview of the model and discuss issues related to timing, and then present the model in detail. In section 3 we examine the regulator's motivation to pursue responsive regulatory policies. We find that one potential factor driving regulatory responsiveness is the efficiency of auditing and enforcement resources. In section 4, we examine social welfare issues

---

[2] Personal discussions with Professor Dr. Eberhard Bohne of the Post Graduate School of Administrative Sciences, Speyer, Germany.

[3] The role the regulator plays in our model is restricted to policing existing environmental statutes, not designing them. As such, our regulator is not a social planner.

pertaining to responsive regulation. While conventional wisdom might assert that voluntary environmental investments will improve social welfare, we find that the welfare effect is ambiguous. A switch from unresponsive to responsive regulation may actually reduce social welfare. In section 5, we present a non-technical summary of the analysis, while section 6 offers concluding remarks and policy implications.

2   THE MODEL

2.1   Overview and timing

We present a two-stage game consisting of two players: a risk-neutral regulator whose task it is to monitor and enforce existing environmental statutes, and a risk-neutral regulated firm motivated to minimize its expected compliance costs. The key to our analysis is the regulatory response to the firm's investment.[4] We assume the regulator minimizes the sum of the *expected* environmental cost of non-compliance and the cost of regulatory monitoring and enforcement.[5] The details of the model will be presented below, but for now consider a firm that generates an environmental cost when it fails to comply. Given that compliance is costly, it is reasonable to assume that in the absence of any monitoring and enforcement activity the firm will not comply.[6] Hence, prior to the realized compliance event, monitoring will act to reduce the expected level of environmental damage arising from non-compliance. The expected environmental damage from non-compliance will, of course, also be determined by the firm's compliance efforts.

Given the complexity of existing environmental statutes, it is often difficult for firms to achieve compliance with certainty. Like Heyes (1996), we assume the firm undertakes actions to raise the probability of compliance. Specifically, we allow the firm two choice variables (both of which influence its compliance probability). The first is a level of environmental

---

[4] The regulator's objective in our model is a modification of one presented in Greison and Singh (1990).

[5] Note that we adopt a more circumscribed objective function than in chapter 4, where the regulator weighed environmental benefits along with industry profits and consumer surplus. That analysis dealt with the broader issue of what regulatory standards to set. Here we are interested in the more focused issue of compliance with the standards that have already been chosen.

[6] Note that in making this assumption, we are ruling out "win–win" motivations for making the voluntary investment. See Palmer, Oates, and Portney (1995) for a detailed study that suggests that examples of true "win–win" investments are rare at best.

investment, z, that reduces compliance effort costs. Examples include investment in a new technology, or the creation of an environmental audit department. The second is a level of compliance effort, e. Effort may embody labor resources devoted to conducting a self-audit, staying current on changes in various environmental statutes, or making sure that abatement technologies are kept in working order.

The crucial difference between the firm's two choice variables is as follows. The environmental investment is assumed to be fixed and observable prior to the regulator's choice of monitoring resources, while effort is not observable prior to the regulator's decision. An illustrative example is ISO 14001 certification. To obtain certification, companies must establish environmental audit procedures, and produce materials detailing these procedures and other environmental plans of action, which must be handed over to the certification organizations. This activity is costly and observable. After the plans have been developed, however, the managerial effort required to carry them out successfully is both ongoing and difficult to observe.

We present our model under two different policy regimes. In the first regime, the firm minimizes its compliance costs by jointly choosing its compliance effort and an observable environmental investment. At the same time, the regulator chooses its optimal level of monitoring and enforcement effort. Thus, the regulator does not respond to the firm's investment decision. We characterize this regulation as *unresponsive*. In the second regime, the regulator determines its regulatory effort *in response to* the level of environmental investment chosen by the firm. Therefore, the second regime is modeled as a two-stage game. In stage I, the firm determines an optimal level of environmental investment taking into consideration the regulator's optimal stage II response. In stage II, the regulator establishes its monitoring and enforcement effort, and the firm determines its optimal compliance effort. As such, we characterize this regulatory regime as *responsive*.[7]

Since the primary motivation for the firm to undertake voluntary investments is the regulatory response, it is worth noting why we do not explicitly

---

[7] The reader will recognize that under both regulatory regimes, the firm and regulator simultaneously determine their respective optimal compliance and monitoring strategies. As pointed out in both Greison and Singh (1990) and Bose (1995), this avoids the problem of assuming a credible commitment to enforcement strategies by the regulator. In models where the regulator moves first, strong assumptions regarding precommitment by the regulator are required, as its strategies might be suboptimal *ex post*. Moreover, at no time is the firm's environmental investment selected subsequent to compliance effort. This recognizes that investment has stronger commitment power than monitoring effort.

model the regulator's decision to adopt the responsive regulatory regime. Usually the announcement of a responsive regulatory policy will precede the environmental investments made by the firm.[8] As we shall see, in our model the regulator benefits from offering a responsive enforcement policy. To be sure, the regulator may incur some costs to make such responsiveness credible, e.g. establishing and promoting such a program. However, if such costs exceeded the expected benefits (e.g. higher compliance, or greater site cleanup), then a responsive policy would not be offered. Since we are interested in examining the impact of regulatory responsiveness, we shall assume that the regulator has decided that the expected benefits arising from this action exceed the associated costs, and without loss of generality we set those costs to zero.

2.2 Model details

2.2.1 The regulator

Define the function $m(r)$ as the probability that the regulator will monitor a firm *and* impose a costly penalty in the event of non-compliance. It is convenient to think of the variable r as including the effort level the regulator directs towards monitoring and enforcement. We assume that $m(r)$ has the following properties: $m_r > 0$, $m_{rr} < 0$, $m(0) = 0$, and $\lim_{r \to \infty} m(r) = 1$. We shall assume here, and throughout the model, that all third- and higher-order derivatives are zero.

An important assumption that affects regulatory and firm actions is that if the firm is monitored and found to be in violation, then the environmental cost, c, will be remediated by the amount gc, where $g \in (0, 1]$ is the proportion of environmental cost that is recovered or remediated.[9] Examples

---

[8] This might not always be the case, since firms may engage in voluntary investments and then lobby for responsiveness.

[9] If $g = 0$, then no remediation takes place. The assumption of partial remediation seems more applicable to water and land pollution than to air pollution. However, the basic flavor of our results will hold even in the case of fugitive air emissions as long as the regulator obtains some *benefit* from conviction, such as altering subsequent firm behavior or receiving a portion of fine revenues collected. For instance, consider a 1997 case brought by the EPA and the State of New Jersey against Citgo Asphalt Refining Co. for CAA violations involving excessive SO_2 releases (*Enforcement and Compliance Assurance Accomplishments Report FY 1997*, p. B-10). The settlement resulted not only in a civil penalty of $1.23 million but a requirement that Citgo's violating plant reduce SO_2 emissions by a sizable 125 tons per year. McKinney and Schoch (1998) discuss how such actions facilitate improvements in local ambient air quality, much as remediation of a toxic spill would improve local soil quality.

include river, lake, and groundwater cleanup efforts, forest reseeding, and Superfund and brownfields cleanup.

The stated mission of the EPA is to "protect human health and to safeguard the natural environment – air, water, and land – upon which life depends."[10] With this in mind, we assume that part of the regulator's objective is to minimize the expected cost to the environment resulting from violations. The expected environmental cost, denoted as $\bar{c}$, is dependent on the probability of monitoring and remediation, $m(r)$, and the probability of non-compliance, $p(e, z)$, described in detail below. Specifically, we can write $\bar{c} = m(r)p(e, z)(c - gc) + (1 - m(r))p(e, z)c$. The term $m(r)p(e, z)(c - gc)$ measures the expected cost to the environment when a violating firm is caught. The term $(1 - m(r))p(e, z)c$ measures the expected cost to the environment from failing to capture a non-compliant firm. It is easy to show that the expected environmental cost expression reduces to $\bar{c} = [1 - m(r)g]p(e, z)c$.

The parameter g can have several interpretations. It can represent a physical property of the environmental damage done, e.g. the lower is g the more permanent is the environmental damage. It can also have a policy interpretation. For instance, for many Superfund sites, involved parties will often negotiate to determine how much cleanup is going to be required (see Sullivan 1995, p. 236). Moreover, from a modeling perspective, we will show that g has ramifications for the degree of the regulator's response to a firm's compliance activities.

We assume that in addition to minimizing expected environmental costs, $\bar{c}$, the regulator is also concerned with the costs associated with monitoring and enforcement, γ. Thus, the regulator's objective is given by:

$$\min_r E(C_{reg}) = (1 - m(r)g)\, p(e, z)c + \gamma(r, \alpha). \qquad (5.1)$$

As discussed above, the first term represents the expected environmental cost of non-compliance. The function $\gamma(r, \alpha)$ captures the regulator's monitoring and enforcement costs, where α is a monitoring cost efficiency parameter.[11] The properties of γ are as follows: $\gamma_r > 0$, $\gamma_{rr} > 0$, $\gamma_\alpha < 0$, and $\gamma_{\alpha\alpha} > 0$, and $\gamma_{r\alpha} < 0$. Hence, α influences monitoring and enforcement costs by reducing the marginal cost of monitoring and enforcement effort.

---

[10] See www.epa.gov for the EPA's mission statement.

[11] The cost of monitoring and enforcement could also be captured through a budget constraint. This would generate a shadow cost of increasing monitoring activities in the regulator's objective function, which would serve the same role as the cost term we include directly in the regulator's objective.

Specifically, an *increase* in α will have the effect of *reducing* the marginal cost of regulatory effort.

Since we will examine the impact of changes in α below, some discussion of the efficiency parameter is in order. As noted by Russell, Harrington, and Vaughan (1986, p. 78), monitoring any type of pollutant involves various phases which include sample collection, transportation, and analysis. At each phase, there are different choices open to the inspector, largely dictated by the type of pollutant analyzed. For example, certain samples might necessitate a special transport method so as to keep temperature constant, while other types of pollutants can be analyzed on site. Moreover, the sample analysis might require detailed biochemical analysis, whereas other pollutants can be analyzed visually, or at least using less sophisticated techniques. Hence, as monitoring efficiency varies widely, so will monitoring costs.[12] As Russell, Harrington, and Vaughan (1986) write,

These variations in general will result in differences in the cost, precision, and accuracy of the monitoring methods, and these, in turn, will affect the likelihood of accurately identifying a violation ... and therefore, the cost of enforcement. (1986, p. 77)

Increased statutory complexity, expansion of regulated substances, etc. can also affect monitoring and enforcement efficiency by adding to the regulator's monitoring costs. Geographic differences in monitoring efficiency may arise as well, e.g., it may be more difficult to monitor plants in less accessible areas. The parameter α is designed to capture these kinds of variations.

2.2.2   The firm

We now consider a representative regulated firm motivated to minimize expected environmental compliance costs by choosing a level of compliance effort, e, and a level of environmental investment, z. The function $p(e, z) \equiv prob(\textit{the firm is in violation})$ captures this notion, and is assumed to have the following properties: $p(0, z) = 1$, $p(e, 0) = 1$, $p_e < 0$, $p_{ee} > 0$, $p_z < 0$, $p_{zz} > 0$, $p_{ez} < 0$, $\lim_{e \to \infty} p(e, z) = 0$, and $\lim_{z \to \infty} p(e, z) = 0$. The first conditions state that in the absence of any environmental investment or compliance effort, it is certain the firm will fail to comply. However, for non-zero levels of z and e we assume that the more effort put forth by the firm, the

---

[12] Russell, Harrington, and Vaughan (1986) present results from an RFF (Resources for the Future) survey conducted in the mid-1980s that show that sampling inspection costs averaged $955 per visit and had a standard deviation of $932.

less likely it will violate a given environmental statute (with diminishing returns to effort). Likewise, environmental investments reduce the probability of non-compliance (again with diminishing returns). Moreover, we assume that environmental investments will increase the marginal impact that additional effort has on reducing the probability of non-compliance. Finally, we assume that infinite amounts of environmental investment or compliance effort will result in certain compliance.

Turning our attention to cost issues, we assume that the effort costs of compliance (and hence the marginal cost of compliance) can be reduced by environmental investments. Define the compliance cost function as follows: $\Psi(e, z) + vz$ where $\Psi_e > 0$, $\Psi_{ee} > 0$, $\Psi_z < 0$, $\Psi_{zz} > 0$, $\Psi_{ez} < 0$, and $v > 0$. That is, effort costs are increasing in e (at an increasing rate). The investment, z, has the effect of reducing effort costs (at a decreasing rate) as well as the marginal compliance cost of effort. For example, the more internal auditing equipment (or the more sophisticated the auditing equipment) purchased, the more productive are the firm's compliance efforts (i.e. the easier it is to determine and correct a violation).[13] Finally, we assume the marginal cost of the environmental investment, v, is exogenous and constant.

The firm also faces statutory costs when it fails to comply. If the firm is found to be in non-compliance, it is assessed a penalty equal to $F + \Gamma(gc)$. F is a pure monetary fine assumed to be set exogenously by a legislative body such as the US Congress. $\Gamma(gc)$ is the cleanup or remediation cost the firm faces and will vary with the type of damage done, where $\Gamma_i > 0$, $\Gamma_{ii} > 0$. Following standard EPA practice, we assume that the firm incurs the costs of remediation.[14]

The firm is assumed to choose compliance effort and environmental investment levels so as to minimize its total expected compliance costs:

$$\min_{e,z} C_f = \Psi(e, z) + vz + p(e, z)m(r)\,(F + \Gamma(gc)). \tag{5.2}$$

Total expected compliance costs, C_f, are simply the sum of the costs of compliance $\Psi(e, z) + vz$ and the expected penalty $p(e, z)m(r)(F + \Gamma(gc))$.

---

[13] Given that the firm's environmental investment might include highly sophisticated abatement capital, it is reasonable to assume that such purchases could increase the firm's marginal effort costs. If this were the case, however, the firm would tend to lower its effort level, which would have the effect of lowering its compliance probability. Since the environmental investment is considered voluntary, it is natural to assume that the direct effect of the investment on compliance probability (which is to raise that probability) dominates the indirect effect through the reduction in effort. If the direct effect dominates, all of the model's qualitative results hold.

[14] According to US EPA (1998d, pp. 2–6), one of the principles underlying the EPA's enforcement program is that violators should pay for and correct any damage caused.

2.3   The unresponsive regulatory regime

We first examine a benchmark case in which the regulator chooses its optimal monitoring and enforcement strategy, and the firm simultaneously chooses compliance cost minimizing levels of e and z. Maximizing the firm's objective (5.2) yields the following first-order conditions:

$$\Psi_e + p_e m(r) \left(F + \Gamma(gc) \right) = 0, \tag{5.3}$$

$$\Psi_z + p_z m(r) \left(F + \Gamma(gc) \right) + v = 0. \tag{5.4}$$

The first condition states that the firm will expend effort up to the point where the marginal cost of effort equals its marginal benefit (in the form of a reduced expected penalty for non-compliance). The second condition states that the optimal level of environmental investment will be the amount where the marginal cost of the environmental investment equals its marginal benefits in terms of effort cost reduction and reductions in the expected fine. Equation (5.4) is of particular interest because it illustrates that in the benchmark case the benefits to environmental investment are non-strategic in nature; that is, they do not arise from changes in regulatory behavior. As we shall see below, this is not the case under responsive regulation.

Optimization of the regulator's objective (5.1) yields

$$-m_r p(e, z) gc + \gamma_r = 0, \tag{5.5}$$

which states that auditing efforts will be allocated up to the point where the marginal cost of those resources, γ_r, equals the expected marginal benefit, $cg m_r p(e, z)$, in the form of a reduction in the expected environmental costs arising from a unit increase in monitoring effort. Solving (5.4) and (5.5) simultaneously yields Nash equilibrium solutions for e, r, and z in the unresponsive game: $r^{ur}(v, \alpha, F, c, g)$, $e^{ur}(v, \alpha, F, c, g)$, and $z^{ur}(v, \alpha, F, c, g)$. (We will often suppress the dependence of r^{ur}, e^{ur}, and z^{ur} on the exogenous parameters to simplify notation.)

2.4   The responsive regulatory regime

The timing of the responsive game is as follows: in stage I the firm chooses z, and in stage II the firm chooses e and the regulator simultaneously chooses r. Hence, we seek a subgame-perfect Nash equilibrium for r and e by solving the model backwards from its second stage.

2.4.1 Stage II

The firm

The firm's objective in stage II is to select an effort level that minimizes its expected costs of compliance (5.2). This yields the first-order condition (5.3), which in turn defines the firm's "effort" best response function $\widehat{e}(r; z, F, c, g)$. As we show in the appendix (p. 140), totally differentiating (5.3) produces a set of predictions regarding how the firm's compliance effort changes when other variables in the model change. For instance, the firm will respond with more effort if regulatory effort, r, or the fine, F, is increased. Furthermore, an increase in environmental investment, z, increases compliance effort as well, since z reduces marginal effort costs. Finally, the firm will exert more effort when cleanup costs (which are rising in c and g) are greater. All of these results are intuitively sensible.

The regulator

The regulator's stage II objective is to choose monitoring resources to maximize (5.1), which yields (5.5). Using (5.5) to define the regulator's "effort" best response function $\widehat{r}(e; z, \alpha, c, g)$, it is straightforward to derive a set of predictions regarding regulatory "effort" that parallel the results for the firm. For example, the more effort the firm devotes to compliance in equilibrium, the fewer resources the regulator devotes to monitoring that firm in equilibrium.[15] The reason is straightforward. The greater the firm's effort directed towards compliance, the less likely the firm will be in violation. The less likely a violation, the lower will be the expected cost to the environment. Hence, the expected return from monitoring the firm is reduced, and the regulator will respond optimally by reducing its (costly) monitoring effort. Similarly, the regulator will reduce the resources it devotes to monitoring the firm if the firm increases its environmental investment z. In addition, greater monitoring efficiency, α, reduces the marginal cost of monitoring, so to maintain resource optimality, r must rise. Furthermore, monitoring

---

[15] Note that the efforts on the part of both the firm and the regulator are unobservable to the other party. Thus, one might wonder how one player's effort level can be said to "respond" to that of the other player. In a strict sense, there is no direct "response" to the efforts of the other player. Nevertheless, each player understands the underlying structure of the other's costs, and is thus able to compute the optimal level of effort for the other player to expend. Whenever there is a shift in one player's cost structure, the other player optimally adjusts his effort level. Thus, the *equilibrium* levels of effort expended by each player appear to respond to those of the other player, even though there is no direct observation of the other player's effort.

and enforcement efforts will rise if the expected benefits to those activities rise, as occurs if c and g increase. This is because the regulator views monitoring and enforcement as a means to reduce environmental damage, either because it will raise firm compliance, or because a convicted violator will be forced to undertake damage remediation.

The stage II Nash equilibrium

The simultaneous solution of the firm's and regulator's best response functions determines a stable Nash equilibrium in firm and regulator efforts, $e^*(z, \alpha, F, c, g)$ and $r^*(z, \alpha, F, c, g)$. Notice that in contrast to the unresponsive policy regime, equilibrium levels e^* and r^* are a function of z since, under this regulatory regime, z is determined in the first stage of the game.

The most important thing to recognize about regulatory behavior at stage II is that r^* is reduced when z rises, i.e. the regulator reduces resources allocated to monitoring the firm after the firm undertakes an observable environmental investment. (This is demonstrated in (5.32) in the appendix.) This result shows that a regulatory policy promising responsiveness to voluntary environmental investments is credible. Because it reduces the marginal cost of compliance effort, an increase in z increases firm effort for any given level of monitoring effort, r. Hence, the firm's best response function shifts to the right. Moreover, this increase in effort implies an increased likelihood that the firm will achieve compliance which, in turn, reduces expected environmental costs. Because monitoring is costly, the regulator will find it optimal to reduce its monitoring and enforcement intensity for any given level of compliance effort, e. Hence, the regulator's best response function shifts down and to the left. The result is a reduction in the equilibrium level of monitoring effort, r^* (see figure 5.1).

While the impact of an increase in z on the regulator's choice of r is clear, its impact on the firm's compliance effort is ambiguous. This is so because z has both direct and indirect effects on the firm's effort choice. Since the environmental investment reduces the marginal costs of effort, such investment tends to raise effort *ceteris paribus*. However, environmental investments serve also to directly raise the probability of compliance. This, in turn, causes a reduction in regulatory effort, *ceteris paribus*. This second response creates an indirect effect on compliance effort because reductions in r lower the expected fine, $m(r)F + \Gamma(gc)$. This, however, reduces the firm's cost of non-compliance, thus offering an incentive to reduce compliance effort. Thus, the overall impact on e^* from a change in z is ambiguous.

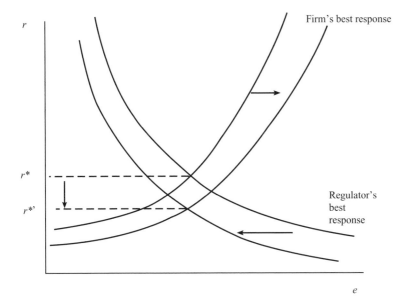

Figure 5.1   Effect of a change in z

Since these two effects are opposing we assume, in the remainder of the chapter, that $\partial e^*/\partial z$ is small.[16]

The other comparative static results are intuitive. An increase in monitoring and enforcement efficiency, α, lowers regulatory costs and thus strengthens the regulator's incentives to engage in enforcement activities. Hence, regulatory efforts and firm compliance efforts increase in equilibrium.

Increases in environmental costs, c (as well as the proportion of cleanup, g), result in a greater compliance effort unambiguously. An increase in c (or g) induces more compliance effort on the part of the firm (for any given level of r) since higher cleanup costs increase the benefits of compliance. Moreover, increases in c (or g) increase the regulator's benefit to monitoring and enforcement (for any given level e) since avoiding and/or recovering

---

[16] Specifically we assume that $\partial e^*/\partial z$ is small relative to $|\partial r^*/\partial z|$. If $\partial e^*/\partial z$ is positive and large relative to $|\partial r^*/\partial z|$ then some of the results we derive below will not hold (see appendix). This case would arise when the environmental investment greatly reduces the marginal cost of the firm's effort, but the resulting increase in the firm's compliance probability elicits only a small decrease in regulatory monitoring effort. In this case, however, it is difficult to argue that the firm's environmental investment is driven by the regulator's offer of responsiveness. Since our focus in this chapter is on the impact changes in enforcement behavior will have on firm environmental investments, we do not consider this possibility and instead focus on situations where the primary benefit to increased z comes from reduced r.

environmental damage is desirable. Hence, equilibrium compliance effort, e^*, increases. However, the equilibrium effect on the level of monitoring effort, r^*, is ambiguous. The direct effect of higher environmental costs (or greater cleanup) is for the regulator to expand enforcement activity. At the same time, higher cleanup costs induce more compliance effort on the part of the firm. This second shift induces an indirect effect on (costly) enforcement activity since, with greater compliance effort, expected environmental cost is reduced. Therefore, the benefit to enforcement expenditure is lower.

Finally, an increase in the monetary fine for non-compliance, F, unambiguously raises firm compliance efforts since larger penalties increase the benefit to avoiding conviction. The equilibrium level of monitoring and enforcement, however, falls. Since the increased fine induces higher compliance effort, it reduces the expected risk to the environment. This reduces the marginal benefit of monitoring. Thus, the regulator will find it optimal to reduce its monitoring and enforcement intensity.

2.4.2   Stage I

Subgame perfection implies that the firm can see through to the stage II equilibrium outcome. Therefore, in stage I the firm will choose a level of environmental investment, z, given e^* and r^*. Thus, the stage I objective for the firm is:

$$\min_z E(C_f) = \Psi(e^*, z) + vz + p(e^*, z)m(r^*)\,(F + \Gamma(gc))\,. \quad (5.6)$$

The resulting first-order condition is[17]:

$$\Psi_z + p_z m(r^*)\,(F + \Gamma(gc)) + v = -p(e^*, z)m_r \frac{\partial r^*}{\partial z}\,(F + \Gamma(gc)) > 0. \quad (5.7)$$

Defining the optimal solution to (5.7) as z^*, analysis of this condition leads directly to Proposition 9.

Proposition 9: *Under responsive regulation, the firm realizes additional benefits to environmental investments relative to the unresponsive regulatory regime,* ceteris paribus.

---

[17] Here we have made use of the envelope theorem, i.e. we have simplified the first-order condition by making use of the fact that $\partial e^*/\partial z = 0$, since the firm chooses its compliance effort optimally in light of its own environmental investment.

Proposition 9 embodies the well-understood strategic overinvestment possible in two-stage models (see Shapiro 1992) and implies that the firm, when faced with a credible offer of regulatory responsiveness, will increase its environmental investment activity. The difficulty in directly comparing the optimal environmental investment levels between the unresponsive and responsive regulatory regimes using standard comparative static techniques is that doing so involves making comparisons across two different models. However, following a procedure outlined by Brander and Spencer (1983), such a comparison can be made by applying the mean value theorem. Doing so leads to Proposition 10.

Proposition 10: *Responsive regulation induces the firm to increase its environmental investment relative to its optimal investment under an unresponsive regulatory regime, i.e.* $z^* > z^{ur}$, *ceteris paribus.*

In the terminology of the strategic investment literature, Proposition 10 illustrates that the firm's voluntary investment commits it to be "tough." The investment is characterized as "tough" because it commits the firm to raise its compliance effort. Since the regulator's best response function is downward sloping (indicating a strategic substitute), its strategic response is to play "soft," that is, to reduce its monitoring resources. As in the strategic investment literature the firm overinvests in z, relative to the level it would choose if there was no strategic response, since the regulator's response is favorable to the firm.[18]

3   REGULATORY EFFICIENCY AND RESPONSIVE REGULATION

We have shown that a switch to responsive regulation will induce the firm to increase its level of voluntary investment. In this section we examine, in light of the firm's behavior, whether the regulator would want to offer responsive regulation. To answer this question we can simply examine the

---

[18] A taxonomy of strategic investment based upon animal analogies such as the "fat cat effect" and the "puppy dog ploy" is given in Fudenberg and Tirole (1984). In our case, the firm pursues a "top dog strategy" in which its investment induces it to achieving a higher level of compliance, thus generating a favorable strategic response from the regulator. Tirole (1989, sections 8.3 and 8.4) provides several examples of strategic investment using this taxonomy.

impact of the firm's decision on the regulator's payoff. That is

$$\frac{dE\left(C_{reg}\right)}{dz} = (1 - m(r)cg)\, p_e \frac{\partial e^*}{\partial z} + (1 - m(r)g)\, p_z c$$

$$+ \left[\gamma_r - m_r c g p\right] \frac{\partial r^*}{\partial z}. \qquad (5.8)$$

Under our assumption that $\partial e^*/\partial z$ is small, and noting that the final term in (5.8) is zero from (5.5), we see that the regulator benefits from offering a responsive regulatory regime. This result follows from the fact that under a responsive regulatory regime the firm undertakes a greater level of environmental investment thereby reducing the firm's detrimental environmental impact.[19]

Since the regulator clearly benefits from responsive regulation, one might ask why responsive regulation is not the norm. Although this question is beyond the scope of the current chapter, it is worth noting that we have not modeled any fixed costs associated with the offer of switching to a responsive regulatory program. Such costs are likely to exist because the regulator must be able to verify that the firm's investment does result in a credible commitment to increase its compliance efforts. Verification will likely include the collection and review of proposals submitted by the firm.

If the regulator does face some fixed costs to adopting responsive regulation, such as program setup costs, it is also natural to ask in which industries are we most likely to see the offer of responsive regulation. The following corollary addresses this question.

Corollary 1: *The degree of regulatory responsiveness to the firm's compliance efforts ($\partial \widehat{r}/\partial e$), is inversely proportional to monitoring efficiency (α), ceteris paribus.*

Recall that a *decrease* in α implies that monitoring resources are *less* efficient. Corollary 1 illustrates that a decrease in α makes the regulator's best response function more negatively sloped. This result suggests a regulatory agency will be more responsive to environmental investments in those cases where its monitoring resources are less efficient. Note that this effect is mediated through a two-step process. Environmental investments commit the firm to make greater compliance effort, and (as Corollary 1

---

[19] The regulator could only be worse off under a responsive environmental regime if firm effort decreased enough in response to the environmental investment to increase the probability that the firm is in violation, i.e. $\partial e^*/\partial z$ is a sufficiently large negative number. This is an unlikely event (recall that the direct effect of an increase in z on e is positive) and one that we have ruled out via our assumption that $\partial e^*/\partial z$ is small.

shows) this increase in effort is rewarded with a reduction in regulatory monitoring effort. All other things equal, the more responsive is $\hat{r}$ to e, the more willing is the firm to undertake environmental investments that commit it to raising its compliance effort. As noted in subsection 2.2, monitoring may vary across industries for many reasons. Corollary 1 indicates that we would not expect responsive regulation to have much impact on environmental investment activity aimed at SO_2 reductions in the electric utility sector because existing technologies, which continuously monitor stack emissions, are very efficient. The model predicts regulatory responsiveness to have a greater impact on environmental investments aimed at reductions in chemical releases, which are more difficult to track or detect.

We have examined both firm and regulatory motivations for engaging in, and offering, responsive regulation, respectively. We now turn to the normative aspects of responsive regulation.

4 SOCIAL COSTS AND RESPONSIVE REGULATION

In Proposition 10 we established that the firm will increase its level of environmental investment under a responsive regulatory regime. In this section we examine how this action, prompted by the regulator's offer of responsiveness, impacts the social cost of the firm's activities. First, we examine how the firm's choice of environmental investment impacts social costs under the unresponsive regime. In doing so we show that it is relatively straightforward to set the fine F such that the firm's choice of environmental investment coincides with that which minimizes social costs. It should be noted that we purposely do not model the fine as a regulatory choice parameter because fines are generally determined by the legislative or judicial branches of government. Second, we examine the impact of a switch to responsive regulation under the assumption that the fine is unchanged from its optimal level in the unresponsive case. We find that the firm undertakes too much environmental investment from a social welfare perspective. This is because its investment serves to lower the firm's expected fine. However, in the social welfare calculus, the fine is a pure transfer. Penalties assessed on the firm can be thought of as representing a social benefit in that the money extracted is typically paid to a state or federal general fund account that can be used to finance environmental cleanup, natural resource reclamation projects, or be used in other ways to enhance social welfare (see Kleit, Pierce, and Hill 1998). Since these benefits represent exactly costs borne by the firm when paying its fines, the net effect on social welfare is zero.

This overinvestment result strongly suggests that the fine must be adjusted as the regulatory regime changes. However, the modification to the penalty structure is difficult to implement in practice since, as we show, the degree of adjustment varies according to level of environmental investment the firm undertakes.

The expected social cost of the firm's activities under unresponsive regulation can be written as[20]

$$E(SC) = \Psi(e^{ur}, z) + vz + [m(r^{ur})F + m(r^{ur})\Gamma(cg)]\,p(e^{ur}, z)$$
$$+ \gamma(r^{ur}, \alpha) + [cg(1 - m(r^{ur}))]\,p(e^{ur}, z) - m(r^{ur})Fp(e^{ur}, z).$$
$$(5.9)$$

The term contained within the first set of braces on the right-hand side of (5.9) represents the firm's expected costs, while the term in the second set of braces represents the regulator's costs. From these two costs we subtract the expected fine since, as discussed above, it constitutes a social benefit.

Optimization of (5.9) with respect to z yields

$$[(1 - m(r^{ur}))cg + m(r^{ur})\,\Gamma(cg)]\,p_z + \Psi_z + v = 0. \qquad (5.10)$$

The firm's choice of investment under the unresponsive regime is given by (5.4), which can be rewritten as

$$[m(r^{ur})F + m(r^{ur})\Gamma(cg)]\,p_z + \Psi_z + v = 0.$$

Comparing the first-order condition above to (5.10) we see that the level of fine, $\hat{F}$, that induces the firm to minimize social costs solves

$$m(r^{ur})\hat{F} = (1 - m(r^{ur}))cg. \qquad (5.11)$$

Note that the optimal fine is independent of z. The same is not true under responsive regulation.

Expected social costs under responsive regulation are

$$E(SC) = \{\Psi(e^*, z) + vz + [m(r^*)F + m(r^*)\Gamma(cg)]\,p(e^*, z)\}$$
$$+ \{\gamma(r^*, \alpha) + [cg(1 - m(r^*))]\,p(e^*, z)\} - m(r^*)Fp(e^*, z).$$
$$(5.12)$$

---

[20] Notice that while F is a pure transfer, remediation is not. The value of the remediation itself, gc, is assumed different from the cost of cleanup, $\Gamma(gc)$, the firm incurs to remediate the damage.

Using (5.1) and (5.2) we can rewrite (5.12) as

$$E(SC) = C_f + E(C_{reg}) - E(F), \qquad (5.13)$$

where $E(F) = m(r^*)Fp(e^*, z)$ denotes the expected fine.

Using this notation we see that the first-order condition defining the level of investment that minimizes expected social costs can be written as

$$\frac{\partial C_f}{\partial z} + \frac{\partial E(C_{reg})}{\partial z} - \frac{\partial E(F)}{\partial z} = 0, \qquad (5.14)$$

or equivalently

$$\frac{\partial C_f}{\partial z} = -\frac{\partial E(C_{reg})}{\partial z} + \frac{\partial E(F)}{\partial z}. \qquad (5.15)$$

Note that the left-hand side of (5.15) is derivative of the firm's objective function. Consequently, if the right-hand side of (5.15) is negative we know from the firm's second-order condition for optimization that the firm's choice of z will exceed the social cost optimum. Straightforward calculations reveal that

$$\frac{\partial C_f}{\partial z} = [pcgm_r - \gamma_r]\frac{\partial r^*}{\partial z} - cg(1 - m(r^*))p_e\frac{\partial e^*}{\partial z} - [cg(1 - m(r^*))]p_z$$

$$+ m_r pF\frac{\partial r^*}{\partial z} + m(r^*)Fp_e\frac{\partial e^*}{\partial z} + m(r^*)Fp_z \qquad (5.16)$$

using (5.5) and rearranging terms we see that

$$\frac{\partial C_f}{\partial z} = [-cg(1 - m(r^*))p_e + m(r^*)Fp_e]\frac{\partial e^*}{\partial z}$$

$$+ [-cg(1 - m(r^*)) + m(r^*)F]p_z + m_r pF\frac{\partial r^*}{\partial z}. \qquad (5.17)$$

Finally, substituting (5.11) into (5.17) and recalling our assumption that $\partial e^*/\partial z$ is small, we see that

$$\frac{\partial C_f}{\partial z} \simeq \left\{\left[-(1 - m(r^*))cg + \frac{m(r^*)}{m(r^{ur})}[(1 - m(r^{ur}))cg]\right]p_z\right\}$$

$$+ \left\{m_r p\frac{[(1 - m(r^{ur}))cg]}{m(r^{ur})}\frac{\partial r^*}{\partial z}\right\}. \qquad (5.18)$$

Clearly the term in the second set of large braces in (5.18) is negative.[21] Recalling that $m_r > 0$, and that, for a given fine F, $r^* < r^{ur}$, we see that $m(r^*)/m(r^{ur}) < 1$, and that $(1 - m(r^*))cg > (1 - m(r^{ur}))cg$. These conditions imply that the term in the first set of large braces is also negative. Thus, $\partial C_f/\partial z < 0$ (for small $\partial e/\partial z$) which implies that the firm

---

[21] Note that $\partial r^*/\partial z < 0$ when $F = \hat{F}$.

overinvests in z from a social cost minimizing perspective. These results constitute the proof of Proposition 11.

Proposition 11: *If F is set to the level that induces the firm to choose a social cost minimizing level of investment under unresponsive regulation, then the switch to responsive regulation will result in an overinvestment in z.*

Proposition 11 establishes that a switch to responsive regulation will lead the firm to undertake too much investment in z if the fine facing the firm is one set to induce the social cost minimizing level of investment under unresponsive regulation. This result follows from the fact that the firm's investment choice is driven by its desire to lower its expected fine. From a social cost perspective, however, the fines are viewed as a transfer since the fine revenues flowing to general revenues denote a positive social benefit.

If we drop our assumption that $F = \hat{F}$, we see from (5.17) that the specific result of overinvestment contained in Proposition 11 will hold whenever F is sufficiently large. The firm might under invest in z following a switch to responsive regulation if the fine is sufficiently small. This is so because the firm, in investing in z, provides the social benefit of a reduction in the likelihood of environmental damage (the term $-cg(1 - m(r^*))p_e$ in (5.17)) but it does not take this benefit into account in its choice of z. In any event, an adjustment of the optimal fine is in order when the regulator offers responsive regulation. However, in practice these adjustments will be difficult to undertake since the optimal fine under responsive regulation will be a function of the firm's choice of voluntary environmental investment.[22]

5 NON-TECHNICAL SUMMARY

In this chapter, we have examined how regulatory responsiveness can motivate firms to undertake voluntary environmental investments. This provides an additional motivation for corporate environmental improvement beyond those of preemption and influencing regulatory standards, which we discussed in chapters 3 and 4. Here we allowed the firm to achieve regulatory compliance through a mix of environmental investments and compliance effort. We showed that if environmental investments lower the marginal cost of compliance effort, then such investments – if observable by the regulator – serve as a credible commitment by the firm to improve

---

[22] The optimal fine under responsive regulation is defined by F such that the right-hand side of (5.17) is zero. In order to find a closed-form solution for F one must choose specific parametric forms for each of the model's functions.

its compliance rate. Thus, if the regulator observes such investments, it rationally reallocates its resources away from monitoring the firm and toward other productive uses.

Despite the fact that regulatory responsiveness conserves on regulatory resources, we showed that a shift to a responsive regime might not be socially desirable unless it is coupled with a revision of the existing penalty structure for violations. Otherwise, there is a chance that regulatory responsiveness will actually induce too much environmental investment, from a social perspective, as the firm exerts excessive effort trying to avoid being fined. Thus, a shift to a responsive regime should be undertaken as part of a broader reevaluation of environmental policy, rather than as an isolated act.

6   CONCLUSION

Instances of corporate voluntary environmental investments have been rising in recent years. Many of these voluntary investments seem to be aimed at reducing the costs of complying with existing regulations. Moreover, regulatory agencies themselves are expressing a greater willingness to respond to *firm-specific* investments. Two examples are the EPA's StarTrack program and changes in its general Audit Policy. We have shown that, under reasonably general firm and regulatory objectives, this responsiveness can give rise to voluntary environmental investments.

We have illustrated that the degree of observed regulatory responsiveness may be sensitive to monitoring and enforcement costs, since this influences the regulator's expected benefits from monitoring and enforcement. If monitoring resources are highly cost efficient, then the regulator will be less responsive to a firm's voluntary environmental investments. Hence, our model not only establishes plausible conditions under which such responsiveness is likely, it also provides some rationales for why we do not see universal application of responsive regulatory programs.

Next, we focused on the question of whether voluntary environmental investments motivated by regulatory responsiveness are welfare enhancing. Somewhat surprisingly, we find that, despite the fact that all agents in the model act voluntarily, their actions may reduce social welfare. The reason is that the firm might invest in too much (costly) compliance effort in order to reduce the expected fines it pays for non-compliance. This becomes more likely the larger are the fines that will be imposed for non-compliance. Furthermore, this effect is enhanced by regulatory responsiveness. Finally, we have shown that if the regulator receives direct compensation from the successful conviction of violators it will be even more responsive under a responsive regulatory regime, which raises the value of voluntary environmental investment to the firm.

Decker (2000b) extends the model of responsive regulation to a multifirm setting. In his model, firms' interactions lead to strategic environmental investments designed to shift regulatory focus onto rival firms. A Prisoners' Dilemma emerges in which each firm overinvests in environmental compliance, relative to the case of a single firm. Whether this raises or lowers social welfare cannot be determined in general, as a result of the same mix of factors that arise in the present chapter.

APPENDIX

Comparative statics of the firm's compliance effort decision with respect to various other variables can be found by totally differentiating (5.3), to yield:

$$\frac{\partial \widehat{e}}{\partial r} = -\frac{p_e m_r \left(F + \Gamma(gc)\right)}{\Psi_{ee} + p_{ee} m(r) \left(F + \Gamma(gc)\right)} > 0, \tag{5.19}$$

$$\frac{\partial \widehat{e}}{\partial z} = -\frac{\Psi_{ez} + p_{ez} m(r) \left(F + \Gamma(gc)\right)}{\Psi_{ee} + p_{ee} m(r) \left(F + \Gamma(gc)\right)} > 0, \tag{5.20}$$

$$\frac{\partial \widehat{e}}{\partial F} = -\frac{p_e m(r)}{\Psi_{ee} + p_{ee} m(r) \left(F + \Gamma(gc)\right)} > 0, \tag{5.21}$$

$$\frac{\partial \widehat{e}}{\partial c} = -\frac{p_e m(r) g\Gamma_c}{\Psi_{ee} + p_{ee} m(r) \left(F + \Gamma(gc)\right)} > 0, \tag{5.22}$$

$$\frac{\partial \widehat{e}}{\partial g} = -\frac{p_e m(r) c\Gamma_g}{\Psi_{ee} + p_{ee} m(r) \left(F + \Gamma(gc)\right)} > 0. \tag{5.23}$$

Comparative statics of the regulator's allocation of resources to monitoring can be obtained by totally differentiating (5.5), to yield:

$$\frac{\partial \widehat{r}}{\partial e} = \frac{gcm_r p_e}{\gamma_{rr} - gcm_{rr} p(e, z)} < 0, \tag{5.24}$$

$$\frac{\partial \widehat{r}}{\partial z} = \frac{gcm_r p_z}{\gamma_{rr} - gcm_{rr} p(e, z)} < 0, \tag{5.25}$$

$$\frac{\partial \widehat{r}}{\partial \alpha} = -\frac{\gamma_{r\alpha}}{\gamma_{rr} - gcm_{rr} p(e, z)} > 0, \tag{5.26}$$

$$\frac{\partial \widehat{r}}{\partial c} = \frac{gm_r p(e, z)}{\gamma_{rr} - gcm_{rr} p(e, z)} > 0, \tag{5.27}$$

$$\frac{\partial \widehat{r}}{\partial g} = \frac{cm_r p(e, z)}{\gamma_{rr} - gcm_{rr} p(e, z)} > 0. \tag{5.28}$$

Total differentiation of conditions (5.3) and (5.5) yields a set of comparative statics predictions about the equilibrium levels of compliance effort and regulatory effort. Total differentiation with respect to r and e yields the following matrix of second-order partials

$$D = \begin{bmatrix} \gamma_{rr} - gcm_{rr}(r)\,p(e,z) & -gcm_r\,p_e \\ p_e m_r\,(F + \Gamma(gc)) & \Psi_{ee} + p_{ee}m\,(F + \Gamma(gc)) \end{bmatrix}. \tag{5.29}$$

Furthermore, the determinant

$$\det D = (\gamma_{rr} - gcm_{rr}(r)\,p(e,z))\,(\Psi_{ee} + p_{ee}m\,(F + \Gamma(gc)))$$
$$+ (p_e m_r)^2\,gc\,(F + \Gamma(gc)) \tag{5.30}$$

is positive. Total differentiation with respect to $z, \alpha, g, c,$ and F yields the following system of equations

$$[D]\begin{bmatrix} \partial r^* \\ \partial e^* \end{bmatrix}$$

$$= \begin{bmatrix} cgm_r\,p_z & -\gamma_{r\alpha} & 0 & gm_r\,p & cm_r\,p \\ -(\Psi_{ez} + p_{ez}m\,(F + \Gamma(gc))) & 0 & -p_e m & -p_e m\Gamma_c g & -p_e m\Gamma_g c \end{bmatrix}$$

$$\times \begin{bmatrix} \partial z \\ \partial \alpha \\ \partial F \\ \partial c \\ \partial g \end{bmatrix}. \tag{5.31}$$

Application of Cramer's Rule yields:

$$\frac{\partial r^*}{\partial z} = \frac{gcm_r\left\{ \begin{array}{l} p_z\,(\Psi_{ee} + p_{ee}m\,(F + \Gamma(gc))) \\ -p_e\,(\Psi_{ez} + p_{ez}m\,(F + \Gamma(gc))) \end{array} \right\}}{\det D} < 0, \tag{5.32}$$

$$\frac{\partial e^*}{\partial z} = \frac{\left\{ \begin{array}{l} -(\gamma_{rr} - gcm_{rr}(r)\,p(e,z))\,(\Psi_{ez} + p_{ez}m\,(F + \Gamma(gc))) \\ -(p_e m_r\,(F + \Gamma(gc)))\,(gcm_r\,p_z) \end{array} \right\}}{\det D} \lesseqgtr 0, \tag{5.33}$$

$$\frac{\partial r^*}{\partial \alpha} = \frac{-\gamma_{r\alpha}\,(\Psi_{ee} + p_{ee}m\,(F + \Gamma(gc)))}{\det D} > 0, \tag{5.34}$$

$$\frac{\partial e^*}{\partial \alpha} = \frac{\gamma_{r\alpha}\,p_e m_r\,(F + \Gamma(gc))}{\det D} > 0, \tag{5.35}$$

$$\frac{\partial r^*}{\partial F} = \frac{-p_e^2\,gcmm_r}{\det D} < 0, \tag{5.36}$$

$$\frac{\partial e^*}{\partial F} = \frac{-\left(\gamma_{rr} - g\,cm_{rr}(r)\,p(e,z)\right)p_e m}{\det D} > 0, \tag{5.37}$$

$$\frac{\partial r^*}{\partial c} = \frac{m_r g p\left(\Psi_{ee} + p_{ee} m\left(F + \Gamma(gc)\right)\right) - \left(p_e g\right)^2 cmm_r \Gamma_g}{\det D} \lessgtr 0, \tag{5.38}$$

$$\frac{\partial e^*}{\partial c} = \frac{-g\Gamma_c p_e m\left(\gamma_{rr} - g\,cm_{rr}(r)\,p(e,z)\right) - m_r^2 g p p_e\left(F + \Gamma(gc)\right)}{\det D} > 0, \tag{5.39}$$

$$\frac{\partial r^*}{\partial g} = \frac{m_r c p\left(\Psi_{ee} + p_{ee} m\left(F + \Gamma(gc)\right)\right) - \left(p_e c\right)^2 gmm_r \Gamma_c}{\det D} \lessgtr 0, \tag{5.40}$$

$$\frac{\partial e^*}{\partial g} = \frac{-c\Gamma_g p_e m\left(\gamma_{rr} - g\,cm_{rr}(r)\,p(e,z)\right) - m_r^2 c p p_e\left(F + \Gamma(gc)\right)}{\det D} > 0. \tag{5.41}$$

Proposition 9: *Under responsive regulation, the firm realizes additional benefits to environmental investments relative to the unresponsive regulatory regime, ceteris paribus.*

Proof: Recall from (5.4) that, under the unresponsive regulatory regime, expected compliance costs are minimized when the firm chooses $z = z^{ur}$ such that $\Psi_z + p_z m(r)\,(F + \Gamma(cg)) + v = 0$ (with the second-order condition that the left-hand side of (5.7) is rising in z). Under responsive regulation, expected compliance costs are minimized when the firm chooses $z = z^*$ such that (5.7) holds. Since the right-hand side of (5.7) is positive due to responsive regulation: i.e. $\partial r^*/\partial z < 0$, the firm forgoes additional benefits from investing $z = z^{ur}$.[23]   ∎

Proposition 10: *Responsive regulation induces the firm to increase its environmental investment relative to its optimal investment under an unresponsive regulatory regime, i.e. $z^* > z^{ur}$, ceteris paribus.*

Proof: Our proof will make use of the Mean Value Theorem.

The Mean Value Theorem

Let $f(x)$ be a continuously differentiable function defined over the set of real numbers R^2 and let x^* and x^{ur} be two points on this function. Then

---

[23] This proof is similar to Brander and Spencer (1983).

there exists a point x^c such that

$$\Delta f = f(x^*) - f(x^{ur}) = \frac{\partial f}{\partial x}|_{x=x^c}(x^* - x^{ur}), \tag{5.42}$$

where $x^c = x^{ur} + \theta(x^* - x^{ur})$ and $\theta \in (0, 1)$.   ∎

First, define $\Delta z = z^* - z^{ur}$ where z^* and z^{ur} are environmental investments in the responsive and unresponsive cases, respectively. Let $f(x)$ be $\partial E^*(C_f)/\partial z$ for both z^* and z^{ur}. Then we can apply (5.42) as follows (dropping the C_f argument for notational convenience):

$$\Delta\frac{\partial E^*}{\partial z} = \frac{\partial E^*}{\partial z^*} - \frac{\partial E^*}{\partial z^{ur}} = \frac{\partial^2 E^*}{\partial z^2}|_{z=z^c}(z^* - z^{ur}). \tag{5.43}$$

Rearranging terms we can get

$$(z^* - z^u) = \frac{\frac{\partial E^*}{\partial z^*} - \frac{\partial E^*}{\partial z^{ur}}}{\frac{\partial^2 E^*}{\partial z^2}|_{z=z^c}}. \tag{5.44}$$

From (5.7) we know that $\partial E^*/\partial z^* = 0$ and $\partial E^*/\partial z^{ur} = p m_r(\partial r^*/\partial z)$ $(F + \Gamma) < 0$. Therefore, the numerator of (5.44) is positive. Since cost minimization requires that $\partial^2 E^*/\partial z^2|_{z=z^c} > 0$, we can conclude that $z^* - z^{ur} >$ ∎

A word on $\partial^2 E^*/\partial z^2$ is in order. When expanded, we find that

$$\frac{\partial^2 E^*}{\partial z^2} = [\Psi_{ze} + (p_{ze}m + p_e m_r)(F + \Gamma)]\frac{\partial e^*}{\partial z} \tag{5.45}$$
$$+ [(2p_z m_r + p m_{rr})(F + \Gamma)]\frac{\partial r^*}{\partial z}$$
$$+ p m_r(F + \Gamma)\frac{\partial^2 r^*}{\partial z^2} + \Psi_{zz} + p_{zz}m(F + \Gamma).$$

Close inspection of (5.45) highlights a particular problem with two-stage models that existence and uniqueness can be difficult to establish (see Brander and Spencer 1983). Note that the terms to the right of the first "+" sign in (5.45) are positive but the effect $[\Psi_{ze} + (p_{ze}m + p_e m_r)(F + \Gamma)]\partial e^*/\partial z$ has on (5.45) is indeterminate due to the ambiguous nature of $\partial e^*/\partial z$. Note, however, that (5.45) will be positive if (1) $\partial e^*/\partial z$ is negative, or (2) $\partial e^*/\partial z$ is "small" relative to the other terms, particularly $\partial r^*/\partial z$. The idea that $\partial e^*/\partial z$ is small is reasonable. The two effects that z has on r both work to reduce r. However, when z is increased, e is made more efficient, prompting an increase in effort. However, regulators will back off on enforcement when z is increased, offering an incentive to reduce e. These off-setting effects can make the overall effect that z has on equilibrium effort, e^*, small. The possibility that $\partial e^*/\partial z$ is negative, while less desirable and less likely, can be rationalized by noting that both e and z have the same effect on p and then might serve as substitutes for one another. Irrespective of the rationale, we will restrict our attention to those cases where $\partial^2 E^*/\partial z^2$ is positive.

Corollary 1: *The degree of regulatory responsiveness to the firm's compliance efforts $(\partial\widehat{r}/\partial e)$, is inversely proportional to monitoring efficiency (α), ceteris paribus.*

Proof: Differentiating (5.24) with respect to α yields[24]

$$\frac{\partial^2\widehat{r}}{\partial e\partial\alpha} = \frac{cgp_e m_{rr}(\partial\widehat{r}/\partial\alpha)}{\gamma_{rr} - cgpm_{rr}} > 0, \tag{5.46}$$

which implies that a decrease in monitoring efficiency makes the regulator's best response function more negatively sloped ∎

Proposition 11: *If F is set to the level that induces the firm to choose a social cost minimizing level of investment under unresponsive regulation, then the switch to responsive regulation will result in an overinvestment in z.*

Proof: Treating the monetary fine, F, as a pure transfer, expected social costs can be defined as[25]

$$E(SC) = c(1 - m(r^*)g)\,p(e^*, z) + \gamma(r^*, \alpha) + \Psi(e^*, z)$$
$$+ vz + p(e^*, z)m(r^*)\Gamma(gc). \tag{5.47}$$

The optimal investment solution to (5.47) solves[26]

$$\left[c(1 - m\left(r^*\right)g) + m\left(r^*\right)\Gamma\left(gc\right)\right]p_z + \Psi_z + v$$
$$= -(-gcpm_r + \gamma_r + pm_r\Gamma)\frac{\partial r^*}{\partial z}$$
$$- \left(c(1 - m\left(r^*\right)g)\,p_e + \Psi_e + m\left(r^*\right)p_e\Gamma\right)\frac{\partial e^*}{\partial z}, \tag{5.48}$$

---

[24] Notice that at this stage, α does not influence e because we are focusing only on the regulator's reaction function, not the Nash equilibrium. Hence, the only place where α enters is through m_r.

[25] Notice that while F is a pure transfer, remediation is not. The value of the remediation itself, gc, is assumed different from the cost of cleanup, $\Gamma(gc)$, the firm incurs to remediate the damage.

[26] One might think of this exercise as a social planner mandating a technology standard for the firm such that the level of environmental investment minimizes (5.47).

which reduces to

$$\left[c(1 - m\left(r^*\right)g) + m\left(r^*\right)\Gamma\left(gc\right)\right]p_z + \Psi_z + v$$
$$= -pm_r\Gamma\left(gc\right)\frac{\partial r^*}{\partial z} - \left(c(1 - m\left(r^*\right)g)p_e + \Psi_e + m\left(r^*\right)p_e\Gamma\left(gc\right)\right)\frac{\partial e^*}{\partial z}.$$
(5.49)

Under an *unresponsive* regulatory regime, where $\partial r^*/\partial z = 0$ and $\partial e^*/\partial z = 0$, the level of environmental investment that minimizes social cost solves

$$\left[c(1 - m\left(r^*\right)g) + m(r*)\Gamma\left(gc\right)\right]p_z + \Psi_z + v = 0.$$
(5.50)

To see that additional investment induced by regulatory responsiveness may not improve social welfare, note that the term $-\left(c(1 - m\left(r^*\right)g)p_e + \Psi_e + mp_e\Gamma\left(gc\right)\right)\partial e^*/\partial z$ is ambiguous in sign. Hence, the right-hand side of (5.49) has an indeterminate sign. It follows immediately that a social planner may desire less environmental investment under a responsive regulatory regime. ∎

PART III

Government voluntary programs

6 | An institutional analysis of voluntary environmental agreements

1 INTRODUCTION

Part II of this book focused on industry-led corporate environmentalism. Thus far, we have treated industry as pro-active, and regulators as reactive in the face of voluntary actions by business. This, however, is an incomplete picture. Regulators around the world increasingly rely on "voluntary" programs for environmental improvement. These programs may take a variety of forms, and this part of the book explores these various forms in detail. We begin in this chapter with an institutional analysis of the factors motivating regulatory interest in voluntary programs. The analysis in this chapter is based on Maxwell and Lyon (2001). Chapter 7 studies "negotiated agreements" between regulators and industry, which are particularly popular in Europe and Japan. Chapter 8 analyzes "public voluntary agreements," (PVAs) which are the preferred form of government-initiated voluntary programs in the USA. Chapter 9 probes the structural details of PVAs, focusing on the critical role that government provision of information plays in these programs.

Voluntary approaches to the control of environmental problems increased greatly in popularity during the 1990s, throughout the OECD countries. According to OECD (1999), by the end of the decade there were over 300 negotiated agreements in the EU countries, over 30,000 local negotiated agreements in Japan, and over forty PVAs in the USA (see OECD 1999, p. 9). The increased popularity of voluntary agreements (VAs) of various sorts has prompted a growing body of academic literature aimed at examining various efficiency and social welfare aspects of VAs.[1] While these studies suggest several reasons why regulated firms and regulatory agencies might benefit from VAs, none has focused on explaining why these supposed benefits have led to the intense interest in VAs only recently. In fact, when one reads the existing literature on VAs, one is struck by the question: "Why is it that VAs rose to prominence only in the early 1990s, when the

---

[1] Lyon and Maxwell (2002) present a detailed review of the economics literature on voluntary agreements.

economic justifications for VAs seem timeless?" Developing a preliminary answer to this question is the goal of the present chapter.

While theoretical models provide useful insight into the causes and consequences of VAs, we believe that an institutional approach is required to explain the *timing* of the shift toward VAs in particular countries. In this chapter, we pursue such an approach, focusing on the case of the USA, since that is what we know best. We leave it to other researchers to adapt this approach to the particular situations of other countries. Nevertheless, we consider in the concluding section 4 the extent to which the factors we identify here help to explain the use of VAs in Europe and Japan.

The use of VAs began in the USA in the early 1990s. To date, over fifty such agreements have been created, as shown in table 6.1.[2] As is apparent in table 6.1, there were fifty-four PVAs, and just two negotiated agreements. This provides an interesting contrast with the situation in the EU and Japan, where negotiated agreements have been more common. The vast majority of VAs in the USA deal with environmental issues of pollution prevention and climate change.

VAs are an example of institutional change in US environmental regulations. Here we are speaking of institutions in the sense of North (1990). That is, institutions are the "rules of the game." Put another way, institutions are humanly devised constraints, both formal and informal, that shape human and organizational interactions. The term "command-and-control" regulation has traditionally been used to encompass any form of environmental regulation that is not market-based, e.g. Best Available Technology (BAT) requirements, product prohibitions, or emission standards.[3] VAs represent an institutional change away from traditional command-and-control regulation, which has dominated (and continues to dominate) US environmental policy. We will use the institutional framework set out in North (1990) to analyze the rise of VAs in the USA in the early 1990s.[4]

Institutional change arises when relative prices change, making existing institutional arrangements suboptimal for at least some of the organizations that are powerful enough to bring about change. Thus, in order to examine

---

[2] See chapter 9 for a more detailed description and analysis of these programs. In particular, the appendix to chapter 9 (p. 255) offers a brief description of all major US VAs with corporate partners to date.

[3] For a detailed discussion and critique of the phrase "command-and-control," see Russell (2001, pp. 188–192).

[4] Our analysis has also benefited from a reading of the Institutional Analysis and Development (IAD) framework developed by Elinor Ostrom and others at the Workshop in Political Theory at Indiana University. Polski and Ostrom (1998) provides an overview of the IAD framework, and discusses how one might apply it to policy analysis.

the rise of VAs in the USA, we must first identify those organizations that are heavily affected by environmental regulations and that have the ability to shape environmental rules and regulations.

In section 2, we discuss the groups that are relevant for our analysis, focusing in particular on how they have benefited from command-and-control regulation.[5] The groups we identify are regulated industries, national environmental groups, the EPA and state-level regulatory agencies, and the Congress. By understanding the benefits each group derives from traditional regulation, we are able to contrast these benefits with those that arise from VAs.

In section 3 we turn our attention to the question of why US VAs arose in the early 1990s. We identify the benefits (if any) that each of our four groups derive from the use of VAs, arguing that the EPA and regulated firms have been the primary beneficiaries of VAs. Then we identify internal and external shocks to the existing command-and-control framework that prompted the EPA and regulated firms to promote the use of VAs. The shocks we point to are: increasingly complex and unrealistic regulations, technological change and scientific discoveries that have made existing laws practically unenforceable, growing political resistance to regulations that are costly and difficult to enforce, shrinking regulatory budgets, and the rise of citizen action lawsuits that targeted both polluters and the EPA.

We argue that regulated firms and the EPA benefit from the use of VAs, but in quite different ways. Firms benefit from negotiated agreements because they avoid the costly political battles that accompany new legislation. They also benefit from PVAs that may subsidize corporate efforts to cut costs or enhance corporate image through favorable publicity. The EPA can benefit from negotiated agreements, in principle, since they may secure environmental benefits without the uncertainty that accompanies attempts to pass new legislation.[6] In addition, EPA benefits from PVAs because they allow the agency to make modest strides toward environmental improvement even when it lacks statutory authority to impose mandatory controls; at the same time, PVAs continue to provide a prominent role for EPA

---

[5] Groups that derive no benefit from the dominant form of regulation generally lack the power to change the regulatory regime, unless there has been a significant shift in political climate since the enactment of the original regulations.

[6] In practice, however, negotiated agreements are rare in the USA. In the European context, negotiated agreements are often used to preempt new legislative proposals. In the USA, however, the separation of the legislative and executive branches of government means that an agreement between industry and the EPA cannot guarantee that Congress will eschew legislation on the same subject.

Table 6.1 US voluntary agreements, 1991–2002

			Public Voluntary Agreements					
		Year	Climate Change	Pollution Prevention	Air Quality	Environmental Quality	Health & Safety	Negotiated Agreements
1	Green Lights[a]	1991	•					
2	WasteWise	1992	•					
3	AgSTAR	1993	•					
4	Climate Wise	1993	•					
5	ENERGY STAR Office Equipment	1993	•					
6	Natural Gas STAR	1993	•					
7	Ruminant Livestock Methane Efficiency Program	1993	•					
8	State and Local Climate Change Outreach Program	1993	•					
9	US Initiatives on Joint Implementation	1993	•					
10	CFC Substitutes	Post-1993	•					
11	HFC-23 Reductions	Post-1993	•					
12	Seasonal Gas Use for the Control of Nitrous Oxide	Post-1993	•					
13	Coalbed Methane Outreach	1994	•					
14	ENERGY STAR Buildings	1994	•					
15	Landfill Methane Outreach Program	1994	•					
16	ENERGY STAR Homes	1995	•					
17	ENERGY STAR Transformer Program	1995	•					
18	Transportation Partners	1995	•					
19	Voluntary Aluminium Industrial Partnership	1995	•					
20	Environmental Stewardship Initiative	1997	•					
21	Mobile Air Conditioning Climate Protection Partnership	Post-1998	•					
22	PFC Emission Reduction Partnership for the Semiconductor Industry	Post-1998	•					
23	SF6 Emission Reduction Partnership for the Magnesium Industry	Post-1998	•					
24	SF6 Emission Reduction Partnership for Electric Power	1999	•					
25	Combined Heat and Power Partnership	2000	•					
26	Commuter Choice	2001	•					
27	Green Power Partnership	2001	•					
28	Climate Leaders	2002	•					
29	"33/50" program	1991		•				

		Public Voluntary Agreements					Negotiated Agreements
	Year	Climate Change	Pollution Prevention	Air Quality	Environmental Quality	Health & Safety	
Design for the Environment	1991		•				
Environmental Accounting Project	1992		•				
Green Chemistry	1992		•				
Water Alliances for Voluntary Efficiency	1992		•				
Pesticide Environmental Stewardship Program	1993		•				
Voluntary Standards Network	1993		•				
Environmental Leadership Program	1994		•				
Waste Minimization National Plan	1994		•				
Indoor Environments Program	1995		•				
Hospitals for a Healthy Environment	1998		•				
Green Engineering	Post-1998		•				
National Waste Minimization Partnership Program	Post-1998		•				
Sustainable Futures Initiative	2002		•				
Improving Air Quality through Land Use Activities	1997			•			
Indoor Air Quality	Post-1998			•			
Voluntary Diesel Retrofit Program	Post-1998			•			
Indoor Air Quality Tools for Schools	2000			•			
Green Vehicle Guide	2001			•			
Clean Air Transportation Communities	2001			•			
SmartWay Transport	2003			•			
Environmental Technology Verification Program	1995				•		
National Environmental Performance Track	2000				•		
Industry Sector Performance Programs	2003				•		
Consumer Labeling Initiative	1996					•	
Sun Wise School Program	2000					•	
Common Sense Initiative	1994						•
Project XL	1995						•

Note: [a] Table 6.1 lists programs by initial year of operation, within each group.

employees through such activities as data collection, information diffusion, and the facilitation of communication between firms about opportunities for abatement. The biggest losers from the use of VAs appear to be national environmental groups, who lose the opportunity to influence EPA priorities and actions through litigation. Environmental champions in Congress may view VAs as undesirable, since unilateral actions may preempt the opportunity for Congressional leaders to take credit for new environmental laws. However, we suspect the vast majority of Congressmen are indifferent toward VAs, or even view them as a convenient way to deflect criticism from environmental constituents disappointed when Congress fails to pass their favored bills.[7]

2   THE ORGANIZATIONS THAT SHAPE US ENVIRONMENTAL REGULATIONS

The economic organizations (and their political entrepreneurs) that are affected by an institution are the agents of institutional change. Thus, to understand how VAs came about in the USA we must first examine those organizations that have two features: they are affected by environmental policy and they have the ability to bring about changes in the policy. We identify four such organizations: regulated firms, national environmental groups, the EPA and state regulatory agencies, and lawmakers (the Congress).

It comes as no surprise to economists that the current system of command-and-control regulation is not only inefficient, but, despite this inefficiency, difficult to change.[8] As Noll and Owen (1983) point out, any new regulation creates interests with a stake in maintaining the new status quo, and they will oppose efforts to deregulate or make substantial changes in the regulations. As Peltzman (1976) points out, the benefits of regulation tend to be shared by a variety of interest groups that have the power to write or influence regulation. However, once all organizations with power to change the regulation agree, through the political process, on how to share the surplus that the regulation generates, change will be rare. In fact, change will arise only from external shocks that alter the bargaining power of the organizations, making it beneficial for some organizations to seek to rewrite the rules.

---

[7] See Hansen (1999) for a formal model in which VAs can deflect criticism away from legislators.

[8] This section of the chapter has benefited from a careful reading of Zywicki (1999), which focuses on explaining the lack of change in US environmental policy.

We identify four types of organizations that are powerful enough to influence US environmental regulation and enforcement. We examine each of these organizations in turn, taking care to illustrate the surplus they capture from the current command-and-control system. In section 4 we will examine how shocks during the mid-to-late 1980s altered the relative bargaining power of these organizations, causing a subset of the organizations to attempt to "rewrite" the rules in the form of VAs.

2.1 Regulated industry

Conventional wisdom holds that industry strongly opposes regulations, since they increase operating costs and reduce managerial discretion. Indeed, this is likely true in the majority of cases, although the academic literature has demonstrated that under certain conditions industry can actually profit from being regulated.[9] More importantly, though, industry is likely to have preferences about the form of regulation when some form of regulation becomes inevitable. In addition, different firms within an industry are likely to take very different views toward particular regulatory proposals.

When introductory environmental economics textbooks compare command-and-control regulation to incentive-based alternatives, such as marketable permit systems or pollution taxes, they focus on the efficiency of the latter. If the regulated firms compete in a competitive industry, these models show that all firms may benefit from more efficient forms of regulation. In practice, however, environmental regulation, just like any other regulation, often creates winners and losers. Those firms that benefit from environmental regulation have powerful incentives to resist regulatory change. Industries can benefit both directly and indirectly from existing command-and-control regulations.

While in some instances certain industries may benefit directly from command-and-control regulations (e.g. the waste disposal industry benefits directly from federal regulations that favor end-of-pipe waste disposal solutions rather than front-of-pipe process changes), the indirect benefits arising from command-and-control regulation are very likely much larger. Simply put, current command-and-control regulations serve as an effective barrier to entry in many industries, for many reasons. Buchanan

---

[9] For example, Maloney and McCormick (1982) show that all firms in an industry can gain from regulations that raise the marginal cost of production more than they raise the average cost.

and Tullock (1975) point out that many regulated industries likely prefer direct command-and-control regulation over incentive-based regulation. They show that incentive-based regulations work to price pollution as an input in production, encouraging efficient use of the input. As a result, the "rights" to pollute tend to flow to firms and industries that can use them most efficiently. However, these firms may have to pay for emission permits or for environmental taxes, in addition to internal expenditures on pollution control. Furthermore, in equilibrium, overall pollution costs will be lower and a more competitive equilibrium featuring lower overall rents will tend to result. Hence firms may prefer a command-and-control regulatory regime.

Empirical studies have found support for this theory. Maloney and McCormick (1982) provide some empirical evidence that both Occupational Safety and Health Administration (OSHA) and EPA regulations of cotton dust and copper smelting served as barriers to entry. Pashigian (1985) finds that politicians from existing and declining industrial regions voted for environmental legislation that tended to protect home-state industries from competition from regions experiencing rapid growth. Portney (1990) reinforces the point in the environmental area by noting that the National Ambient Air Quality Standards (NAAQSs) disallow the deterioration of air quality in regions that currently exceed the standards. This protects existing firms from entry by new firms and ensures that industries will not shift their location even if such shifts would improve air quality generally. Finally, Dean and Brown (1995) provide cross-sectional evidence that pollution regulation tends to serve as a barrier to entry.

In general, command-and-control regulations tend to favor established larger firms over smaller startups. Often abatement capital is lumpy, requiring installation of expensive equipment (e.g. scrubbers) no matter the scale of production. Indeed, in general the quantity and complexity of environmental regulations along with the uncertainty of environmental liability serve as an effective barrier to entry to smaller producers.

2.2   National environmental groups

The primary concern of national environmental interest groups is to ensure government and industry undertake actions to improve the environment. Since these groups are less concerned with economic efficiency, the reasons why they prefer centralized command-and-control regulation are numerous. First, although command-and-control regulations may be less efficient than market-based or tax-related forms of regulation, they are generally a quicker means of attacking pollution problems. For example, technology-forcing regulations are relatively simple to enforce: new capital equipment is easy to monitor, and once installed there is little scope for management disinterest to undermine the resulting pollution reductions. Second, command-and-control regulations are generally better at locking-in environmental improvements. As Moe (1989) argues:

> by directing bureaucratic behavior themselves via detailed formal requirements –
> even if these requirements were technically ill-advised and took a toll on agency
> performance – the [environmental] groups were removing crucial decisions from
> the realm of future influence by business. This was tremendously valuable, and
> they were willing to pay a price for it. As a result, they purposefully created bizarre
> administrative arrangements that were not well suited to effective regulation. (See
> Moe 1989, pp. 325–326)

Third, it is easier to monitor compliance with command-and-control regulations than with other forms of regulation. This feature is of special importance to national environmental groups, because almost every environmental statute contains "citizen suit" provisions that allow for citizens or groups to sue private parties for non-compliance with statutes.[10] Several environmental groups have been increasingly successful in suing under these provisions. While in many cases environmental groups do not receive direct compensation from suits won, their legal fees are covered, providing incentives to pursue legal actions. Furthermore, environmental groups have been very active in lobbying for "technology-forcing" regulations that have become a common feature of command-and-control regulations. Portney (1990) notes that these regulations are increasingly unrealistic, and non-compliance is inevitable. Once non-compliance results, environmental groups sue for compensation or remedial action, while having legal fees covered as part of the judgment.

For all of the foregoing reasons, command-and-control regulations tend to be favored by national environmental groups.

2.3   The EPA and state regulators

Under most federal environmental legislation (including the CAA and CWA) the EPA is charged with setting standards that will result in the

---

[10] The increasing frequency of lawsuits against the EPA has been a major factor motivating the adoption of VAs. We elaborate on this point in section 3 below.

attainment of regulatory goals. For the most part, state regulatory agencies are charged with monitoring and enforcement of federal regulations. The EPA, along with the Department of Justice, serves as an enforcement back-stop.

The EPA and its state-level counterparts, as any government bureaucracy, have multiple objectives, as we discussed in chapter 2. In addition to direct concern about the environmental benefits of the programs they administer, and (possibly to a lesser extent) the costs programs impose on industry, they are naturally concerned with seeking larger budgets and greater power. In order to justify their budgets, these environmental agencies must be active and useful. Hahn (1994) notes that "The EPA recognized that the key to its growth lies in expanding the list of environmental issues that need attention and in writing regulations in such a way as to provide a greater need for the EPA." Traditional regulation provides such a role for the EPA and its state-level counterparts. Firms engage in self-reporting of emissions to the EPA and these reports are backed up by monitoring and enforcement by state agencies and in some cases the EPA.

Regardless of EPA's own preferences, there are a number of environmental situations in which the agency is constrained to take a very circumscribed approach. Some major pieces of environmental legislation focus solely on environmental goals, without regard for cost. For example, the CAA Amendments of 1977 require EPA to set NAAQS for seven major pollutants; the cost of meeting the standards was not supposed to be a criterion in setting the standards. Similarly, the CWA declared that all US waters were to be "fishable and swimmable" by 1983, and that discharge of pollutants into navigable waters was to be halted by 1985; clearly these goals do not reflect costs. In addition, as the foregoing quote from Moe (1989) indicates, some pieces of legislation have been written with very detailed directives that greatly constrain EPA discretion in tackling environmental problems. In some circumstances, then, EPA may prefer to avoid operating under the confining strictures of legislation. Not surprisingly, these may well be the same circumstances in which industry finds legislation to be unduly costly or inefficient.

Another concern for EPA is that formal legislation leaves the agency open to suits alleging failure to enforce environmental laws. As discussed earlier, the stringency of many laws and the growing sophistication of new technology mean that certain statutory requirements (e.g. "safe" levels of emissions) may be nearly impossible to fulfill, leaving EPA vulnerable to continual lawsuits from disaffected parties.

2.4 The Congress

Lawmakers have two main constituencies, voters and interest groups directly affected by proposed laws. Members of Congress can benefit by passing environmental legislation that pleases one or both of these constituencies. To please voters, regulations are often written with simple, absolutist goals in mind. As mentioned above, the federal CWA dictates that lakes and streams should quickly be made "swimmable" and "fishable," and the Clean Air Act requires ambient air quality standards to be set at a level that is "safe" for public health. Vague and general goals, along with low budget allocations for monitoring and enforcement, tend to favor regulations that specify particular technologies, the installation of which is relatively easy to monitor. For example, according to Buck (1996, p. 109), "[t]he original 1972 [Clean Water Act] legislation proved very difficult to implement, and EPA agreed to new methods of control. Codified in the 1977 amendments, the Best Available Technology (BAT) is used to determine effluent limitations...There is no requirement of a balancing between the costs and benefits of effluent reduction." As we argued above, such technology-based regulations are often less efficient than, say, effluent taxes, but they may be preferred by environmental interest groups (since they are easy to enforce) and by industry interest groups (because they create entry barriers that shield incumbent members from increased competition).

At a secondary level, members of Congress can engage in rent extraction by threatening to replace existing legislation or to add new laws. Direct rent extraction occurs when threatened parties contribute to Congressional campaigns through political action committees, or when affected firms lobby Congressional members, providing them with honoraria, free trips to conferences, etc. To the extent that command-and-control regulation leaves industry greater rents, the threat of extraction is also higher under this mode of regulation. Even if the threat to legislate is never actually fulfilled, the mere ability to credibly threaten legislative action can be valuable to Congressional representatives, especially those who are leaders in a particular legislative area.

We have detailed the various ways in which organizations powerful enough to affect the writing and enforcement of environmental regulations may benefit from those regulations. To demonstrate that VAs represent an institutional change in US environmental policy, we must show two things. First, that some organization with the ability to effect such change in the regulatory arena can benefit from the changes embodied in voluntary environmental agreements, and second that those benefits had arisen within a reasonable time interval prior to the early 1990s (when most VAs were established in the USA).

3   THE RISE OF VOLUNTARY AGREEMENTS

According to Dixit (1996), institutions are generally designed to reduce uncertainty and to minimize transactions costs. However, it is clear that the establishment of institutions and institutional change does not occur behind a veil of ignorance. Dixit makes this point with a striking example. While the authors of the US Constitution strove to establish the principle of equality among men in order to preempt the establishment of the rigid class system they had just fought to escape, they saw fit to leave the lucrative practice of slavery untouched.

North (1990) describes the process of institutional change as follows. There is first a change in relative prices. This change leads one or more of the parties to an exchange to perceive that they could do better with an altered agreement or contract. Changes in relative prices usually result from an outside shock. This shock may help or harm all parties involved in an agreement, but more than likely the shock will affect each party differently. Such shocks alter the relative bargaining power of the parties involved and/or impose extra transactions costs on a subset of parties. These changes then lead to a desire to rewrite the rules, formal or informal, that govern the interaction of the parties.

The change we focus on here is the rise of VAs in the early 1990s in the USA. As discussed above, there are four types of organizations with the potential to alter environmental laws: industry, environmental groups, Congress, and the EPA. All four benefited in one way or another from the use of traditional command-and-control regulation. However, the two main participants in VAs are the affected industry and the regulator. Environmental groups and Congress, in contrast, tend to be marginalized by the use of VAs. What benefits did industry and the EPA expect to achieve through the use of VAs? From industry's perspective, VAs are appealing for several reasons: they tend to be non-binding, typically do not require the level of regulatory paperwork and other burdens associated with formal rules, and may involve subsidies for desired behavior instead of the threat of penalties for bad behavior. The benefits for regulators are somewhat less obvious but are also important. Perhaps most important is that VAs promise to free regulators from the virtually impossible demands that can be imposed by well-meaning but overly ambitious legislative language.

What changes in the relative prices associated with US regulatory institutions prompted EPA and the industries it regulates to explore VAs as an alternative to traditional regulation? We identify four such changes: (1) a growing body of environmental law that is broad, increasingly complex, and costly to enforce, (2) technological innovation and scientific discoveries, (3) regulatory budget cutbacks, and (4) the increasing use (and effectiveness) of "citizen suits."

While some of these changes, such as mounting legislation, have evolved gradually, we argue that the confluence of these four changes reached critical proportions during the mid-to-late 1980s, leading to the adoption of VAs in the early 1990s. Portney's (1990) review of US environmental policy between 1970 and 1990 provides an excellent description of the four changes we have enumerated.

3.1   Growing body of environmental legislation

From its inception, the EPA has been charged with implementing the tremendously complex environmental laws passed by Congress. The complexity of these laws often lies in the simplicity of their wording. As mentioned, Congress tends to be absolutist in its approach to environmental legislation. Federal air and water laws, for example, required the setting of literally thousands of discharge standards, the establishment of comprehensive monitoring standards, and other important tasks, while at the same time allowing only 180 days for the completion of many tasks (see Portney 1990, p. 22). Portney notes that many assignments were left undone seventeen years after legislation was passed, and offers the following characterization of the EPA: every year the EPA works harder and harder to stay on top of the laws passed by Congress, while at the same time falling further behind.

3.2   Technological innovation and scientific discoveries

Since the formalization and centralization of US environmental policy in 1970, technological progress has affected firms and regulators in numerous ways. Abatement equipment has become increasingly sophisticated and costly, and new industrial facilities are often required to utilize the best technology available. The growing costs of abatement mean that industry is willing to allocate growing amounts of resources to political pressure activity, further increasing the costs of regulatory action. These two effects reinforce one another, giving industry strong incentives to attempt to preempt the legislative process.

The EPA is also affected by technological change, though in a somewhat different way. Innovations in monitoring technology, along with a growing body of literature on the physiological and toxicological effects of industrial pollution, have led to two stark conclusions: first, current levels of industrial emissions are "unsafe," and, second, there may be no "safe" level of emissions! These facts, especially the latter, cause the EPA tremendous difficulty in carrying out its mission. As Portney (1990) notes: "Since Congress did not contemplate such [possibilities], the EPA administrator is caught between the apparent mandate of the law and the realities of science and economics." One result of this situation is that the EPA appears to be ineffective in fulfilling its political role, which may lead to political criticism and even to reductions in its budget allocation. Another result is that environmental interest groups have assumed growing control of the environmental agenda through the use of litigation, which we discuss in more detail below.

In light of the challenges scientific and technological changes pose for the EPA, it should not be surprising that there is growing caution in many quarters toward the use of new command-and-control regulations in areas where there is substantial scientific or technological uncertainty. Indeed, the areas where VAs have been most popular – including climate change, toxic pollution, and solid waste recycling – are ones where such uncertainty is rife. With regard to climate change, there is a growing consensus that the phenomenon is occurring, and that human action contributes to the process, but much less is known about the exact extent to which human activity is responsible, and the meteorological processes that mediate global warming. With regard to toxic pollution, there are numerous chemicals suspected of being toxic to humans that have not yet been adequately tested, and for which it is thus very difficult to promulgate reasonable emissions standards. With regard to solid waste recycling, especially for such complicated products as automobiles, the logistics required for a thorough-going system of cradle-to-grave controls are complex and the optimal technological approach still uncertain. In all of these cases, premature legislation could easily lock environmental agencies into a highly inefficient set of regulations.

3.3   Budget cutbacks

While it is clear that the optimal response to many scientific discoveries may be to rewrite existing pieces of legislation, another possible response could be to increase the EPA's budget and/or work force, thus allowing the agency to craft new approaches to measuring the environmental and health effects of pollution, develop improved methods of monitoring and enforcement, sponsor new research on mitigation opportunities, and support the dissemination of compliance information throughout the affected industries. With greater resources, one might hope to ensure that the growing challenges faced by the agency could be effectively met. In reality, however, the EPA's resources have not kept pace with the demands placed upon it. As figures 6.1 and 6.2 show, both the size of the EPA labor force and its overall real budget declined in the early 1980s, almost certainly hampering the EPA's capabilities. In 1983, the General Accounting Office (GAO) delivered a critical report of the EPA's enforcement record.[11] The report noted that in some cases enforcement action was not taken for years after non-compliance had begun.

Note that the graphs in figures 6.1 and 6.2 actually understate the extent of cutbacks at the EPA during the 1980s, because the post-1980 figures include spending and personnel devoted to the administration of the Superfund program. Portney (1990) estimates that, excluding Superfund spending, by 1990 the EPA's budget had fallen by 15 percent from its 1980 level. Figures 6.1 and 6.2 illustrate the trend in EPA's budget and labor force assuming this 15 percent reduction. In summary, while the demands upon EPA have grown substantially over time, labor resources at the agency have risen only modestly, and EPA funding has remained virtually unchanged since the 1980s.

3.4   Rising cost of litigation against EPA

Shortly after the publication of the 1983 GAO report, several major environmental groups, citing lax enforcement by the EPA, began to sue for the right to use self-monitoring data (which are public information) as the basis of citizen law suits against non-compliant polluters. Russell (1990) reports that these efforts were generally successful. Through a series of

---

[11] General Accounting Office, *Waste Water Dischargers Are Not Complying with EPA Pollution Control Permits*, RECED-84-53 (Washington, DC, 1983).

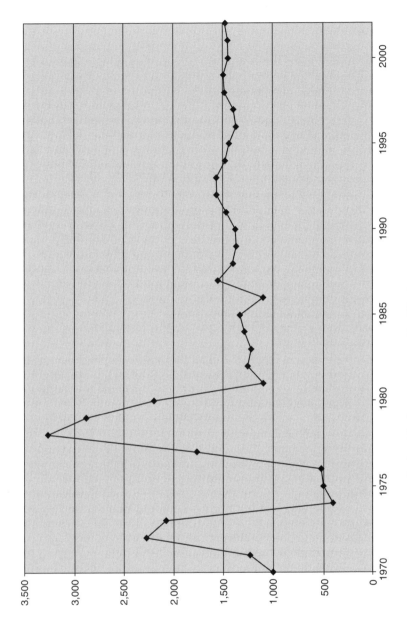

Figure 6.1 EPA non-Superfund real budget, 1970–2002 ($ million)

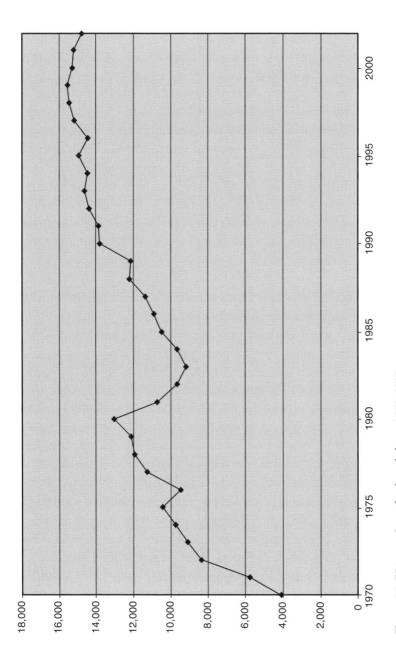

Figure 6.2 EPA non-Superfund work force, 1970–2002

cases, the courts ruled against defendant firms on most legal challenges designed to block the use of self-monitoring data. Also, following the release of the GAO report, national environmental groups began to sue the EPA for failure to enforce its own regulations. Farber (1992) notes that "The major environmental groups, most notably the Sierra Club and the Natural Resources Defence Council, have participated in scores of major law suits against the EPA and other government agencies."[12] This body of law has shifted the balance of power in the political economy game towards national environmental groups and the Congress (since their laws are being more fully enforced), weakening the positions of both the EPA and industry. While Russell does not provide details of timing, it is quite reasonable to postulate that if environmental groups began suing for the right to use self-reported data in 1984, a sufficient body of legal precedent could not have emerged for a number of years. Indeed, the data indicate that although environmental groups filed a total of only ten lawsuits against the EPA in 1988, that number had risen to fifty-one by 1991.

Figure 6.3 shows the number of new lawsuits filed against the EPA by environmental groups over the period 1979–2000, classified by the lead statute under which the suit was brought.[13] Suits under the CAA and the CWA were by far the most common. It is important to recognize that figure 6.3 does not reveal the full burden of lawsuits on EPA resources, since it takes several years for most suits to be fully resolved. Figure 6.4 presents a range of estimates of the total number of "live" lawsuits by environmental groups that were ongoing at each point between 1983 and 2000. The figure shows the number of new suits filed, along with three different moving averages of the total suits in process at a given time. The moving average calculations variously assume three years, four years, or five years for the estimated average time to resolve a lawsuit. Regardless of the duration assumed, however, the broad picture is the same: the number of environmental group suits consuming EPA resources rose dramatically in the early 1990s, reaching a rough steady-state level of between 150–175 active lawsuits by the middle of the decade.

Environmental groups were not the only organizations that began to pelt the EPA with a growing number of legal actions. Figure 6.5 shows

---

[12] Farber (1992), as quoted in Zywicki (1999).

[13] These data were obtained from the Department of Justice through a Freedom of Information Act request. In figure 6.3, the statutes are abbreviated as follows: CAA = Clean Air Act; CWA = Clean Water Act; NEPA = National Environmental Policy Act; CERCLA = Comprehensive Environmental Response, Compensation, and Liability Act (Superfund); and RCRA = Resource Conservation and Recovery Act.

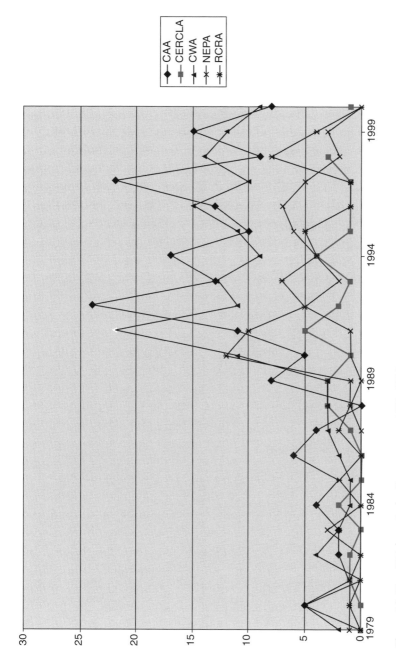

Figure 6.3 New EPA lawsuits by Green groups, 1979–2000

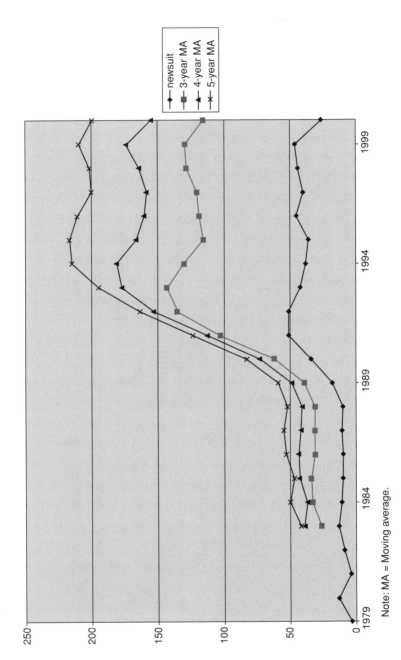

Figure 6.4 Estimated total EPA lawsuits by Green groups, 1979–2000

Note: MA = Moving average.

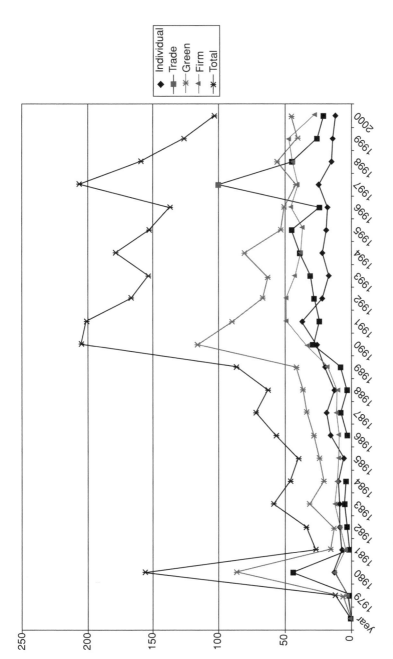

Figure 6.5 New lawsuits against EPA, 1979–2000

the number of new lawsuits filed against the EPA by type of plaintiff, including individuals, firms, trade associations, and green groups. Figure 6.5 shows that individual firms file more suits against EPA every year than do environmental groups, and trade associations file almost as many as do environmental groups. Furthermore, the growth in litigation against EPA occurs in a similar pattern for all categories of plaintiffs: all subjected EPA to a growing number of suits in the late 1980s, reaching a rough steady state of approximately 175 *new* lawsuits per year by 1990. Examination of the underlying data shows that the decline in new suits that is apparent from 1998–2000 results solely from a reduction in suits by trade associations under the CAA. The huge spike in lawsuits by trade associations in 1997 appears to have been a response to changes in the CAA involving standards for ground level ozone ("smog") and particulate matter.[14]

We reiterate that the burden of lawsuits on EPA is a function not of the number of new lawsuits filed, but of the total active suits at any one time. Thus, figure 6.6 shows a range of estimates for total active lawsuits against EPA over the period 1979–2000. Calculated in a fashion identical to that used in figure 6.4, figure 6.6 shows that by the early 1990s the number of active suits against EPA had stabilized at around 700 at any one time. This figure declined somewhat by the end of the decade, but by any measure the EPA was being forced to allocate resources to addressing hundreds of ongoing suits.

The four changes that took place during the mid-to-late 1980s raised the cost of traditional regulatory approaches, and placed increasing control over the regulatory agenda in the hands of litigants from both environmental groups and industry. The shift toward greater reliance on VAs can be seen as an attempt to lower regulatory costs and to wrest control from environmental groups. We have argued above that this change was of particular benefit to industry, but that EPA also stood to benefit in light of its increasing difficulties in implementing existing legislation. From table 6.1, it is clear that in the USA the great majority of voluntary initiatives take the form of PVAs. There is reason to believe that Congress, as well as industry and the EPA, would find such plans attractive. They increase industry's willingness to expend political resources opposing new regulations, in hopes of obtaining government assistance through public voluntary programs.[15] This increased willingness to spend money on the political process tends

---

[14] The EPAs website contains information on the changes to the CAA that were finalized in July 1997; see http://www.epa.gov/oar/oaqps/ozpmbro/ for details.

[15] For a full explication of this point, see chapter 8.

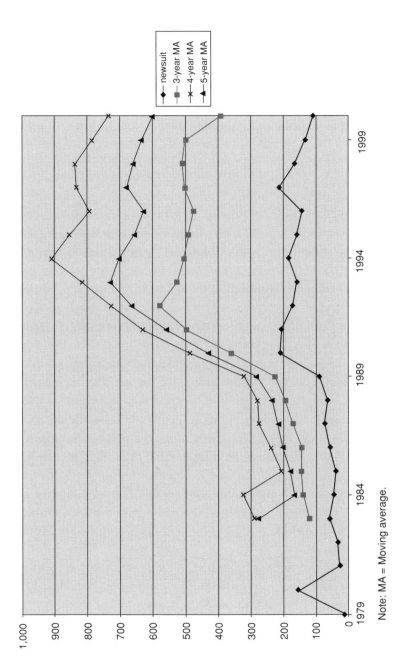

Note: MA = Moving average.

Figure 6.6 Estimated total lawsuits against EPA, 1979–2000

to enrich Congressional war chests. Furthermore, as we show in chapter 8, the emergence of public voluntary programs reduces industry's motivation to engage in self-regulation that would preempt the legislative process altogether, another outcome that may benefit Congress.

If one examines the structure of most US PVAs, one observes at least four regularities.

(1) PVAs tend to arise in the absence of a strong regulatory threat, as we discuss in detail in chapter 8. As we have argued above, resistance to regulation may come from several quarters. Industry allocates more resources to resisting regulation as the cost of incremental regulatory policies continues to rise. At the same time, the EPA finds new regulations increasingly costly to enforce, and spends increasing amounts of time defending its actions in court; as a result, it too has reason to resist new legislative requirements.

(2) Whether industry resistance alone is enough to block new legislation, or whether EPA efforts reinforce this resistance, PVAs can serve a useful role for regulators. They may allow at least a modicum of environmental improvement even in areas where EPA lacks statutory authority. From a more self-serving perspective, EPA can use PVAs to expand its scope of authority and to legitimize further budget appropriations. For example, most such programs involve membership certification by the EPA. In addition, they often include information-sharing among participating firms, the EPA, and environmental abatement experts. The EPA plays an important role in such information-based activities, by facilitating meetings among interested parties, documenting and validating the claims of industry members, and, in some cases, through its own internal research efforts. Chapter 9 discusses these activities in greater detail.

(3) Because PVAs are not legally binding, by their very nature they present litigation difficulties for environmental groups while shielding EPA and industry from the costs of defending themselves in court. Not surprisingly, VAs have been widely criticized by national environmental groups and smaller environmental watchdogs.[16]

---

[16] For example, the Environmental Justice and Climate Change Initiation, a coalition of twenty-eight advocacy groups, argues that "Voluntary agreements between government and business exclude the people who are affected by those agreements ... In a democracy, people should have a say in the decisions that affect their lives. By moving the decision making process into the elite world of CEO's and lobbyists for industries, our communities lose." For further details, see http://www.ejcc.org/releases/030212.html.

(4) VAs leave in place existing regulations, and the rents they create, thereby avoiding political opposition.[17] Furthermore, in the case of environmental problems that are not currently subject to legislative mandates, VAs leave in place rents that might be threatened by new regulations, which again enhances their political attractiveness.

As predicted by proponents of institutional change theory, VAs appear to reduce the transaction costs and uncertainty associated with EPA–industry interactions, while leaving in place previous regulations. Transaction costs are reduced in a variety of ways. In the case of negotiated agreements, costs of lobbying for legislation and participating in EPA rulemaking activities are eliminated, and firms enjoy greater flexibility in their abatement activities, especially when they involve pollution problems that may involve multiple "media" (e.g. water, air, and land). In the case of PVAs, transaction costs are reduced when their introduction helps make the passage of legislation so unlikely that it is simply not proposed.[18] With either type of VA, uncertainty is reduced by removing the possibility of litigation that surrounds mandatory regulatory requirements. Industry and EPA both share in both of these forms of savings.

While the EPA and industry might like to go beyond the introduction of VAs, and actually rewrite some existing regulations, such change would likely require the active participation of Congress. This participation is unlikely since Congress would derive little benefit from revisions of current laws and would be left open to the criticism that existing laws were being weakened. At the same time, political realities make it extremely unlikely that Congress would legislate against the use of VAs unless they were proven to be ineffective.

A major benefit VAs deliver to the EPA is the ability to alleviate outside pressure from environmental groups. These pressures are particularly severe when the EPA's budget constraint is tightly binding, and monies spent on litigation have a high opportunity cost. One might therefore hypothesize

---

[17] The one exception to this rule is Project XL which, at least in one case, did seek to relax existing regulations. However, Project XL is focused at the individual firm level. Therefore any regulatory relaxation that takes place would be firm-specific, which does not repeal the general anticompetitive effects of existing regulations. For more information on the Project XL proposal by Intel Corporation, see Boyd, Krupnick, and Mazurek (1998).

[18] Of course, the possibility of offering a PVA will not always eliminate legislative proposals, and if it does not, a costly round of political battling will occur. In this case, we might expect to see discussion of PVAs arise only after legislative efforts have been tried, but failed. Indeed, this is what happened in the case of the Clinton Administration's proposed BTU tax, as we discuss in chapter 8.

that as budgets become less constrained, relative to the EPA's obligations, VAs will lose favor. To date, however, this hypothesis is not testable. As figure 6.1 shows, the EPA's real budget has remained roughly unchanged since the 1980s as its obligations have grown. Thus, the conditions supporting the use of VAs appear to remain in place.

The second Bush Administration's approach to climate change has continued the reliance on voluntary programs that was emphasized by the Clinton Administration. There is one interesting difference, however. While Clinton relied upon PVAs, Bush has emphasized "voluntary" commitments by industry to achieve an 18 percent reduction in greenhouse gas intensity (i.e. emissions per unit of economic activity).[19] The Bush approach more closely resembles a negotiated agreement designed to preempt legislation than a PVA created out of a lack of legislative threat. This change probably reflects two factors. First, the political climate in the USA on the issue of climate change has become more sympathetic to government action since large corporations such as Alcoa and others have spoken out publicly in favor of government action. The formation of the Chicago Climate Exchange by a group of private firms further signaled that at least some segments of industry are prepared to begin taking action to reduce greenhouse gas emissions. Second, the Bush Administration has received strong political support from traditional energy industries, broad swathes of which are likely to see climate change legislation as a costly encroachment on their profitability. Hence, Bush has greater incentives to try and preempt legislation than did Clinton, whose political allegiances lay elsewhere.

4   CONCLUSIONS

Voluntary environmental agreements represent a change in the existing institutional structure of environmental regulation in the USA. In this chapter we took an initial step in examining this change by appealing to the economic theory of institutions and institutional change. This theory tells us that the first step in examining institutional change is to examine the players that have the power to effect change. To this end, we have identified four such groups: regulated industries, the EPA, national environmental groups, and the Congress. Keeping in mind that VAs arose in the USA in the early 1990s, we identified several external factors which worked to alter

---

[19]   For details on the administration's climate change plans, see its "Climate Change Fact Sheet" at http://www.whitehouse.gov/news/releases/2003/04/20030409-11.html.

the relative returns these four groups derived from the existing regulatory institutions. We have argued that these factors – mounting legislative pressures, budget cutbacks, increasing litigation, and scientific discoveries – combined to increase the power of national environmental groups and the Congress, and weaken the other two groups.

Institutional change analysis suggests that when an outside shock upsets the balance of power in an existing institution, affected players might work to alter the rules, that is, to change the institution. It appears that the EPA and affected members of regulated industries may be attempting to use VAs as a way to win back some of the power they have lost under the traditional regulatory structure. It is clear that VAs grant these two groups much more power than Congress or national environmental groups, both of whom are blocked from participation in many VAs.

Our institutional analysis focused on the USA, and would not carry over directly to countries in the EU or to Japan. While it is widely recognized that VAs are numerous in both these locations, and that negotiated agreements play a much larger role there than in the USA, there has been no analysis of the timing of adoption of these agreements in Europe and Japan. We believe that the approach we have adopted here can be utilized in other countries, but there is no reason to expect the precise nature of the story to be the same. One obvious difference, for example, is that parliamentary democracies can more readily threaten new legislation, since they fuse the executive and legislative branches of the government. This factor is consistent with the greater use of negotiated agreements – which we view as a response to a regulatory threat – outside the USA.

Despite the important differences in political structure between the USA, Europe and Japan, we nevertheless expect some of the central features of the US situation to have parallels abroad. In particular, we have depicted VAs as in part a response to the rising costs of traditional regulatory tools. This is a phenomenon that is likely true in most developed nations, and one that motivates interest in alternative institutional means for dealing with environmental problems.

7 | Negotiated agreements

1 INTRODUCTION

As we explained in chapter 6, both firms and regulators may have incentives to negotiate around the process of creating new legislation and regulation. Our model of self-regulation in chapter 3 focused on the incentives of firms to preempt the regulatory process, leaving the regulator as a passive "black box" whose objectives were not specified. Here we develop a model in which the regulator's objectives are clearly stated, and negotiated agreements (NAs) emerge out of bargaining between the regulator and an industry association. This model, with a more pro-active regulator, reflects situations where the regulator has significant bargaining power. In fact, the analysis of chapter 3 can be thought of as a special case of a negotiated agreement in which industry holds all the bargaining power.

Negotiated agreements are more common in the nations of Europe and Japan than in the USA, perhaps because of the corporatist structure of many of these countries, which allows industry to negotiate as a unit with government. In addition, the parliamentary structure of the democracies of these nations ensures that the legislative and executive branches of government are of the same political party, potentially making legislative threats more credible.

This chapter presents a model of NAs that parallels in a number of ways the analysis of self-regulation introduced in chapter 3. In both cases, regulation is a function of interest group pressure, and the level of environmental protection is below the welfare maximizing level. At the same time, there are several differences in the two models. In particular, this chapter allows for uncertainty regarding the imposition of legislation, and incorporates a pro-active regulator who can bargain for a portion of the surplus created by regulatory preemption. In addition, we examine how industry heterogeneity affects the structure of negotiated agreements. Most importantly, we find that as with self-regulation, negotiated agreements that arise under the threat of regulation produce voluntary action that preempts the threat and is welfare-enhancing.

2 NEGOTIATED AGREEMENTS WITH ENDOGENOUS LEGISLATIVE THREAT

In this section, we present a simple model in which industry bargains with a regulator to create an NA that preempts the imposition of a mandatory regulation. The exposition follows closely the analysis of Glachant (2003a).[1]

Consider a model with three players: a polluting industry, a non-governmental organization (NGO) with "green" preferences, and a regulator. The industry has a total fixed cost of abatement $c(z)$, where z is the level of abatement achieved. This cost is the sum over all firms in the industry of achieving the aggregate abatement level z. Because abatement is costly, the industry will lobby against it if there is a legislative proposal for emissions control; we model industry's objective as minimizing the expected costs of pollution control. The "green" group will lobby in favor of emissions controls, with utility that is increasing in abatement activity; for simplicity, we assume the green group's utility is equal to z. Finally, the regulator's objective is to maximize the net social welfare associated with controlling z, which is given by $W(z) = z - c(z)$. Obviously the first-best level of abatement, z^*, is simply determined by $c'(z^*) = 1$.

The game unfolds in three stages. First, industry and the regulator can bargain over a level of abatement. If they reach agreement on some abatement level $\tilde{z}$, then no legislative proposal is put forward, and the game ends. The second stage is reached if negotiation breaks down, in which case the regulator can put forward a legislative proposal for a level z^M of mandatory emissions control. In the third stage, which is reached if the regulator makes a proposal, industry and the green lobby invest in rent-seeking expenditures designed to influence whether the proposal passes or fails. If it passes, we assume it is enforced perfectly and costlessly. As is typical in such models, we solve the game in reverse order, beginning with the rent-seeking stage.

2.1 The rent-seeking stage

In the rent-seeking subgame, the industry and the green lobby invest in rent-seeking expenditures to influence the likelihood that the regulator's legislative proposal z passes. We seek a Nash equilibrium, in which the

[1] For an analysis of efficiency and welfare issues associated with a NA negotiated under an exogenous legislative threat, see Segerson and Miceli (1998).

industry acts cooperatively to choose an aggregate rent-seeking expenditure L to maximize its expected payoff, taking the aggregate rent-seeking contribution M of the green lobby as given, and conversely. Let the probability that legislation passes be given by

$$\rho(M, L) = \rho_0 + (1 - \rho_0)\frac{\lambda M}{\lambda M + L}.$$

Then for the industry, the maximization problem is

$$\max_{L} -\rho(M, L)c(z) - L.$$

The first-order condition for this problem is

$$(1 - \rho_0)\frac{\lambda M}{(\lambda M + L)^2}c(z) = 1. \tag{7.1}$$

For the green lobby, the maximization problem is

$$\max_{M} \rho(M, L)z - M,$$

with solution given by

$$(1 - \rho_0)\frac{\lambda L}{(\lambda M + L)^2}z = 1. \tag{7.2}$$

Taken together, the first-order conditions imply

$$Lz^{M} = Mc(z^{M}).$$

Substituting in $L = Mc(z^{M})/z^{M}$ in (7.2) yields

$$(1 - \rho_0)\frac{\lambda Mc(z)}{(\lambda M + \frac{Mc(z)}{z})^2} = 1.$$

Thus the equilibrium expenditures made by the two groups on rent-seeking are

$$M^{e} = (1 - \rho_0)\frac{z^2\lambda c(z)}{(\lambda z + c(z))^2} \tag{7.3}$$

$$L^{e} = (1 - \rho_0)\frac{z\lambda c(z)^2}{(\lambda z + c(z))^2}. \tag{7.4}$$

Which group will devote more resources to rent-seeking? The green lobby invests more in rent-seeking than does the industry if $M^{e}/L^{e} > 1$, which the above equations show occurs if $z > c(z)$. Now recall that total welfare is $W(z) = z - c(z)$. We have the result that the green lobby will fight harder than the industry if the legislative proposal makes society better off, that is, if the environmental benefits of the proposal are greater than the cost to industry of emissions control. Since the regulator is assumed to maximize social welfare, she will never propose a level of abatement for which the costs are greater than the benefits. Thus, the green group undertakes more rent-seeking activity than does the industry.[2]

For any regulatory proposal z, the equilibrium probability with which the legislative proposal passes is

$$\rho(z) = \rho_0 + (1 - \rho_0)\frac{\lambda M^e}{\lambda M^e + L^e} = \rho_0 + (1 - \rho_0)\frac{z\lambda}{z\lambda + c(z)}. \qquad (7.5)$$

Note that $\rho'(z) < 0$, that is, a more stringent bill is less likely to pass, which accords with intuition.

2.2   The regulatory proposal

If the regulator proposes a bill, she seeks to solve the problem:

$$\max_z \rho(z)[z - c(z)].$$

Note that the regulator must trade off the desire to have a strong bill against the likelihood of passing the proposal, since as we saw above the chance of passage falls the more stringent is the proposal. The first-order condition for the regulator's proposal z^M is

$$\rho(z^M)\left[1 - c'\left(z^M\right)\right] + \rho'\left(z^M\right)\left[z^M - c\left(z^M\right)\right] = 0,$$

which implicitly defines the best level of z to propose. Note that z^M is less than the socially optimal level of abatement z^*, which maximizes $z - c(z)$, because the regulator strategically reduces the stringency of the proposal to increase its chance of passage.[3] We record the above findings in Proposition 12.

Proposition 12: *If there is no NA, then the regulator offers a legislative proposal z^M that is weaker than the socially optimal level z^*. In the ensuing interest group competition, the green lobby expends more political resources M^e in favor of the proposal than the resources L^e expended by industry in opposing the proposal.*

It is interesting to note the parallels between this result and what we found in chapter 3's analysis of self-regulation, despite the differences in modeling

---

[2] Note that this finding is similar to what we derived in our study of self-regulation in chapter 3.

[3] Since $\rho'(z) < 0$, we have $c'(z^M) = 1 + \rho'(z^M)[z^M - c(z^M)]/\rho < 1$, while $c'(z^*) = 1$.

structure across the two chapters. In both cases, the political process produces a level of pollution abatement that is less than socially optimal, and consumer/environmentalists expend more resources in influencing political outcomes than does the industry. Chapter 3 focused on the interaction of interest group pressure in determining policy outcomes, and did not allow for uncertainty over the passage of the mandatory proposal. In that model, the political process produces too little environmental protection because consumers suffer greater free-rider problems than does industry, and because there are diminishing returns to lobbying, which systematically disadvantages the winning group. In the current chapter, in contrast, the welfare maximizing regulator makes the regulatory proposal and does not suffer from any free-riding problems since she is a unitary decisionmaker. Nevertheless, she proposes an abatement level below the social optimum because industry opposition reduces the chance her proposal will pass, and hence she weakens the proposal to improve the chance it passes.

2.3   The bargaining stage

The regulator's proposal establishes a threat point against which the industry and the regulator can bargain, in hopes of finding an outcome that both prefer to mandatory regulations. Suppose that the industry delegates bargaining responsibility to a trade association, as is typical in the European context, so is able to negotiate as a single entity. Let $W(z) = z - c(z)$ be net social welfare and $\Pi(z) = -c(z)$ be aggregate industry profit under the bargaining outcome z. In addition, let W^M and Π^M, respectively, denote expected welfare and industry profits under the regulator's legislative proposal.

There is a sizable literature in economics on bargaining. We will utilize the early model of bargaining developed by Nobel laureate John Nash, since it provides a simple methodology that captures many of the key insights of more complex models.[4] In a seminal paper, Nash identified a set of simple and compelling axioms with which he felt any bargaining solution ought to be consistent. He then showed that the unique outcome consistent with the axioms could be found simply by maximizing an expression that has

---

[4] See Nash (1953). Other researchers have shown that the outcome of Nash's simple model often coincides with the equilibrium from more sophisticated bargaining models in which the parties make alternating offers. For more details on the connections between the Nash solution and other models, see Binmore, Rubinstein, and Wolinsky (1986).

become known as the "Nash product":

$$\left[W(z) - W^M\right]^{\alpha} \left[\Pi(z) - \Pi^M\right]^{1-\alpha}.$$

The parameter α indicates the bargaining power of each player. As α increases, the industry is able to claim a larger share of the total gains from bargaining. The solution to the bargaining problem is given by differentiating the Nash product with respect to z, and rearranging terms to obtain

$$\frac{\alpha}{1-\alpha} \frac{\Pi(\tilde{z}) - \Pi^M}{W(\tilde{z}) - W^M} = \frac{c'(\tilde{z})}{[1 - c'(\tilde{z})]}. \tag{7.6}$$

This leads to a solution $\tilde{z}$, with $\tilde{z} < z^M$, since the firm will never accept a bargaining outcome imposed with certainty that is as stringent as z^M, the regulatory threat, which is not guaranteed to pass.

There are two sources of gains from negotiation in this model, which the industry and the regulator divide between themselves. First, the NA allows industry to avoid the rent-seeking expenditures that would be necessary if legislation were proposed. Second, because abatement costs are strictly convex, industry acts as if it were risk-averse, preferring to avoid the chance of having a stringent regulation imposed, and being willing to agree to a somewhat weaker regulation for certain.

Self-regulation, which we studied in part II of this volume, can be thought of as a special case of negotiation in which the industry holds all the bargaining power. The parameter α traces out what happens as the relative bargaining power of the industry and the regulator shifts. As α decreases, the bargaining power of the regulator becomes small and we approach the self-regulatory outcome in which the industry chooses the level of voluntary abatement that will preempt regulation at least cost. In contrast, as α grows and approaches unity, the firm's bargaining power becomes small and the regulator's demands in the bargaining game converge to z^M, the level she would propose at the legislative stage; thus, the value of a NA disappears as the regulator's power becomes total.

What determines the relative bargaining strength of the two parties? Binmore, Rubinstein, and Wolinsky (1986) discuss this question in the context of dynamic models of bargaining. They consider games in which the players take turns making offers to one another until one party accepts the offer made by the other. Important factors in such models include the length of time between proposals and the risk that negotiations may break down if a player refuses the offer made by the other party. Binmore, Rubinstein, and Wolinsky show that one interpretation of the parameter α is in terms of how long it takes each party to prepare a counter-offer if it rejects the proposal made by the other side. For example, suppose it takes the industry longer to construct a counter-proposal when the industry has more members. Then the industry's bargaining power would be reduced as the number of members in the industry grows. Similarly, the bargaining power of the regulator is diminished if she must comply with a large number of bureaucratic requirements each time she prepares a counter-offer. From this perspective, American laws controlling the regulatory process, such as the 1946 Administrative Procedures Act, may encumber the regulator to the point where she loses the bulk of the bargaining power in settings like that we are considering. This may be at least a partial explanation for why NAs are so much less common in the USA than they are in Europe (box 7.1).

3   PUBLIC PARTICIPATION IN ENVIRONMENTAL NEGOTIATIONS

One criticism that is sometimes leveled at NAs is that they exclude environmental groups from the negotiation process, and hence fail to achieve the best outcomes from an environmental perspective.[5] Indeed, our discussion in chapter 6 showed that US VAs do tend to exclude the participation of environmentalists. In the context of the model we are considering here, however, one might think that this is not a problem because the regulator is assumed to maximize social welfare. Let us consider this issue in more detail.

Suppose the regulator did not play an active role in the negotiation process, and instead simply facilitated the process of negotiation between the green group and the industry, similar to the model of chapter 3. For example, this type of participation is increasingly common in the siting of hazardous waste disposal facilities.[6] How should we expect the bargaining outcome $\tilde{z}$ to change when the green group replaces the regulator at the bargaining table?

Recall that the green group's objective function is simply to maximize environmental benefits z, while the regulator maximizes overall social welfare $W(z) = z - c(z)$. Thus, to reflect the objectives of the green group we can simply rewrite the equilibrium condition (7.6), replacing $W(z)$ with z.

---

[5] For comments along these lines, see chapter 6, n. 16 (p. 172).

[6] Rabe (1994) gives some interesting examples of how direct involvement of environmental groups can facilitate the siting process. DeSimone and Popoff (2000), pp. 150–152, describe the increasing importance the chemical industry ascribes to the use of Community Advisory Panels, which facilitate direct communication between firms and members of the local community.

This yields a new equilibrium outcome $\widehat{z}$ defined by the condition

$$\frac{\alpha}{1-\alpha} \frac{\Pi(\widehat{z}) - \Pi^M}{\widehat{z} - z^M} = \frac{c'(\widehat{z})}{[1 - c'(\widehat{z})]}. \tag{7.7}$$

Compared with the left-hand side of (7.6), the left-hand side of (7.7) clearly has a smaller denominator, and hence a larger overall left-hand side, for any proposed level of z. In order for the equality to hold, the right-hand side must also become larger. It turns out that this requires an increase in z, since the right-hand side of (7.7) is increasing in z.[7] As a result, the level of abatement negotiated by an environmental group is greater than the level that would be negotiated by a regulator. We record this result in Proposition 13.

Proposition 13: *The level of abatement $\widehat{z}$ negotiated with industry by an environmental group is greater than the level of abatement $\widetilde{z}$ negotiated with industry by a regulator.*

The result we have just reached makes sense from an intuitive perspective. The green group will focus more aggressively on environmental improvement, since that is all it cares about. The regulator, in contrast, takes a more measured and cautious bargaining stance, since she is trying to balance environmental gains against costs to industry. In a sense, when the regulator is bargaining, industry costs are represented twice (once in the regulator's objective and once in industry's objective), while environmental benefits are represented only once. Allowing the green group to negotiate directly redresses this imbalance, and allows for a bargaining outcome that is closer to – though still less than – the socially optimal level.[8]

Box 7.1   Common Sense Initiative (CSI) and Project XL

For years companies have complained that the rigid command-and-control orientation of environmental regulations discourages innovations that might produce better environmental performance at lower cost. Furthermore, the piecemeal development of regulatory policy fosters a lack of coordination across various programs that affect particular industries. The Common Sense Initiative (CSI) and Project XL,

---

[7] The derivative of the right-hand side is $c''(z)/[1 - c'(z)]^2 > 0$, so we must increase z to increase the overall value of this side of the equation.

[8] For more details on public participation in environmental decisions, see Beierle and Cayford (2002).

proposed by the Bush and Clinton Administrations, respectively, aim to support companies in achieving superior environmental performance by granting regulatory "flexibility."

The CSI was motivated out of a desire to coordinate pollution reduction activities across different "media" (land, water and air), and is oriented at the industry level. The pilot phase of the program involved six industries: auto manufacturing, computers and electronics, iron and steel, metal finishing and plating, petroleum refining, and printing. A working group was assembled for each industry, with each group meeting for two-day periods roughly four times per year, usually in Washington, DC. It was hoped that the groups would identify opportunities for regulatory reform and streamlining. Unfortunately, after 16 months of meetings, no regulatory changes have emerged. "By all accounts, CSI has not yet fulfilled its promise to achieve regulatory reform and integration primarily because EPA lacks the statutory authority" to conduct programs on a multi-media basis (Davies and Mazurek 1996, p. 25).

Project XL, in contrast to the CSI, is oriented toward individual industrial facilities and their surrounding communities. To provide regulatory flexibility, the EPA agreed to a policy of "discretionary enforcement," under which the agency would not pursue statutory violations at participating plants in recognition of their ongoing plans to implement improvements. One significant problem has been that EPA has not been granted legal authority to waive enforcement of any regulations, leaving participating firms vulnerable to third-party enforcement actions. As a result, only three proposals had been granted approval as of January 1998, three years after the program's inception. The first and perhaps most interesting of the permits applies to Intel's "Fab 12" plant near Phoenix, Arizona, the company's newest Pentium fabrication facility. The XL permit allows Intel to make routine changes in production processes without specific authorization from the EPA, as long as the total emissions of conventional and hazardous pollutants do not exceed plant-wide caps. Importantly, the caps are more stringent than required by federal law. The company places great value on XL's regulatory flexibility, for even modest delays can be extremely costly in the rapidly-evolving computer industry (Boyd, Krupnick, and Mazurek 1998). While it is too early to assess the effectiveness of the program, its more focused approach may enable it to produce better results than CSI.

Sources: Davies and Mazurek (1996); Boyd, Krupnick and Mazurek (1998).

Given that it seems advantageous to have green groups directly involved in the negotiation process, one wonders why typical negotiation processes leave these groups out. There may be a number of reasons. First, the model shows that negotiations with environmental groups will typically require industry to undertake greater abatement than would be the case if the regulator were conducting the negotiations. Hence, industry has obvious incentives to try and keep environmentalists away from the bargaining table. Second, the foregoing analysis assumes there is a single actor representing environmental interests, who does not suffer from free-rider problems or problems coordinating with other environmental groups. Coordination problems may be compounded if different environmental groups take substantially different approaches to certain issues. For example, Greenpeace may prefer to develop a reputation as an uncompromising advocate that sticks to its principles. Environmental Defense, in contrast, may prefer to achieve influence from "within the system," and may be more willing to negotiate with industry. If only one group is willing to negotiate, then it cannot claim to truly represent the entire environmental sector, and industry may not trust the outcomes that are negotiated with only a subset of the relevant groups. Third, meaningful participation in a negotiation process may require a substantial amount of technical understanding of the issues at hand. Green groups may not be able to afford the kind of scientific and engineering expertise that may be needed in these sorts of situations. Fourth, green groups may prefer to avoid such negotiations if they believe industry is unlikely to keep its end of the bargain. They may perceive negotiations as simply a delaying tactic, and may decide to opt out as a result. The model we have been analyzing assumes costless and perfect enforcement of the NA. Relaxing this assumption could change the impact of negotiation in significant ways. Indeed, chapter 6 emphasized the important role environmental groups have played in using litigation to force the EPA to enforce legislative requirements for pollution control. Since negotiated agreements are more difficult to enforce than traditional regulation, environmental groups may prefer to avoid them.

4 NEGOTIATING WITH OLIGOPOLISTIC INDUSTRIES

The foregoing analysis treated the industry as a single, unified actor. As we discussed in chapter 1, this may be a reasonable assumption in many

European contexts, where industry trade associations are often empowered to negotiate on behalf of their members, and have some ability to coerce conformance with the outcomes they negotiate. Even in the USA, where trade associations lack the privileged status granted them by many European countries, it may be possible for the association to impose a certain degree of discipline upon members. The primary mechanism for enforcement is the association's ability to exclude a firm from membership.[9] This is particularly effective if the firm must possess a membership certificate or license in order to obtain government contracts or to otherwise operate successfully in the industry.

Even if industry is empowered to negotiate on behalf of its members, we would expect its negotiating posture to vary with the makeup of the industry. For example, an industry whose members vary widely in size and production cost will probably take a different stance than one whose members are very similar to one another. In the remainder of this section, we discuss two issues that emerge when we explicitly consider the number of members in an industry association. First, we discuss how the industry allocates across its members the burden of conforming with a negotiated agreement. Second, we discuss how heterogeneity across firms in the industry affects the expected outcome of a negotiation (box 7.2).[10]

4.1   Free-riding and coalitions of firms

In a symmetric industry, it is natural to suppose that the industry association simply allocates an equal burden to all members of the industry. Indeed, this is the case we emphasized in chapter 3 when we discussed the role of industry self-regulation. However, it is clear from that chapter that any allocation of burdens that achieves the requisite aggregate reduction in pollution is sufficient to preempt a regulatory threat. In fact, there is an infinite number of possible ways to allocate burdens in such a setting, each

---

[9] For example, in the forest products sector, the American Forestry & Paper Association (AF&PA) has adopted a code of conduct called the Sustainable Forestry Initiative (SFI), and sixteen firms have been expelled from the AF&PA for failure to adhere to the terms of the SFI. See http://www.sfms.com/sfi/htm for more details. Similarly, in the chemical industry, Nash (2002, p. 244) points out that the "NACD [National Association of Chemical Distributors] has a history of suspending and terminating memberships for noncompliance" with its environmental code of conduct.

[10] Our analysis in this section follows closely that of Manzini and Mariotti (2003).

> **Box 7.2   Dutch declaration on Toxic Waste Emission Reductions**
>
> In 1990 the Dutch government produced the National Environmental Policy Plan, which set out a strategy aimed at achieving sustainable development by 2010. As part of this plan, various reductions in the toxic emissions of the Dutch chemical industry were necessary. To meet the necessary emission reductions, government and industry negotiated a declaration on toxic emission reduction targets. Companies that signed the declaration were allowed to pursue an integrated approach to achieving the overall targets. This approach allows companies greater flexibility in introducing new production processes (which may raise some chemical emissions while dramatically reducing others). Non-participating firms (those that did not sign the declaration) were regulated under existing non-integrated regulations. Thus, by agreeing to engage in corporate environmental activities that were overcompliant in nature, companies were granted the reward of additional flexibility in meeting their targets.
>
> Source: European Environment Agency (1997b).

of which is stable in the sense of being a Nash equilibrium. Similar results should apply in the context of a negotiated agreement.

4.2   Heterogeneity among firms

When the firms within an industry vary in terms of size, costs, or other matters, it becomes more difficult for the industry association to allocate burdens across industry members. From the perspective of efficiency, it makes sense for those firms that can abate at lowest cost to undertake the bulk of the abatement burden. This outcome is especially likely if it is possible for industry members to make side payments to one another. If side payments are impossible, we would expect to see a wider dispersion of abatement responsibilities across industry members.

An interesting special case is one where the industry is heterogeneous, and where the negotiation process demands full consensus among industry members before an agreement can be accepted. Manzini and Mariotti (2003) present a model of such situations, with industry members varying in their cost of abatement. Their focus is on the implications of heterogeneity for the stringency of NAs. They take the level of the regulatory threat as exogenous, but model the details of the bargaining process explicitly, including the possibility that legislation will be passed should bargaining break down. In the remainder of this section we present a version of their model.

There are N firms. Demand is $P = a - bQ$, where $Q = \sum_i^N q_i$, and q_i is the output level of firm i. The analysis is conducted in the context of a Cournot game with firms competing in quantities. Let Z^M be the level of abatement that would be required if legislation were passed; this can be taken as the outcome of the political influence game studied in chapter 3 or as the legislative proposal made by the regulator in section 2 above. Before legislation is proposed, the industry can negotiate with the regulator for some level of Z that will serve to preempt the regulatory threat. Let profits for firm i be $\pi_i(Z)$, with $d\pi_i(Z)/dZ < 0$. The regulator's utility in the event of legislation is normalized to zero,[11] but an NA is assumed to provide her with utility $V(Z) > 0$, which is strictly increasing in Z.

Instead of simply imposing the Nash bargaining solution, the negotiation process is modeled explicitly through an alternating offers mechanism. Let the regulator make the first proposal, at a level Z^R per firm. If the industry accepts the offer, then industry members take the needed abatement actions. If it rejects the offer, then legislation occurs with probability $1 - p$, with the mandatory level of abatement Z^M being imposed should legislation pass. If negotiations continue, which occurs with probability p, then the industry makes a counter-proposal, at a level Z^I, and so forth, until an agreement is reached.

We focus on stationary strategies, that is, strategies for which each player takes the same action at identical subgames, regardless of the previous history.[12] This substantially simplifies the analysis.[13] In particular, it implies that the firms immediately come to agreement when they vote on the regulator's proposal or make their own internal proposal.

From the regulator's perspective, the abatement level she will accept from any industry proposal must satisfy the incentive compatibility constraint

$$V(Z^I) \geq pV(Z^R) + (1 - p) \cdot 0.$$

---

[11] Chapter 6 presents a number of reasons why regulators may prefer VAs to mandatory policies.

[12] A subgame is simply the future course of the game, starting from any point at or after the beginning of the game, and contingent on the history up to that point.

[13] Manzini and Mariotti (2003) argue that there is no loss of generality in making this assumption.

Thus, the regulator will accept the industry's proposal of Z^I only if it provides her with at least as much value as she can hope to achieve by refusing the offer and counter-proposing with Z^R, taking into account the risk that legislation will be imposed should she refuse the offer.

Similarly, from industry's perspective, each member i will accept a regulatory offer such that

$$\pi_i(Z^R) \geq p\pi_i(Z^I) + (1-p)\pi_i(Z^M).$$

Thus, each firm will accept the regulator's proposal of Z^R only if it provides her with at least as much profit as she can hope to achieve by refusing the offer and counter-proposing with Z^I, taking into account the risk that legislation will be imposed should she refuse the offer.[14]

To illustrate the solution procedure, we will use very simple functional forms and begin with a symmetric industry. Suppose $V(Z) = Z$ and $\pi_i(Z) = -fZ$ for all i. Then the incentive compatibility conditions are just

$$Z^I = pZ^R \tag{7.8}$$

and

$$-fZ^R = -pfZ^I - (1-p)fZ^M. \tag{7.9}$$

Substitute in for Z^I in (7.9) and simplify to get

$$Z^R = \frac{1}{(1+p)}Z^M. \tag{7.10}$$

Thus, joint solution of the incentive compatibility constraints yields the regulator's optimal proposal in the negotiation game. Equation (7.10) shows that the regulator's equilibrium proposal is determined by the level of the background legislative threat, and the probability with which legislation is imposed should industry refuse the regulator's offer. Since $p > 0$, it is clear that $Z^R < Z^M$, that is, the regulator's proposal is weaker than the mandatory abatement level. This result is consistent with our previous findings in chapter 3 and earlier in this chapter.

Turn now to the case where firms differ in their cost of abatement. Assuming the negotiation process requires industry consensus, the regulator must ensure that her proposal is acceptable to all firms in the industry. As

---

[14] Note that because there is no discounting in this model, industry cannot gain from a strategy of "stonewalling," that is, always refusing a proposal and then making an unacceptable counter-proposal. If industry and the regulator disagree forever, then a representative firm's expected payoff is $\bar{\pi} = (1-p)\pi(Z^M)[1 + p + p^2 + p^3 + \ldots] = \pi(Z^M)$.

Manzini and Mariotti (2003) show, this essentially places all the bargaining power in the hands of the "toughest" or least efficient firm, i.e. the firm that demands the weakest abatement level. If we let this firm be denoted by i^*, then the only relevant incentive constraint within the industry is

$$\pi_{i^*}(Z^R) \geq p\pi_{i^*}(Z^{I^*}) + (1-p)\pi_{i^*}(Z^M).$$

Let (Z^{R^*}, Z^{I^*}) denote the corresponding equilibrium proposals. Then the regulator proposes Z^{R^*}, which is immediately accepted by the industry, which would counter-propose $Z^{I^*} < Z^{R^*}$ in the event the regulator failed to make the expected proposal.

To be more concrete, let firm i's unit cost be $c_i(Z) = c_i + \alpha_i Z$. Then in a Cournot equilibrium, profits are

$$\pi_i = \frac{[a - Nc_i(Z) + \sum_{j \neq i} c_j(Z)]^2}{b(N+1)^2}.$$

Manzini and Mariotti (2003) show that if $V(Z) = Z$, then the equilibrium abatement level is

$$Z^* =$$
$$\frac{(a-C)(1+p) \pm \sqrt{(a-C)^2(1+p)^2 - (1+p+p^2)[2(a-C) - AZ^M]AZ^M}}{A(1+p+p^2)},$$

$$\tag{7.11}$$

where $C = c_i^* + N(c_i^* - \bar{c})$ and $A = \alpha_i^* + N(\alpha_i^* - \bar{\alpha})$. While this expression is rather complicated, the key thing to notice about it is that it is driven by the difference between the highest-cost firm's abatement cost and the average abatement cost for all the other firms. Thus, their key result is that the least efficient firm plays a special role in driving the outcome of the negotiation process. For example, they find that if the marginal abatement cost of firm i^* increases, then the negotiated abatement level falls, while if the cost of any other firm increases, then the negotiated abatement level rises. We record these results in Proposition 14.

Proposition 14: *Consider an oligopoly with N firms, where firm i has abatement cost $c_i(Z) = c_i + \alpha_i Z$, and Z is a uniform standard imposed on all firms in the industry. If the regulator negotiates an agreement with industry, and consensus among all industry members is required, then the equilibrium abatement level is given by (7.11), which is decreasing in the least-efficient firm's abatement cost.*

The main implication of the above analysis is that there is a kind of "lowest common denominator" effect when full consensus is required of the negotiation process. This makes sense intuitively. It is also in accord with conclusions reached by academics who have studied the process of negotiated rulemaking, in which the implementation of mandatory regulations is conducted by a group of stakeholders who meet together. Under the Negotiated Rulemaking Act of 1990, the regulator must use the results of the stakeholder deliberations as the basis for its proposed rule – but only if the stakeholders come to unanimous consensus regarding their final proposal. If so much as one stakeholder objects, then matters revert to a traditional rulemaking process. As Coglianese (2001, p. 441) argues, "Negotiated rulemaking's emphasis on unanimity also makes it more likely that the final outcome will succumb to the lowest-common-denominator problem. The outcome that is minimally acceptable to all the members of a negotiated rulemaking committee will not necessarily be optimal or effective in terms of achieving social goals."

To the best of our knowledge, there is very little academic work that studies the negotiation process when less than full consensus is required from industry.[15] One might expect that a wide range of negotiated outcomes would be possible, in light of the multiplicity of Nash equilibria in the case of self-regulation. Suppose, for instance, that all firms in the industry but one are highly efficient, and that that one uses an obsolete technology with high abatement costs. If consensus is required, then the inefficient firm will drive down the abatement requirement. If that firm were exempted, however, then the abatement level required of the other firms could increase, and it is quite possible that the overall social benefits of the agreement would be greater than before. In practice, however, there is typically a range of costs across the industry members, and it may not be easy to determine who should be exempted. It is easy to imagine some very difficult discussions within the industry association as firms debate which of them should bear the costs of a program designed to benefit the group, and which should be allowed to take a free-ride on the efforts of their rivals. We believe this is an area in which further theoretical work is likely to be fruitful.

5 NON-TECHNICAL SUMMARY

The basic structure of the analysis in this section is as follows. There is a background threat of regulation, which both industry and the regulator would like to preempt through an NA. Should negotiations fail, the

---

[15] Two papers in the area are Carraro and Siniscalco (1993) and Dawson and Segerson (2002).

regulator can propose a mandatory standard to the legislative body. The likelihood that proposed legislation will pass is determined by a rent-seeking competition between industry and a green lobbying group. Recognizing that passage of the bill becomes more difficult when the bill's requirements are tighter, the regulator strategically weakens the legislative proposal to increase the chance that it will pass. Assuming that both industry and the regulator are able to foresee this weakening of the proposal, the negotiation process achieves an abatement level that makes both industry and the regulator better off than they would be if the legislative proposal were put forward. The negotiated outcome will be weaker than the proposal would be, which benefits industry, but it is achieved with certainty, which benefits the regulator. Industry also gains from avoiding the costly rent-seeking process that will ensue should negotiation fail. Thus, the model provides a simple and, we believe, reasonable depiction of the political environment in which NAs arise.

NAs are typically negotiated by an industry trade association, which then implements the agreement by allocating the burden of abatement across its members. When all firms in the industry are identical, this allocation process is simple. When firms differ in their size or their cost of abatement, however, allocation becomes a more delicate task. The efficient outcome would be for firms that can abate cheaply to do a larger share of overall abatement, perhaps with some form of side payments from other industry members. If side payments are impossible, though, it will be more difficult to convince efficient firms to shoulder what may seem to them an unfair share of the overall burden.

When firms are heterogeneous, the industry trade association will take this fact into account in the negotiation process. If the association demands unanimous consensus on any proposed agreement, then the most intransigent firm (typically the one with highest abatement costs) plays a pivotal role in the bargaining process, leading to a "lowest-common-denominator" effect that can cause the ultimate agreement to be weak. Despite the fact that this type of outcome could potentially be avoided if the regulator were to negotiate with just a subset of the industry, it appears more common in practice for the regulator to negotiate with the whole industry, or else to undertake negotiations on a firm-by-firm basis. This is perhaps not surprising since the firms that are targeted by the agreement bear costs avoided by the rest of the industry. One would expect heated disagreements within the industry regarding which firms are to "fall on the sword" for the good of the group, with a good chance that the association will fail to agree on a coalition of the willing.

6 CONCLUSIONS

This chapter has presented a framework for understanding NAs between industry and a regulator. Self-regulation emerges as a special case of this family of agreements, one in which industry has all the bargaining power. While we were able to speculate about why regulators have greater bargaining power in some settings than others, this is an area in which further work remains to be done. It seems clear that, in practice, regulators in Europe are much more likely to participate in NAs than is true in the USA. This may be due in part to the separation of powers within the US political system, which makes regulatory threats less credible, as well as to the European corporatist tradition, in which industry assocations are empowered to devise and implement government policies.

As in our analysis of self-regulation in chapter 3, we find that voluntary efforts to improve the environment are likely to produce weaker results than would be embodied in mandatory requirements, but nevertheless improve overall social welfare. From a modeling perspective, the analysis in this section differs from that in chapter 3 in that it treats the regulator as an active player in the negotiation process, and recognizes that legislation imposing mandatory regulations is uncertain to succeed. As a result, the regulator weakens her legislative proposal in order to increase the likelihood that it passes. This uncertainty creates an opportunity for mutual gains if the regulator and the industry can negotiate an agreement that preempts the legislative threat. Since industry is averse to the risk of legislation, it is willing to accept a regulatory proposal for an abatement program that is more modest but whose parameters are known for certain. This gain from preemption comes in addition to the savings from avoiding the rent-seeking game that follows a legislative proposal. Note that the results of this chapter are qualitatively similar to those we obtained in chapter 3, where a legislative proposal passed with certainty after the influence game and its rent-seeking expenditures. This suggests that while uncertainty is a nice additional feature to incorporate in a political economic model, it is probably not the central part of the story.

One policy implication we can draw from this chapter is that it is essential to have either (a) a strong program for monitoring and ensuring compliance with the NA, and/or (b) an ongoing regulatory threat that will be triggered if industry fails to meet its obligations. Another policy implication that follows from the model is that society benefits when agreements with industry are negotiated by a party that is primarily concerned about the environment, rather than trying to balance environmental and economic goals. For example, environmental groups could be empowered to negotiate directly with industry.

While there are some strong similarities between this chapter and chapter 3, one interesting difference is that the model here assumes that the legislative threat is taken off the table once an NA is reached. This is fine if there is a monitoring and enforcement scheme to ensure that industry follows through on the agreement. In practice, though, such enforcement schemes are woefully uncommon among NAs. Indeed, a number of case studies of NAs have concluded that they produced disappointing results, in large part due to a lack of monitoring and enforcement.[16] In contrast, the analysis of chapter 3 assumed that the threat of interest group pressure remains in force, even after the industry undertakes self-regulatory action, if industry accomplishes too little voluntarily. Thus, self-regulation has a self-enforcing character that may be lacking in an NA.

[16] For details, see European Environment Agency (1997b, vol. II).

8 | Self-regulation, taxation, and public voluntary agreements

1 INTRODUCTION

Chapter 6 explained how regulators benefit from the use of voluntary agreements (VAs), and chapter 7 showed how negotiated agreements (NAs) – used frequently in Europe and Japan – can serve the interests of both industry and regulators. In this chapter, we turn to public voluntary agreements (PVAs), which are commonly used in the USA. Under PVAs, participating firms agree to make good faith efforts to meet program goals established by the regulatory agency; in return, they may receive technical assistance and/or favorable publicity from the government. The present chapter is based on Lyon and Maxwell (2003a) and develops a model of corporate and government behavior in which self-regulation, taxation, and PVAs can be considered in one unified framework. In so doing, we sharpen the discussion of VAs by distinguishing carefully the relative merits of each of these instruments.

As we showed in chapter 3, the preemption of stricter future regulations is a leading motivation for self-regulation. This motivation can also explain corporate participation in voluntary environmental agreements between corporations and environmental regulators, as discussed in chapter 7. Furthermore, chapter 6 showed that the environmental regulator may wish to preempt future regulations if voluntary actions represent a cheaper way of achieving environmental goals. While preemption may indeed explain the adoption of some VAs, it is not uncommon to find PVAs in the *absence* of strong regulatory threats. In fact the US EPA notes that "Governments promote voluntary initiatives for a variety of reasons, including the pilot testing of new approaches and *the absence of legislative authority to establish mandatory programs*" (US EPA 2001, p. 173; emphasis added). If voluntary environmental agreements are not designed to preempt legislation, what then is motivating firm and regulatory adoption of these agreements, and what are the impacts of such agreements on social welfare? This chapter attempts to answer these questions.

We begin by reviewing the political history of the US Climate Change Action Plan (CCAP), which has spawned numerous PVAs. We find that the

CCAP and its progeny arose in the absence of any serious regulatory threats. These programs offer participants a variety of modest benefits, including information about projects undertaken by other firms, and performance and cost data on energy efficiency products sold by a variety of vendors. The chief benefit to regulators appears to have been the improvement in the environmental performance of at least a portion of the industry when statutory authority for mandatory environmental standards did not exist.

We incorporate these stylized facts into a three-stage game that features the possibility of self-regulation aimed at legislative preemption, legislative efforts to impose an environmental tax, or a PVA. The model features a continuum of firms – differentiated according to their abatement costs – which produce a homogeneous good sold at a fixed price, and a welfare maximizing environmental regulator. Firms have the option of adopting an environmental technology that eliminates all environmental externalities. In the first stage of the game, firms choose a level (possibly zero) of voluntary adoption. In the second stage of the game, after observing the unilateral adoptions by the industry, the regulator chooses whether to propose new legislation that would impose a pollution tax or, alternatively, to propose a PVA.[1] If the tax proposal is made, it is put to Congress and passes with some probability less than one. If legislation is successful, the regulator imposes a constrained welfare maximizing pollution tax. Firms that did not choose voluntary abatement in stage one may now decide to adopt the technology and avoid paying the tax, or they may choose not to abate and thereby incur the tax. If legislative efforts fail, the regulator still has the option of proposing a PVA, which is implemented by subsidizing firms' technology adoptions through the use of costly public funds. The level of subsidies is set so as to maximize social welfare.

Our model generates both positive and normative implications. We identify conditions under which industries will undertake self-regulation, and we identify which firms are most likely to participate in public voluntary programs. We also examine in detail the relative merits of taxation and VAs from the regulator's perspective; in particular, we show that the regulator is better off imposing a tax rather than a PVA unless political opposition to the tax is high. The chief normative findings are surprising: PVAs can reduce welfare by increasing industry resistance to socially beneficial tax proposals and by reducing industry incentives to engage in welfare-enhancing self-regulation.

---

[1] In order to economize on the number of agents in the model, we treat the regulator as a part of the executive branch of government and empower it to make tax proposals to the legislature.

The following section discusses in some detail the political backdrop of many US PVAs, setting the stage for the overview of our modeling approach, which is presented in section 3. Our analysis of the model is conducted in two separate sections of the chapter. Section 4 studies the regulator's choice between proposing a tax and proposing a PVA. Section 5 examines the industry's decision regarding self-regulation, and how that affects the regulator's policy decisions. Section 6 provides a non-technical summary of the analysis, and section 7 concludes and discusses policy implications.

2 POLITICS AND PUBLIC VOLUNTARY AGREEMENTS

In this section we provide details of the political backdrop to many US public voluntary environmental agreements and review a related case study of corporate behavior developed by the International Academy of the Environment (IAE). Both of these serve to illustrate the use of PVAs in the absence of regulatory threats.[2] For a broader institutional analysis of the use of PVAs, see chapter 6.

2.1 Background to US public voluntary agreements

Table 6.1 (p. 152) surveys the use of VAs in the USA, and clearly shows that PVAs are the dominant form of VA. A large number of the PVAs arose from the Clinton Administration's CCAP, which we examine in detail below. We argue that these schemes share several important features: (1) they can be implemented at little or no cost to at least some subset of firms, (2) they arose in an area in which the regulatory authorities did not have a statutory mandate to require any actions, and (3) The heterogeneity of the offenders would have made command-and-control regulation complex and costly for regulators to administer.[3]

Most of the climate change VAs aim to increase investments in energy efficiency. Energy efficiency has been supported by the US government,

---

[2] The interested reader is encouraged to consult IAE (1998) for case details.

[3] Our characterization of these programs has been shaped by interviews with a number of current and former EPA officials: James Barnes, former Assistant Administrator; Linda Fisher, former director, Office of Pesticides and Toxic Substances and Office of Pollution Prevention; Skip Laitner, director, Office of Atmospheric Programs; and Bill Rosenberg, former Assistant Administrator for Air during the Bush Administration. We thank all of these individuals for their gracious cooperation.

through a variety of programs, since the 1970s. Most of these emphasize the private benefits to firms and individuals of adopting energy-efficient equipment, and attempt to solve the "market failures" that limit the spread of these technologies. The climate change VAs were begun under the first Bush Administration after President Bush promised to be the "environmental president." Most of them, however, were promulgated as part of the Clinton Administration's efforts to achieve reductions in greenhouse gases after the "Earth Summit" in Rio de Janeiro in June 1992.

In most cases, there does not appear to have been a substantial regulatory "threat" driving the adoption of VAs. In our conversations with current and former EPA officials, none mentioned such threats as important to the creation of VAs, while all pointed out that VAs were typically used by the EPA when the agency had no statutory authority to take formal regulatory actions. Global warming provides a particularly interesting case in point. The first Bush Administration opposed strong actions to combat global warming, and was publicly derided by US environmental groups and by most other nations of the world for its refusal at the "Earth Summit" to agree to a timetable with specific targets for reducing emissions of greenhouse gases. Senator Al Gore was among the Administration's harshest critics, and proposed a carbon tax to combat global warming.

After President Clinton was elected in November 1992, one of his early actions was to announce support for stronger measures to prevent climate change. In the early months of 1993, his Administration floated a variety of proposals to tax energy, including a carbon tax and a broader-based "BTU tax" based on the energy content of fuels as measured in British Thermal Units (BTUs). As described in chapter 1, the political response was fast and furious, and within a few months the Administration had abandoned the BTU tax initiative. When the Administration presented its CCAP later in the year, the focus was shifted away from mandatory regulations to subsidies (including $200 million per year to stimulate the adoption of more energy-efficient technologies) and voluntary programs. The environmental community was not impressed. Alden Meyer, director of the program on climate change and energy at the Union of Concerned Scientists, argued that the plan placed too much emphasis on voluntary measures, "with no prospect of hammers or sticks to bring us into compliance if those don't work."[4]

---

[4]   William K. Stevens, "US Prepares to Unveil Blueprint for Reducing Heat-Trapping Gases," *New York Times*, October 12, 1993, p. C4.

Released in October 1993, the President's CCAP embodied the Administration's commitment to reduce US greenhouse gas emissions to 1990 levels by the year 2000.[5] The plan was based on the premise that government and private enterprise could work together to achieve program goals without harming the economy. The plan involved four major government departments: the Department of Energy (DOE), the Environmental Protection Agency (EPA), the Department of Agriculture, and the Department of Transportation.

The CCAP spawned many public voluntary programs including Green Lights, Climate Wise, Motor Challenge, and ENERGY STAR Buildings, among many others.[6] IAE (1998) examines US corporation Johnson and Johnson's decisions to participate in several of the CCAP's PVAs, including each of those mentioned above. The report clearly indicates that the chief factors motivating Johnson and Johnson were the programs' implicit subsidies to participants.

According to IAE (1998), participation in these programs provided Johnson and Johnson with several benefits. To begin with, participants were provided with case studies detailing the cost savings of program participants. Second, the program administrators commissioned outside consulting firms to provide technical information aimed at aiding the development of a program action plan. The programs also offered seminars at which firms could exchange information about cost savings. Other benefits cited included access to question hotlines, free software, and access to databases of equipment suppliers and financing programs.

This section has attempted to make two key points that are developed more fully in the model of the succeeding sections. First, PVAs are often proposed in the absence of strong legislative threats; indeed, regulatory authorities often use such agreements precisely because they lack statutory authority to undertake more stringent measures. Second, companies join PVAs in order to obtain the (admittedly modest) benefits offered to participants by the government. Such agreements can thus be viewed as subsidies from government to firms, aimed at inducing environmentally friendly actions by the participating firms.

---

[5] According to the US Energy Information Administration, US greenhouse gas emissions in 1990 were 1,682.5 million tons of carbon equivalent. By 2000, they had increased to 1,907 million tons of carbon equivalent, an increase of 224.5 million metric tons, or 13.3 percent. For further details, see http://www.eia.doe.gov/oiaf/1605/ggrpt/executive_summary.html.

[6] For details on these and the other programs introduced under the CCAP, see US Office of Global Change (1997).

3 MODEL OVERVIEW

Drawing on the insights into PVAs presented in section 2, we develop a three-stage game played by a regulator and the firms in an industry. In order to distinguish between unilateral agreements and PVAs, we allow the firms in stage 1 to decide whether or not to unilaterally adopt an environmental technology based on the decision's impact on expected industry profits. In stage 2, the regulator decides whether to propose an environmental tax, and sets its level, τ. In stage 3, if the regulator chooses not to propose a tax, or if the proposed tax is not passed by the legislature, the regulator may propose a PVA involving a subsidy s, paid for by raising costly public funds. We purposely do not assume that voluntary actions are cheaper than actions mandated by law, as doing so would make it too easy to reach simplistic conclusions about the superiority of voluntary measures. We also assume away the possibility of "win–win" solutions in which the adoption of environmentally friendly technology lowers cost; economic analysis is not needed to conclude that these actions are desirable, nor are subsidies required to induce adoption.

The basic setup of our model is based on Lewis (1996). The industry consists of a group of domestic firms that supply an export product that sells at a fixed world price.[7] Firms, which are indexed by θ, differ according to their profitability and their fixed costs of adopting an environmental technology, which is assumed to eliminate all environmental costs associated with production. We assume that θ is distributed over $[\underline{\theta}, \overline{\theta}]$ with cumulative density $F(\theta)$. (The simplest interpretation of θ is as an efficiency parameter.) Following Lewis, we assume that the regulator knows the density $F(\theta)$, but does not know the efficiency of any given firm.[8] We denote by $\pi(\theta)$ the gross profits of a firm of type θ, and we assume that $\pi'(\theta) > 0$, where the ' indicates the first derivative. Further, we assume that $\pi(\underline{\theta}) = 0$. Similarly, $c(\theta)$ is the fixed adoption cost of the environmental technology for a firm of type θ, and we assume $c'(\theta) < 0$.[9]

---

[7] By assuming a competitive global market we leave out consideration of "green consumers." While this is clearly an interesting issue, we eschew it in order to keep our model tractable and because green consumers are arguably fairly unimportant in many markets, especially those for intermediate products. As chapter 1 points out, the empirical support for the notion that green consumerism drives corporate environmental efforts is mixed at best.

[8] This assumption rules out the possibility of firm-specific subsidies. Such subsidies are not common in PVAs (see, e.g., US EPA (2001, section 10)).

[9] The idea is that firms with a high value of the efficiency parameter θ have high profits due to lower costs, and that their higher efficiency will also translate into lower costs of adopting the new technology. This is consistent with the observation that firms undertaking voluntary actions are often the larger, more profitable members of an industry.

We assume each operating firm emits pollutants that create environmental damages of $x > 0$. The net social welfare generated by firm θ prior to the adoption of the environmental technology is $\pi(\theta) - x$. Absent adoption of the environmental technology, the optimal size of the industry is the mass of firms indexed by $\theta \geq \theta^x$, where $\pi(\theta^x) - x = 0$.

In an unregulated equilibrium entry will occur until gross profits are driven to zero. This will cause excessive entry from a social viewpoint and the welfare maximizing regulator will wish to act to prevent or remedy this outcome. This may be done by the imposition of a tax τ set equal to the social cost of pollution. (The cost of proposing and implementing the tax is assumed to be a fixed amount K.[10]) Any firm with costs $c(\theta) < \tau$ will undertake the environmental investment and avoid paying the tax. As Lewis (1996) points out, however, firms have a strong incentive to oppose the tax even if it is set at the optimal level. Let $\Delta(\tau)$ be the aggregate costs imposed on the industry by a tax, and $P(\Delta)$ be the probability that a tax will pass the legislature if it would impose aggregate costs of Δ. We assume that $P(\Delta)$ is declining in Δ at an increasing rate. Like Lewis, we focus on the aggregate losses imposed on the industry, and abstract from issues of coalition formation within the industry; we thus implicitly assume that the industry is able to coordinate its political actions through the use of tools such as a trade association or side payments.[11]

As an alternative to a tax, the regulator may propose a PVA to encourage the adoption of the environmental technology. We assume that the cost K of implementing the VA is the same as the cost of implementing the tax, so as not to have our results hinge on exogenous differences in the cost of the two programs. As we have illustrated in section 2, many PVAs contain features which serve to subsidize the cost of corporate environmental actions. Thus, we follow Carraro and Siniscalco (1996) in modeling the PVA as a subsidy, s, set optimally by the regulator, which is payable to any firm that adopts the

---

[10] The literature offers multiple explanations for such political transaction costs. For example, Glazer and McMillan (1992) present a model in which a legislator who wishes to introduce a bill must bear the costs of investigating the matter carefully, conferring with interest groups, and enrolling like-minded legislators to support the bill. An alternative approach is to focus not on the costs borne by the legislator, but on the costs borne by his constituents who support the bill. This is the approach taken in the Chicago tradition of political economy pioneered by Stigler (1971), Peltzman (1976), and Becker (1983), who identify both the organizing costs faced by interest groups that wish to mobilize for effective political action, and the influence costs incurred by these groups once they have become organized. Both approaches generate a fixed cost of introducing a proposal for government action. We assume the cost of introducing a tax proposal is equal to that of introducing a VA, so as to avoid obtaining results that simply depend upon arbitrary differences in these costs.

[11] The political economic analysis used here is similar to that in chapter 7, but focuses on the role of industry-generated political pressure in an effort to keep the model as simple as possible.

environmental technology. Note that a PVA is a specialized form of subsidy, which can be collected only by firms that stay in business and participate in the PVA. Lewis models an optimal subsidy that is also collected by firms that reduce their emissions by exiting the industry. PVA programs, however, are not optimal subsidies, since only firms that join the program can benefit from them.[12]

We assume the subsidies paid by the regulatory authorities involve costly public funds.[13] In addition, we assume firms that adopted the environmental technology before the PVA was established cannot be excluded from receiving the benefits of participating in the VA, an assumption that is consistent with government practice in the public voluntary programs described in section 2.[14]

To highlight the distinction between PVAs and unilateral industry self-regulation, we include a first stage of the game in which some subset of firms may unilaterally adopt the environmental technology. In so doing, we extend the analysis of chapter 3 by incorporating heterogeneous firms and the possibility of a PVA offered by the regulator. As in chapter 7, we treat the industry as working in concert in its political efforts; we extend that assumption to the coordination of self-regulatory activity as well.[15] Under this assumption, firms with the lowest technology adoption costs will be selected to enter the unilateral voluntary agreement. Thus, we denote by θ^v the firm with the highest technology adoption costs that joins the industry's unilateral voluntary efforts. Then all firms indexed by $\theta > \theta^v$ will also adopt the technology. Alternatively, the industry can choose not to take unilateral actions by setting $\theta^v = \overline{\theta}$.

Section 4 of the chapter explores stages 2 and 3 of the game by examining in detail the regulator's choice between proposing a tax and proposing a PVA. Following standard backward-induction logic, analysis of stage 1 of the game – the industry's choice of a unilateral level of technology adoption – is deferred until section 5.

---

[12] Chapter 9 presents a more detailed analysis of the structure of PVAs, focusing on the role of information provision.

[13] An alternative approach would be to assume that the regulator has a budget constraint that limits the total amount that can be spent on subsidies under a VA. This would generate a Lagrange multiplier that would play a role similar to that of the cost of public funds. Since we do not believe our results would be substantially different either way, we have adopted a cost of public funds for simplicity.

[14] For example, under provisions of the ENERGY STAR Buildings program, firms owning buildings which meet or surpass the program's minimum standards receive public recognition as soon as the firm joins the program.

[15] Chapter 3 discusses the extent to which coordinated levels of self-regulation can be sustained as non-cooperative Nash equilibria.

4   THE REGULATOR'S CHOICE BETWEEN TAXATION AND A PUBLIC VOLUNTARY AGREEMENT

In this section, we focus on the regulator's expected welfare when it proposes an environmental tax and when it proposes a PVA. We work backward through the game, beginning with the stage 3 decision regarding whether to offer a PVA, then turning to the stage 2 decision regarding taxation. Note that the regulator faces these policy choices only in the event that the industry's unilateral actions are not sufficient to preempt government action. Furthermore, as we show in section 5, the industry will choose either a preemptive level of unilateral action, or none at all.

Throughout this section we assume that the industry engages in no unilateral voluntary action, i.e. $\theta^v = \overline{\theta}$. (Section 5 takes up the case of self-regulation.) As a reference point, we note that if government takes no action, social welfare is given by

$$W(\emptyset) = \int_{\underline{\theta}}^{\overline{\theta}} [\pi(\theta) - x] \, dF(\theta), \qquad (8.1)$$

where $\emptyset$ indicates the absence of government action. This expression simply adds up, over all firms in the industry, each firm's net social contribution, which consists of profits less environmental damages. Social welfare is illustrated in figure 8.1. Firms are arrayed along the horizontal axis according to the efficiency index, θ, and the figure plots each firm's profits $\pi(\theta)$, environmental damages x, and net social contribution $\pi(\theta) - x$. The shaded region shows total social welfare $W(\emptyset)$.

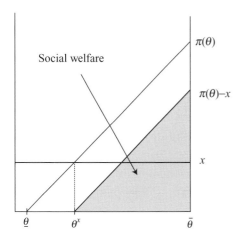

Figure 8.1   Welfare with no government action

4.1   Stage 3: the public voluntary agreement

Should legislative efforts fail, the regulator may incur a fixed cost K and create a PVA consisting of a positive subsidy s, payable to firms which adopt the environmental technology. Recall that we assume the fixed cost of creating a PVA is equal to the cost of proposing an environmental tax, in order to ensure our results are not simply driven by arbitrary differences in these costs. Define θ^s such that $c(\theta^s) = s$; then all firms of type $\theta \geq \theta^s$ adopt the technology. The subsidy is chosen to maximize social welfare.

Since the regulator cannot identify the cost of an individual firm, it must set a single subsidy level that applies to all firms. The regulator's problem is then to choose s to maximize $W^S(s) - K$, where

$$W^S(s) = \int_{\underline{\theta}}^{\theta^s} [\pi(\theta) - x] \, dF(\theta) + \int_{\theta^s}^{\overline{\theta}} [\pi(\theta) - c(\theta) + s] \, dF(\theta)$$
$$- [1 - F(\theta^s)] \, s \, (1 + \lambda), \qquad (8.2)$$

and $\lambda > 0$ indicates that the funds used to subsidize adoption are costly.[16] The first term on the right-hand side of (8.2) indicates the net contribution to social welfare (profits minus environmental costs) from firms operating in the industry that do not adopt the clean technology. The second term on the right-hand side denotes the net contribution to social welfare arising from program participants, who incur the cost $c(\theta)$ of adopting the environmental technology and collect the subsidy payment s. The final term captures the total costs of funding all program participants.

Maximizing (8.2) with respect to s and collecting terms yields:

$$s^* = \frac{x}{1 + \lambda(1 + 1/\eta_V)}, \qquad (8.3)$$

where $\eta_V > 0$ is the percentage change in the number of participants in the voluntary program when the subsidy is increased by 1 percent (i.e. the subsidy elasticity of participation).[17]

Equation (8.3) shows that if public funds were not costly, i.e. if $\lambda = 0$, then the optimal subsidy would simply be equal to the environmental harm done by each firm, i.e. $s^* = x$. This is an intuitively appealing criterion for setting the subsidy level, as it ensures that all firms that can adopt the technology at a cost less than x will do so. When public funds are costly, however, s^* is distorted below x, and too few firms will adopt the environmental

---

[16] A reasonable estimate of λ for the US economy is 0.3 (Laffont and Tirole (1993, p. 38)).

[17] More formally, define the number of participants in the voluntary program as
$V(s) = 1 - F(\theta^s)$. Then $\eta_V = (\partial V/\partial s)(s/V)$.

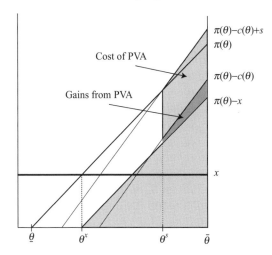

$\pi(\theta)-c(\theta)+s$

$\pi(\theta)$

$\pi(\theta)-c(\theta)$

$\pi(\theta)-x$

Cost of PVA

Gains from PVA

x

$\underline{\theta}$ θ^x θ^s $\bar{\theta}$

Figure 8.2   Welfare gains and costs of public voluntary agreements

technology, relative to the case of costless public funds. At the margin, the regulator faces a tradeoff between inducing additional participation in the program and paying out additional subsidies to inframarginal firms that would participate in the program anyway. These factors are illustrated in figure 8.2. The benefit of a PVA with subsidy level s is represented by the shaded region immediately above the original welfare triangle, which lies between $\pi(\theta) - c(\theta)$ and $\pi(\theta) - x$, and above θ^s. The cost of the program is shown by the uppermost shaded region, which represents the payment s made to all program participants, indexed by $\theta > \theta^s$. As λ gets bigger, the program cost grows while program benefits do not; as a result the regulator scales back on the subsidy.

We can also see that when the elasticity η_V is small and public funds are costly, it becomes very burdensome to raise the level of participation in the program, and the distortion in the subsidy grows. The role the participation elasticity plays in distorting the subsidy can be better understood by recognizing that it reflects the heterogeneity in adoption costs across the firms in the industry. The regulator's goal in designing a subsidy program is to induce as much participation as possible at the lowest possible cost. As the heterogeneity in firm adoption costs grows larger (i.e. the elasticity of participation becomes small), however, it becomes increasingly costly to induce additional firms to participate in the voluntary program.

Overall, social welfare under a PVA increases when the cost of public funds is low and the cost of technology adoption does not vary greatly across firms. In addition, if the regulator is to find it worthwhile to offer a PVA, it is also necessary that the social benefits of the PVA exceed the cost of creating the program. This requires that K be smaller than the net benefits of the adoptions induced by the PVA. We will assume this condition holds throughout the remainder of this section, since otherwise a PVA would never be offered. We will relax this latter assumption in section 5, however, where we examine how changes in K affect the industry's incentives for self-regulation.

4.2   Stage 2: proposal of an environmental tax

In stage 2 of the game, the regulator may propose an environmental tax τ which can be implemented at a cost K, or can choose to create a PVA at the same cost.[18] It is easy to see that any tax proposal will result in losses to the industry. As a result, industry will oppose even a first-best tax, and the optimal tax proposed by the regulator will be distorted away from its first-best level. For clarity of exposition, we start our analysis with the case where there is no political opposition, and then move on to study the regulator's behavior when tax proposals face political resistance.

Absent any political opposition, i.e. if $P(\Delta) = 1$, the regulator's objective is to maximize $W^T(\tau) - K$ by choosing a tax level that will be imposed on all firms, where

$$W^T(\tau) = \int_{\theta^\tau}^{\theta^a} [\pi(\theta) - x + \gamma\tau]\, dF(\theta) + \int_{\theta^a}^{\bar{\theta}} [\pi(\theta) - c(\theta)]\, dF(\theta).$$

(8.4)

The first term on the right-hand side of (8.4) denotes the social value of firms remaining in the industry and paying the tax after its imposition, where the term $\gamma\tau$ captures the benefit the regulator receives from environmental tax revenues. Note that the marginal benefit of tax revenues, γ, is not necessarily identical to the cost of public funds, λ,[19] and in practice may be quite small. The second term denotes the social value of firms that adopt the new technology. We assume that welfare is concave in τ.

---

[18]   As mentioned earlier, we assume this cost of the two programs is equal, so that arbitrary differences in these two costs do not drive any of our results.

[19]   For example, Bovenberg and Goulder (1996) show that the benefits of an environmental tax are much lower if revenues are recycled through lump sum rebates than if the revenues are used to reduce marginal income tax rates.

We turn now to characterizing the optimal tax more explicitly. The regulator's objective (8.4) is maximized by a tax set at[20]

$$\tau^N = \frac{x}{1 + \gamma(1 + 1/\eta_{TB})}. \tag{8.5}$$

The structure of the expression for the optimal tax is very similar to that for the optimal subsidy, as given in (8.3). The key parameter in (8.5) is η_{TB}, the tax elasticity of the tax base. This parameter measures how rapidly the number of firms paying the tax drops off as the level of the tax is increased. If tax revenues had no value to the government, i.e. if $\gamma = 0$, then the optimal tax would simply be equal to the environmental harm done by each firm, i.e. $\tau^N = x$. This is an intuitively appealing criterion, as it ensures that all firms that can adopt the technology at a cost less than x will do so.

When the regulator values tax revenues, matters become more complicated. The regulator faces a tradeoff between two effects when γ is strictly positive. On one hand, there is an incentive to expand the tax base, by reducing the tax level a bit so as to increase the number of firms that are paying the tax. On the other hand, there is an incentive to increase the tax revenues raised from the existing tax base, by raising the tax level. Which of these effects dominates depends on the elasticity of the tax base. If $\eta_{TB} < -1$, then the size of the tax base is highly responsive to the level of the tax. As a result, the regulator distorts τ^N *below* x, in order to keep the tax base large, and expand tax revenues. As a result, too many firms pay the tax, and too few firms adopt the environmental technology, relative to the case when $\gamma = 0$ Conversely, if $0 > \eta_{TB} > -1$, then the size of the tax base is not very responsive to changes in the tax level. In this case, τ^N is distorted *above x*, in order to increase the amount of tax paid by each firm in the tax base. As a result, too few firms pay the tax, and too many firms adopt the environmental technology, relative to the case when $\gamma = 0$.

The welfare gains from taxation, relative to government inaction, come in three parts and are shown in figure 8.3. The shaded region between $\underline{\theta}$ and θ^{τ^N} in the lower left part of figure 8.3 represents social gains from forcing inefficient firms to exit the industry. It is positive because profits are less than x on its range. The shaded region between θ^{τ^N} and θ^a represents the social value of the tax revenues raised from the emissions tax. The social gains from adoptions are represented by the shaded region in the right-hand side of the figure 8.3 between θ^a and $\overline{\theta}$. Those gains represent the fact that the

---

[20] Define the tax base as $B(\tau) = F(\theta^a) - F(\theta^\tau)$, the fraction of firms paying the tax. Then $\partial B/\partial \tau < 0$ is the change in the size of the tax base when the tax is increased by a small amount, and we can define the tax elasticity of the tax base to be $\eta_{TB} = (\partial B/\partial \tau)(\tau/B) < 0$.

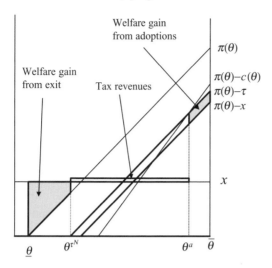

Figure 8.3   Welfare gains from taxation

social cost of technology adoption, $c(\theta)$ is less than the social cost of pollution, x.

We have seen that even when political opposition is not an issue, both the PVA and the tax are distorted by the need to cope with the cost of raising public funds. In the following proposition we evaluate the relative performance of the two instruments, still maintaining the assumption that there is no political resistance.

Proposition 15: *When regulators do not face political opposition from industry, i.e. when $P(\Delta) = 1$, the optimal pollution tax generates greater social benefits than does the optimal PVA.*

Proposition 15 shows that the tax is inherently a more powerful instrument than the PVA. There are two reasons for this. First, as mentioned above, a fundamental limitation of the PVA is that it cannot subsidize firms to exit the industry; firms must stay in business in order to collect any benefits from the PVA program. Thus, a PVA should not be confused with an optimal subsidy program, which would actually subsidize some firms to exit the industry. Second, in a world with costly public funds, a tax that generates public revenues is preferable to a subsidy that drains public coffers. Both effects make a tax preferable to a PVA program, when political pressures are ignored.

In reality, of course, political opposition is important. Industry losses from a tax occur in several different forms. All firms indexed by $\theta \in \left[\underline{\theta}, \theta^{\tau}\right)$

will exit the industry and their profits will be lost. All firms indexed by $\theta \in [\theta^\tau, \theta^a]$ will continue operations, but each firm will incur losses equal to the tax.[21] Firms indexed by $\theta \in [\theta^a, \bar{\theta}]$ will be induced to adopt the environmental technology at cost $c(\theta)$ rather than pay the tax. The sum of these enumerated losses constitutes the total direct costs borne by industry from the tax proposal. However, additional indirect losses are possible due to the loss of potential subsidies from a PVA. Specifically, all firms indexed by $\theta \in [\theta^{s^*}, \bar{\theta}]$ are eligible to receive the subsidy s^*, but will forgo this benefit if the tax is passed. These opportunity costs of a tax must also be taken into account. We will denote the sum of all these different losses to industry as $\Delta(\tau)$. It will come as no surprise that industry losses are increasing in the size of the tax τ.

Since industry losses $\Delta(\tau)$ are positive for any positive tax, industry can always be expected to oppose a tax. This fact alters the regulator's objective function. Specifically, the regulator will optimize the *expected* benefits of the tax, given that legislation favoring the tax will pass only with probability $P(\Delta) < 1$. Thus, in setting the tax the regulator solves the following optimization problem:

$$\max_\tau \overline{W}(\tau) = P(\Delta) W^T(\tau) + [1 - P(\Delta)] W^S(s^*), \qquad (8.6)$$

where s^* is the optimal subsidy to be imposed if the tax does not pass. To solve for τ we will introduce one additional elasticity measure, the tax elasticity of political resistance, which we denote by η_{PR}.[22] The solution to the regulator's optimization problem is then defined by[23]

$$\tau^* = \tau^N + \frac{1}{1+\gamma} \frac{[W^T(\tau^*) - W^S(s^*)]}{\partial B/\partial \tau} \left(\frac{\eta_{PR}}{\tau^*}\right). \qquad (8.7)$$

Recalling that $\partial B/\partial \tau < 0$ and that $\eta_{PR} > 0$, (8.7) shows that political resistance weakens the tax, relative to τ^N, since $W^T(\tau^*) > W^S(s^*)$. The intuition is simple: since the tax is socially beneficial, the regulator lowers the proposed tax so as to increase its chances of passage. As a result, $\tau^* < \tau^N$.

The extent of the distortion away from τ^N depends on two key factors that appear in (8.7): the elasticity of political resistance with respect to taxation, and the net benefit of taxation compared to the PVA. Clearly the political distortion in the tax increases with η_{PR}, i.e. when the political

---

[21] Note that $\pi(\theta^a) - c(\theta^a) = \tau = \pi(\theta^\tau)$ so $\pi(\theta^a) > \pi(\theta^\tau)$. Since $\pi'(\theta) > 0$ it necessarily follows that $\theta^a > \theta^\tau$.

[22] Mathematically, $\eta_{PR} \equiv \frac{-P'(\Delta)}{P(\Delta)} \frac{\tau}{\Delta'(\tau)} > 0$.

[23] Although (8.7) does not yield a closed-form expression for τ^*, it does define implicitly a unique solution.

resistance to a marginal tax increase is strong. As can be seen in the definition of η_{PR}, the political elasticity is greater when $P'(\Delta)$ is large; when the probability of passing a tax, $P(\Delta)$, is small; and when losses rise rapidly with the tax rate, i.e. when $\partial \Delta(\tau^*)/\partial \tau$ is large, either because many inefficient firms would be forced to exit, because many moderately efficient firms would resist paying the tax, and/or because many efficient firms would be forced to adopt the costly new technology. In any case, the higher is the tax elasticity of political resistance, the more the regulator distorts downward the proposed tax.

The second key factor causing political tax distortion is that the more the regulator wants the tax, i.e. the greater is $\left[W^T(\tau^*) - W^S(s^*) \right]$, the more the regulator weakens the tax proposal to increase its chances of passage.

We record these observations in the following lemma.

Lemma 4: *Political distortion causes the regulator to weaken its tax proposal, i.e. $\tau^* < \tau^N$. The distortion increases with the tax elasticity of political pressure and with the net benefit of taxation compared to the VA.*

We have shown that both the PVA and the tax depart from the marginal social cost of pollution due to the distortionary effects of raising tax monies and/or political resistance to taxation. Whether the tax produces better results than the PVA in practice, then, depends upon a number of parameters. The key parameters affecting each of these instruments have been discussed above. In particular, welfare under a PVA improves when the cost of public funds is low and the cost of adoption is low and does not vary greatly across firms. At the same time, welfare under a pollution tax improves when the tax elasticity of political resistance is low. In light of the result established in Lemma 4, it is easy to see the following corollary to Proposition 15.

Corollary 2: *Taxation is a preferable regulatory instrument to a PVA unless political opposition $[1 - P(\Delta)]$ is high.*

Because taxation works at both the upper and lower end of the efficiency distribution of firms, and bolsters rather than drains public coffers, it is inherently a more powerful instrument than a PVA. As a result, it is preferred to a PVA unless the political forces opposing taxation are strong. Indeed, the only reason the regulator might not propose a tax is that making the proposal requires a fixed cost of K, which is not justified if the probability of success is too small. As discussed in section 2, the CCAP appears to be a case where the costs of technology adoption for many firms were relatively low, but where the political resistance to a tax was high because some firms would have been forced out of business and a broad base of firms would have had to pay higher taxes. Thus the PVA proved to be the only feasible policy, even though an energy tax would have been a more potent tool.

As we discussed in chapters 6 and 7, voluntary programs – despite their inherent weaknesses – are becoming more popular. It is interesting, therefore, to examine how welfare is affected when the regulator has the possibility of offering a PVA after legislative efforts fail. As the following proposition notes, the option of offering a PVA may diminish social welfare, and legislatures might wish to commit *not* to use PVAs to achieve some environmental policy goals.

Proposition 16: *If the tax elasticity of political resistance is high, social welfare may be lower when the regulator has the option of offering a PVA.*

The intuition behind Proposition 16 is simple: if firms know a PVA will be offered after a tax fails, they have more incentive to oppose the tax so they can collect the subsidy that is offered under the PVA. If the tax elasticity of political resistance is high, offering the PVA can produce a significant increase in political resistance to the tax, and greatly reduce the chance that the tax proposal will be passed. If the social benefits of the tax are substantially greater than the benefits of the PVA, then this increased political resistance dominates the benefits of the PVA, and expected welfare is higher when the possibility of a PVA is eliminated. Note that as K (the cost of crafting a tax proposal or offering a PVA) rises, the benefits of the PVA fall, while the total subsidy payments under the PVA program remain unchanged. Hence, the option of offering a PVA is less socially valuable the larger is K. Indeed, Proposition 2 (p. 61) shows it is possible that social welfare would be higher if public VAs had never come into existence. Whether a legislature could credibly commit *not* to offer a PVA is questionable, since governments are not known for their commitment abilities. Nevertheless, our results suggest a more cautious approach to the use of public VAs than has been espoused by some.[24]

5 INDUSTRY SELF-REGULATION

The previous section studied stages 2 and 3 of the game, involving the regulator's decision regarding which policy instrument to wield. This section

---

[24] For example, IAE (1998) highlights the benefits voluntary programs appear to offer and urges serious consideration of expanding their use in the future. Our results suggest that policymakers should also be cognizant of the opportunity costs of making such programs available.

studies stage 1 of the game, in which the industry decides whether and to what extent it will unilaterally adopt the environmental technology, taking into account how its decision will affect the likelihood and level of the tax, as well as the likelihood of the public voluntary program. Thus we must examine not only the impact of unilateral activities on industry profitability, but also on the regulator's response. Because the technical analysis of these effects is involved, the formal analysis is relegated to the appendix (p. 219). Here we provide the intuition behind the results in a less formal fashion. We examine whether the industry will undertake unilateral self-regulation, and the welfare consequences if self-regulation occurs. We also study how offering a PVA affects incentives for industry self-regulation.

This section of the chapter extends the analysis of chapter 3 in two main ways. First, we allow for uncertainty regarding the passage of new legislation if no self-regulation occurs. Second, we allow the regulator to employ a PVA if legislation does not pass. Thus, we distinguish sharply between unilateral action by industry and a PVA offered by the government, something that has not been done in previous formal models. In addition, this chapter focuses on the imposition of a tax instead of the regulatory standards considered in chapter 3.

To begin with, we change our notation to make all of our expressions for welfare contingent upon the level of unilateral adoption by industry. As discussed earlier, we imagine the industry working in concert in its preemption efforts. Under this assumption, the firms with the lowest technology adoption costs will enter the unilateral voluntary agreement, since this set of firms can achieve preemption at the lowest total cost to the industry. Thus, we denote by θ^v the firm with the highest technology adoption costs (lowest efficiency) that joins the industry's unilateral voluntary efforts. Then all firms indexed by $\theta > \theta^v$ will also adopt the technology. If the industry opts to take no unilateral actions, it simply sets $\theta^v = \bar{\theta}$. Throughout this section we will write $W(\emptyset, \theta^v)$ for the level of social welfare when the regulator takes no action, $W^T(\tau, \theta^v)$ to indicate social welfare under a tax τ, $W^S(s^*, \theta^v)$ for social welfare under the optimal PVA, and $\overline{W}(\tau, \theta^v)$ for expected social welfare when the regulator proposes a tax of τ. Note that all of these expressions are conditional on the level of self-regulation, θ^v. The formal definitions of each of these expressions are in the appendix; see (8.12)–(8.16).

For purposes of this section, we assume that if there is no unilateral action by the industry, then the regulator prefers to propose a tax rather than institute a PVA. If this were not so, then the industry would have no motive for taking unilateral action. As we show below, unilateral action is unprofitable for the industry unless it serves to preempt government action. While preempting a tax is desirable for the industry, preempting a government handout is not. Hence, if the PVA is preferred by the regulator when $\theta^v = \bar{\theta}$, then the industry will take no self-regulatory action.

We turn next to the impact of self-regulation on the regulator's benefits of offering a PVA. The benefits of a PVA, relative to doing nothing, are

$$W(s^*, \theta^v) - W(\emptyset, \theta^v) = \int_{\theta^{s*}}^{\theta^v} [x - c(\theta)] \, dF(\theta) - \lambda s^* [1 - F(\theta^{s*})] - K.$$

$$(8.8)$$

The benefit of offering the PVA is given in the first term on the right-hand side of (8.8). This shows the net social benefits, summed over all firms that join the PVA, of incurring cost $c(\theta)$ to reduce environmental degradation by x. The second term indicates the aggregate subsidy payments that must be made to all firms that join the PVA, while the third term represents the fixed cost of creating and administering the program.

It is easy to show that if enough firms undertake unilateral action in stage 1, then the regulator does not propose a PVA. Denote by θ^{-s} the critical value of θ^v at which the regulator will forgo the public voluntary program. Then $\theta^{-s} > \theta^{s*}$ is the value of θ^v that sets (8.8) to zero:

$$\int_{\theta^{s*}}^{\theta^{-s}} [x - c(\theta)] \, dF(\theta) = \lambda s^* [1 - F(\theta^{s*})] + K. \qquad (8.9)$$

Clearly the regulator will find it optimal to propose the public voluntary program only as long as $\theta^v > \theta^{-s}$. Note that even if $K = 0$, it is possible for unilateral voluntary efforts to preempt PVAs.

It is also important to note that the optimal subsidy is independent of the number of firms that engage in the unilateral voluntary agreement (i.e. independent of θ^v). The regulator sets s by maximizing (8.8), but it is clear by inspection that θ^v has no impact upon the marginal effect of an increase in s. Hence, as long as the regulator decides to offer the PVA at all (i.e. as long as $\theta^v > \theta^{-s}$), s^* is not a function of θ^v.[25] We thus obtain the following lemma.

Lemma 5: *The regulatory benefits arising from a PVA are strictly decreasing in the number of voluntary adoptions (hence, increasing in θ^v) and reach zero at $\theta^v = \theta^{-s}$.*

Lemma 5 shows that unilateral voluntary activity on the part of the industry (which reduces θ^v) will not enhance the likelihood that the regulator will

---

[25] Note that optimization of (8.8) yields the same s^* as optimization of (8.2).

provide the public voluntary program.[26] Nor do these efforts affect the level of the subsidy. Furthermore, as long as voluntary activities do not preempt the PVA, firms will receive the same compensation no matter the timing of the adoption. Clearly, then, incentives for unilateral voluntary action exist only because of the threat of taxation. Put another way, if $P(\Delta) = 0$ the industry has no incentive to engage in voluntary activity.

Next we examine industry incentives to engage in unilateral voluntary activities when faced with both the possibility of a tax and the possibility of a subsequent PVA. To examine the impact of unilateral initiatives on the possibility of a tax we examine the net benefits to the regulator of offering the tax, relative to its next-best option. These net benefits are:

$$\overline{NW}\left(\tau^*, \theta^v\right) = \begin{cases} \overline{W}(\tau^*, \theta^v) - W^S(s^*, \theta^v) & for\, \theta^v \geq \theta^{-s} \\ \overline{W}(\tau^*, \theta^v) - W(\emptyset, \theta^v) - K & for\, \theta^v < \theta^{-s} \end{cases}.$$

(8.10)

Equation (8.10) reflects the fact that as long as unilateral voluntary efforts do not preempt the PVA, the relevant alternative to the tax is the stage 3 agreement. However if industry unilateral efforts do preempt the PVA, then the relevant regulatory alternative is one of inaction. Note that both the tax proposal and the PVA require the regulator to incur the cost K, so this cost cancels out when one is subtracted from the other. Thus, the fixed cost K appears only in the lower part of (8.10), since inaction requires no fixed costs.

We have seen that industry has no incentive to engage in unilateral voluntary actions absent a tax. Thus, two possible motivations for unilateral voluntary actions exist. First, unilateral actions that do not preempt the tax might nevertheless raise expected industry profits above those associated with no unilateral voluntary agreement, perhaps by weakening the tax that is eventually proposed. Second, unilateral action might preempt the tax and industry profits following preemption may exceed the expected profits associated with no unilateral voluntary agreement.

Unless the benefits of revenue recycling are large, then expected welfare under a tax proposal always increases with more industry self-regulation. The reason is that greater self-regulation reduces the political resistance to a subsequent tax proposal, thereby allowing the regulator to propose

---

[26] This could change in a model with asymmetric information about the distribution of firms' costs. If the regulator is poorly informed regarding the potential costs of technology adoption, then unilateral adoptions could signal that a VA program would be cost effective, and might encourage the regulator to offer such a program. For a related model, see section 4.

a stiffer tax, one closer to the social optimum.[27] However, greater self-regulation does not raise the social benefits of a PVA; in fact, greater industry self-regulation means the subsidy program is increasingly providing unnecessary subsidies to firms that have already adopted the clean technology without government assistance. Thus, as self-regulation increases, a tax proposal looks increasingly desirable, from a social perspective, relative to a PVA. From industry's perspective, this means that self-regulation is undesirable unless it is extensive enough to preempt the proposed tax – otherwise, self-regulation increases the likelihood of a tax and decreases the likelihood of a subsidy.[28]

It is easy to see that preemption is possible for a large enough K. Consider a K large enough that the regulator is almost indifferent between proposing a tax and not; in this case, a small amount of voluntary adoption will reduce the incremental benefit of taxation enough to preempt tax legislation. For a smaller K, preemption is still feasible, but requires a larger amount of self-regulation. Yet it is not enough to establish that it is feasible to preempt the tax proposal; we must also consider whether preemption is profitable for the industry. In the appendix, we prove Proposition 17, which establishes conditions under which feasible preemption is also profitable.

Proposition 17:   *If preemption is feasible, it is also profitable for large enough* K.

This result extends that of chapter 3, where we studied the profitability in a setting where there is no possibility of a PVA. The relationship between K and the extent of unilateral action is shown in figure 8.4. At high levels of K, legislation is effectively "blockaded" due to the excessive fixed cost of implementing it. As K falls, a point is reached where a small amount of unilateral action is sufficient to preempt a tax, and industry finds this action profitable. As K falls further, proposing the tax becomes more attractive, so the level of unilateral action needed for preemption rises. Beyond a certain point, however, the requisite level of unilateral action becomes

---

[27] If the benefits of revenue recycling are large, however, then voluntary adoptions can reduce expected welfare because fewer firms will be paying the tax. This can happen only when γ is large, which Bovenberg and Goulder (1996) show is unlikely to be the case.

[28] In chapter 3 we showed that unilateral action that fails to preempt is unprofitable in a setting without the possibility of a PVA. Our point in this section is that a similar result arises in many situations even when a PVA is possible. We show in the appendix that a sufficient, though not necessary, condition for this is that the welfare benefits of tax revenues are small (i.e. γ is small).

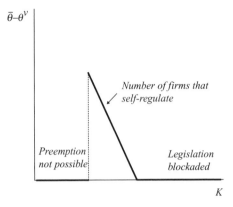

Figure 8.4   Extent of self-regulation

too expensive, and industry is unwilling to undertake it. This is shown in figure 8.4, where there is a sharp, discontinuous, drop in unilateral activity.

Our analysis of self-regulation has implications for welfare as well as for industry behavior. Indeed, throughout our analysis we have assumed that the industry is able to coordinate in fighting a tax proposal and in taking unilateral action that would preempt the tax. An important policy question is whether such cooperation should be allowed. The answer turns on whether $W(\emptyset, \theta^{-\tau}) > \overline{W}(\tau^*, \overline{\theta}) - K$, i.e. whether welfare is higher when the industry's unilateral action preempts the tax proposal or when the industry takes no unilateral action and the regulator proposes the optimal tax. We address this question in Proposition 18.

Proposition 18: *Expected social welfare is higher when unilateral industry action preempts government action.*

The proposition shows that self-regulation enhances social welfare. The reasoning behind this result is very similar to that used to establish Proposition 4 in chapter 3. As shown in the proof in the appendix, expected welfare with the tax increases with unilateral abatement, so self-regulation raises the welfare level that the regulator can claim by proposing a tax. If the regulator allows the tax proposal to be preempted, it must be the case that welfare is even higher under preemption than it would be if the tax were imposed when there is no unilateral action.

Given that self-regulation enhances welfare, it is important to examine how PVAs affect the incentives for industry to undertake unilateral actions. This is the focus of our final Proposition 19.

Proposition 19: *PVAs reduce the industry's incentives to engage in preemptive self-regulation, and consequently may reduce social welfare.*

The proposition shows that when the regulator is expected to offer a PVA should a tax fail to pass, industry self-regulation may be discouraged, with negative effects on social welfare. This result extends that of Proposition 16, which showed that making the PVA available could reduce welfare in a setting where self-regulation is not possible. Proposition 19 goes on to show that the availability of the PVA may induce industry to eschew self-regulation, and that this change in industry behavior can harm welfare.

6   NON-TECHNICAL SUMMARY

In this chapter, we have examined the regulator's choice between proposing an environmental tax and offering a PVA program. We showed first that if no tax is imposed, then the regulator may still wish to offer a PVA, assuming that the benefits of doing so are greater than the fixed costs of setting up the program. We also showed that when raising public funds is costly, as is typically the case, then the PVA will provide weaker subsidies than would be socially optimal. As a result, some firms will fail to adopt the new abatement technology even though their adoptions would be socially beneficial.

We went on to show that an emissions tax is an inherently more powerful instrument than a PVA, because it can induce inefficient firms to exit the industry and can raise tax revenues, in addition to inducing efficient firms to adopt the new abatement technology. However, industry will put up political resistance to a proposal for new taxes, and knowing this the regulator will weaken its tax proposal to increase the chance the proposal passes. If political resistance is too great, the regulator may be better off to skip proposing the tax and go straight to introducing a PVA program.

Despite the potential usefulness of PVA programs as regulatory instruments, we showed that the very existence of a regulatory option to offer a PVA can make society worse off. The reason is that if industry knows that a PVA will be offered when a tax proposal fails, it will have greater incentives to fight the tax proposal. Such increased expenditures on rent-seeking are socially wasteful, yet may be encouraged when the regulator has an option to offer a PVA when a tax is voted down. Furthermore, rent-seeking efforts of this kind make it less likely that a socially desirable tax will be implemented.

Following our comparison of taxes and public voluntary programs, we turned to an examination of industry incentives for self-regulation. We showed that self-regulation reduces the social benefits of offering a PVA program, since many firms that would have been swayed by the subsidy have already adopted the new technology. Since initiating a PVA program is costly, the regulator may be less likely to initiate a PVA if industry has already undertaken substantial self-regulatory efforts. As a result, industry may be reluctant to self-regulate, for fear of preempting a government subsidy program. However, we also showed that if the cost to the regulator of introducing the tax program is high enough, then industry can profitably self-regulate and preempt the threat of an emissions tax. Furthermore, we showed that when such preemption occurs, society benefits. As a result, we identified another social cost of PVA programs: they reduce industry's incentive to engage in socially beneficial self-regulation.

7 CONCLUSIONS AND POLICY IMPLICATIONS

We have presented a model of environmentally friendly technology adoption in which a broad array of instruments – industry self-regulation, PVAs, and legislatively imposed taxes – can be jointly considered. Our analysis in this chapter is somewhat at odds with the conventional view of PVAs, which sees them as a more efficient instrument than traditional approaches to pollution control, and hence something to be encouraged. We do not deny that this is possible in some circumstances, but we emphasize that it is not a general conclusion. Previous work has often failed to distinguish carefully between self-regulation and PVAs, and thus reaches misleading policy conclusions. In particular, it is often thought that VAs emerge only under pressure of strong legislative threats, and that PVAs should be promoted as efficient alternatives that are superior to politically unpopular taxes and inflexible standards. Our more general analysis reaches very different conclusions: PVAs are often weak instruments that are used precisely because strong legislation is infeasible due to industry's political resistance. We argue that this view aptly characterizes the most numerous group of public voluntary programs in the USA, namely those developed by the EPA for issues of global warming. Furthermore, we show that PVAs may reduce welfare by preempting self-regulation that would have been better.

Section 6 provided a non-technical summary of our analysis of PVAs and their impact on corporate and regulatory behavior. Here we highlight the major policy implications arising from this analysis. The most important lesson of this chapter is that PVAs typically arise from weakness, not from strength. They should not be regarded as some new and superior policy instrument. Rather, they should be viewed as a limited tool that may be useful in settings where more powerful policy instruments are infeasible. Indeed, policymakers should approach PVAs with caution, since their very availability may increase industry resistance to the use of more powerful regulatory tools. This resistance increases because the hope of obtaining a subsidy (through a PVA) strengthens industry's resolve to fight traditional regulatory tools of taxes and standards, which impose direct costs on the industry.

There is a second risk associated with the increased use of PVAs by policymakers. Just as they may undermine more stringent regulatory tools, they may undermine industry's incentives to undertake environmental improvement under its own initiative. Instead, industry may prefer to wait until government offers a "carrot" before agreeing to improve its environmental performance. Industry may have incentives to preempt the imposition of a tax or standard, but it does not want to risk preempting a handout.

APPENDIX

Proposition 15: *When regulators do not face political opposition from industry, i.e. when $P(\Delta) = 1$, the optimal pollution tax generates greater social benefits than does the optimal PVA.*

Proof: We begin by comparing the optimal PVA and the optimal tax when $\lambda = \gamma = 0$, in which case $s^* = \tau^* = x$. We then consider how the comparison changes when $\lambda > 0$ and $\gamma > 0$.

Define $\hat{\theta} = c^{-1}(x)$. Then when $\lambda = \gamma = 0$ and $s^* = \tau^* = x$, social welfare under the PVA is

$$W^S\left(s^* = x\right) = \int_{\underline{\theta}}^{\hat{\theta}} \left[\pi\left(\theta\right) - x\right] dF\left(\theta\right) + \int_{\hat{\theta}}^{\bar{\theta}} \left[\pi\left(\theta\right) - c\left(\theta\right)\right] dF\left(\theta\right)$$

and social welfare under the tax is

$$W^T\left(\tau^* = x\right) = \int_{\theta^\tau}^{\hat{\theta}} \left[\pi\left(\theta\right) - x\right] dF\left(\theta\right) + \int_{\hat{\theta}}^{\bar{\theta}} \left[\pi\left(\theta\right) - c\left(\theta\right)\right] dF\left(\theta\right).$$

The only difference between these two expressions is that the tax induces exit by firms with $\theta \in [\underline{\theta}, \theta^\tau]$. These exits are socially beneficial, since these firms had profits that were less than the social cost of their emissions. Hence $W^T(\tau^* = x) > W^S(s^* = x)$.

Now consider what happens when $\lambda > 0$ and $\gamma > 0$. Let us abuse notation slightly by writing $W^T(\tau, \gamma)$ and $W^S(s, \lambda)$ to indicate explicitly the dependence of welfare on γ and λ under a tax and PVA, respectively. In terms of this notation, the foregoing paragraph proved that $W^T(\tau^*, 0) > W^S(s^*, 0)$. Recalling that the regulator sets τ optimally for a given γ, and sets s optimally for a given λ, denote by τ_i^* the optimal tax when $\gamma = \gamma_i$, and denote by s_i^* the optimal subsidy when $\lambda = \lambda_i$. It is easy to see from (8.4) that $\partial W^T/\partial \gamma > 0$. Then for $\gamma_1 > \gamma_0$ it is immediate that $W^T(\tau_1, \gamma_1) > W^T(\tau_0, \gamma_1) > W^T(\tau_0, \gamma_0)$. Hence, social welfare under an environmental tax is greater the larger is γ. In similar fashion, it is easy to see from (8.2) that $\partial W^S/\partial \lambda < 0$. Then for $\lambda_1 > \lambda_0$, it is immediate that $W^S(s_1, \lambda_1) < W^S(s_1, \lambda_0) < W^S(s_0, \lambda_0)$. Hence, social welfare under a PVA is smaller the larger is λ. Pulling these observations together, we have shown that when the regulator does not face political resistance from industry, $W^T(\tau^*, \gamma) > W^S(s^*, \lambda)$ for all $\gamma > 0$ and $\lambda > 0$.   ∎

Lemma 5: *The regulatory benefits arising from a PVA are strictly decreasing in the number of voluntary adoptions (hence, increasing in θ^v) and reach zero at $\theta^v = \theta^{-s}$.*

Proof: From (8.8), it is easy to see that the net benefit of the PVA is increasing with θ^v so long as $x - c(\theta) > 0$ for all $\theta \in [\theta^{s*}, \theta^v]$. Since $c'(\theta) < 0$, it is sufficient to show that $x - c(\theta^{-s}) > 0$. As shown above, we know $\theta^{-s} > \theta^{s*}$. Furthermore, $\theta^{s*} = c^{-1}(x/(1+\lambda) + \lambda/(1+\lambda)(c'(\theta^s)[1 - F(\theta^s)]/f(\theta^s)) > \theta^{sw} \equiv c^{-1}(x/(1+\lambda))$, which is the social welfare optimum under costly public funds. The inequality holds because $\lambda/(1+\lambda)(c'(\theta^s)[1 - F(\theta^s)]/f(\theta^s) < 0$, due to the fact that $c'(\theta^s) < 0$. This restates the observation that (8.3) shows that too few firms adopt the abatement technology, relative to the social optimum. Since $c'(\theta) < 0$, we know that $c^{-1}(\cdot) < 0$ as well. Since $x/(1+\lambda) < x$, we then have $c^{-1}(x/(1+\lambda)) = \theta^{sw} > c^{-1}(x) \equiv x$. Hence $\theta^{-s} > \theta^{s*} > \theta^{sw} > \theta^x$, and $c(\theta^{-s}) < x$.   ∎

Proposition 16: *If the tax elasticity of political resistance is high, social welfare may be lower when the regulator has the option of offering a PVA.*

Proof: Consider a reference case in which government either taxes or takes no action. Expected social welfare is $\overline{W}^{NVA}(\tau) = P(\Delta)[W^T(\tau) - K] + [1 - P(\Delta)]W(\emptyset)$. To this reference case compare a case in which the regulator can offer a PVA if a tax proposal fails, the expected welfare of which is $\overline{W}^{VA}(\tau) = P(\Delta)[W^T(\tau) - K] + [1 - P(\Delta)][W^S(s^*) - K]$. The benefit of the latter case is that offering a PVA *ex post* is preferable to no government action, i.e. $W^S(s^*) - K > W(\emptyset)$. The cost is that industry losses from a tax – relative to the subsidy offered under a PVA – are greater in the latter case. As a result, political resistance is greater in the latter case, and $P(\Delta)$ is smaller. If the political elasticity η_{PR} is high enough, the reduced probability of passing tax legislation more than offsets the *ex post* gains from being able to offer a PVA. In that case, welfare would be higher if the regulator did not have the option of offering the PVA *ex post*. ∎

The remaining proofs deal with the case of industry self-regulation. In this case, our definition of industry losses due to taxation must be generalized to incorporate the various possible levels of self-regulation, as represented by θ^v. To do so, we introduce $\Phi(x, y)$, an indicator variable taking on the value 1 if $x < y$, and 0 otherwise. Now the industry loss function becomes

$$\Delta(\tau) = \int_{\underline{\theta}}^{\theta^\tau} \pi(\theta)\, dF(\theta) + \int_{\theta^\tau}^{min\{\theta^a, \theta^v\}} \tau\, dF(\theta)$$

$$+ \Phi\left(\theta^{-s}, \theta^v\right)\left(\Phi\left(\theta^a, \theta^v\right)\int_{\theta^a}^{min\{\theta^{s*}, \theta^v\}} c(\theta)\, dF(\theta) + \int_{\theta^{s*}}^{\bar{\theta}} s\, dF(\theta)\right)$$

$$+ \Phi\left(\theta^v, \theta^{-s}\right)\left(\Phi\left(\theta^a, \theta^v\right)\int_{\theta^a}^{\theta^v} c(\theta)\, dF(\theta)\right). \tag{8.11}$$

Next we present the formal expressions for the welfare measures used in the remaining proofs. The general expression for welfare when the government takes no action is

$$W(\emptyset, \theta^v) = \int_{\underline{\theta}}^{\theta^v} [\pi(\theta) - x]\, dF(\theta) + \int_{\theta^v}^{\bar{\theta}} [\pi(\theta) - c(\theta)]\, dF(\theta), \tag{8.12}$$

where all firms indexed by $\theta \geq \theta^v$ voluntarily adopt the pollution technology. If a PVA is offered after some firms have undertaken voluntary adoptions, social welfare is given by[29]

$$W^S(s^*, \theta^v) = \int_{\underline{\theta}}^{\theta^{s*}} [\pi(\theta) - x]\, dF(\theta) + \int_{\theta^{s*}}^{\theta^v} [\pi(\theta) - c(\theta) + s^*]\, dF(\theta)$$

$$+ \int_{\theta^v}^{\bar{\theta}} [\pi(\theta) - c(\theta) + s^*]\, dF(\theta) - [1 - F(\theta^{s*})]\, s^* (1 + \lambda). \tag{8.13}$$

---

[29] The reader will note that the second and third terms on the right-hand side of (8.13) could be combined so as to eliminate the dependence of the expression on θ^v. We keep the two terms independent for notational consistency. All other welfare functions are dependent on θ^v and are presented as $W(\cdot, \theta^v)$.

If the legislature passes the tax proposal following the voluntary technology adoptions of some firms, social welfare is given by

$$W^T \left(\tau^*, \theta^v \right) = \int_{\theta^{\tau^*}}^{min\{\theta^v, \theta^a\}} \left[\pi \left(\theta \right) - x + \gamma \tau^* \right] dF \left(\theta \right)$$

$$+ \int_{min\{\theta^v, \theta^a\}}^{\bar{\theta}} \left[\pi \left(\theta \right) - c \left(\theta \right) \right] dF \left(\theta \right). \qquad (8.14)$$

Finally, subsequent to some level of voluntary technology adoption,[30] the expected level of welfare from proposing the optimal tax is

$$\overline{W} \left(\tau^*, \theta^v \right) = P \left(\Delta \right) W^T \left(\tau^*, \theta^v \right) + \left[1 - P \left(\Delta \right) \right] W^S \left(s^*, \theta^v \right) \qquad (8.15)$$

if the level of voluntary adoption has not preempted the PVA, and is otherwise

$$\overline{W} \left(\tau^*, \theta^v \right) = P \left(\Delta \right) W^T \left(\tau^*, \theta^v \right) + \left[1 - P \left(\Delta \right) \right] W \left(\emptyset, \theta^v \right). \qquad (8.16)$$

Lemma 6: *If a greater number of firms adopt under the tax than under the PVA, or if γ is sufficiently small, then $\theta^{-\tau} < \theta^{-s}$.*

Proof: We present this proof in two parts. The first part examines the case in which $\theta^a < \theta^{s^*}$ and the second considers $\theta^a > \theta^{s^*}$.

$\theta^a < \theta^{s^*}$

In this case more firms will adopt under the tax than under the PVA. As discussed in the text, we assume that $\overline{W}(\tau^*, \bar{\theta}) > W^S(s^*, \bar{\theta})$, which also implies that $W^T(\tau^*, \bar{\theta}) > W^S(s^*, \bar{\theta})$. However, for all $\theta^v \geq \theta^{s^*} \geq \theta^a$ it follows from (8.2) and (8.4) that $dW^S(s^*, \theta^v)/d\theta^v = 0$ and $dW^T(\tau^*, \theta^v)/d\theta^v = 0$. Thus $W^T(\tau^*, \theta^v) > W^S(s^*, \theta^v) \; \forall \theta^v \in (\theta^{s^*}, \bar{\theta})$. Now recall from (8.9) that $\theta^{-s} > \theta^{s*}$, so $W^T(\tau^*, \theta^{-s}) > W^S(s^*, \theta^{-s})$, and therefore $\overline{W}(\tau^*, \theta^{-s}) > W^S(s^*, \theta^{-s})$, which implies $\theta^{-\tau} < \theta^{-s}$.

$\theta^a > \theta^{s^*}$

In this case, voluntary adoptions resulting in $\theta^v < \theta^a$ will cause the regulator to alter the optimal tax. Our goal is to identify the level of voluntary adoptions at which the government prefers to abandon a particular policy (either tax or PVA) in favor of the inaction option, whose social value is given

---

[30] The expression for industry losses due to a tax becomes more complex when we consider the possibility of self-regulation. The full mathematical expression for the industry loss function is presented as (8.11).

by (8.12). Thus, we seek the levels of θ^v at which $\overline{W}(\tau^*, \theta^v) = W(\emptyset, \theta^v)$ and $W^S(s^*, \theta^v) = W(\emptyset, \theta^v)$. Since $\overline{W}(\tau^*, \bar{\theta}) > W^S(s^*, \bar{\theta})$, we know that $W^T(\tau^*, \bar{\theta}) > W^S(s^*, \bar{\theta})$. In addition, we know that $W^S(s^*, \theta^v)$ is constant for $\theta^v \in (\theta^{-s}, \bar{\theta})$, and that $W^T(\tau^*, \theta^v)$ is constant for $\theta^v \in (\theta^a, \bar{\theta})$. Furthermore, we know that $\overline{W}(\tau^*, \theta^a) > \overline{W}(\tau^*, \bar{\theta})$ since the optimal tax when $\theta^v = \theta^a$ imposes lower losses on industry than does the optimal tax when $\theta^v = \bar{\theta}$, hence inducing less political resistance and raising the probability the tax is passed. It follows that $\overline{W}(\tau^*, \theta^a) > W^S(s^*, \theta^a) = W^S(s^*, \bar{\theta})$. Given that $W(\emptyset, \theta^v)$ is decreasing in θ^v (rising in the number of voluntary adoptions) over the relevant range we can ensure $\theta^{-\tau} < \theta^{-s}$ by showing that $d\overline{W}(\tau^*, \theta^v)/d\theta^v < 0$ for $\theta^v \in (\theta^{-s}, \theta^a)$, i.e. $\overline{W}(\tau^*, \theta^v)$ is always above $W^S(s^*, \theta^v)$ on the relevant range. From (8.14) and (8.15) we see that

$$\frac{d\overline{W}(\tau^*, \theta^v)}{d\theta^v} = P(\Delta) \left[\frac{dW^T(\tau^*, \theta^v)}{d\theta^v} \right]$$
$$+ P'(\Delta) \frac{d\Delta}{d\theta^v} \left[W^T(\tau^*, \theta^v) - W^S(s^*, \theta^v) \right]. \quad (8.17)$$

If $W^T(\tau^*, \theta^v) > W^S(s^*, \theta^v)$, the second term will be negative since $P'(\Delta) < 0$ and $d\Delta/d\theta^v > 0$, as can be seen by differentiating (8.11). Recall that we know that $W^T(\tau^*, \theta^a) > W^S(s^*, \theta^a)$, and that $dW^S(s^*, \theta^v)/d\theta^v = 0$ for all $\theta^v \in (\theta^{-s}, \theta^a)$, thus as long as $dW^T(\tau^*, \theta^v)/d\theta^v < 0$ over the relevant range, both the first and second terms in (8.17) are negative for all $\theta^v \in (\theta^{-s}, \theta^a)$.

To establish the sign of $dW^T(\tau^*, \theta^v)/d\theta^v$, we note that

$$\frac{dW^T(\tau^*, \theta^v)}{d\theta^v} = \frac{\partial W^T(\tau^*, \theta^v)}{\partial \tau^*} \frac{\partial \tau^*}{\partial \theta^v} + \frac{\partial W^T(\tau^*, \theta^v)}{\partial \theta^v} \quad (8.18)$$

which, substituting in for the partial derivative of (8.14) can be rewritten as

$$\frac{dW^T(\tau^*, \theta^v)}{d\theta^v} = \frac{\partial W^T(\tau^*, \theta^v)}{\partial \tau^*} \frac{\partial \tau^*}{\partial \theta^v} + \left[c(\theta^v) - x + \gamma \tau^* \right] f(\theta^v). \quad (8.19)$$

Note that the second term is negative for γ sufficiently small. The first component of the first term is positive given our assumption that $W^T(\tau, \theta^v)$ is concave in τ and our result in Lemma 4, which shows that τ^* falls short of the welfare maximizing level due to political resistance. Thus, we see that $dW^T(\tau^*, \theta^v)/d\theta^v < 0$ when $\partial \tau^*/\partial \theta^v < 0$.

To establish the sign of $\partial \tau^*/\partial \theta^v$, observe that by totally differentiating the first-order condition governing the choice of τ^* we obtain

$$\frac{\partial^2 \overline{W}(\tau^*, \theta^v)}{\partial \tau^{*2}} d\tau^* + \frac{\partial^2 \overline{W}(\tau^*, \theta^v)}{\partial \tau^* \partial \theta^v} d\theta^v = 0, \quad (8.20)$$

and therefore

$$\frac{d\tau^*}{d\theta^v} = -\frac{\partial^2 \overline{W}(\tau^*,\theta^v)/\partial\tau^*\partial\theta^v}{\partial^2 \overline{W}(\tau^*,\theta^v)/\partial\tau^{*2}}. \tag{8.21}$$

Since $\overline{W}(\tau^*,\theta^v)$ is concave, we see that the denominator of (8.21) is negative, and thus $d\tau^*/d\theta^v < 0$ if the numerator is positive. Differentiating (8.17) with respect to τ and evaluating at τ^* yields

$$\frac{\partial^2 \overline{W}(\tau^*,\theta^v)}{\partial\tau^*\partial\theta^v} = P(\Delta)\frac{\partial^2 W^T(\tau^*,\theta^v)}{\partial\tau^*\partial\theta^v} + P'(\Delta)\left[\frac{\partial\Delta}{\partial\theta^v}\frac{\partial W^T(\tau^*,\theta^v)}{\partial\tau^*}\right.$$

$$+\frac{\partial^2\Delta}{\partial\tau^*\partial\theta^v}\left[W^T(\tau^*,\theta^v)-W^S(s^*,\theta^v)\right]\bigg]$$

$$+P''(\Delta)\left[\frac{\partial\Delta}{\partial\theta^v}\frac{\partial\Delta}{\partial\tau^*}\left[W^T(\tau^*,\theta^v)-W^S(s^*,\theta^v)\right]\right]. \tag{8.22}$$

It is straightforward to show that all terms in the large square brackets on the second and third lines of (8.22) are positive. Furthermore, we know $P'(\Delta) < 0$ and $P''(\Delta) < 0$, so (8.22) is positive if the first term is small enough in magnitude. Using (8.14) one can show that $\partial^2 W^T(\tau^*,\theta^v)/\partial\tau^*\partial\theta^v = \gamma f(\theta^v)$. Thus, we see that for sufficiently small γ, $\partial^2 \overline{W}(\tau^*,\theta^v)/\partial\tau^*\partial\theta^v < 0$. Thus, from (8.21), $d\tau^*/d\theta^v$ is also negative for sufficiently small γ. Finally, from (8.19) we have that for sufficiently small γ, $dW^T(\tau^*,\theta^v)/d\theta^v < 0$. ∎

The following lemma, along with Proposition 17, addresses the desirability for industry of engaging in a unilateral voluntary agreement under the threat of taxation.

Lemma 7: *Expected industry profits are increasing in θ^v, and therefore decreasing in the number of firms that voluntarily adopt, for all $\theta^v \in \left[\theta^{-\tau},\bar{\theta}\right]$.*

Proof: Expected profits for the industry, as a function of Δ, are

$$\Pi(\Delta) = P(\Delta)\left(\int_{\theta^\tau}^{\bar{\theta}} \pi(\theta)\,dF(\theta) - \int_{\theta^\tau}^{min\{\theta^a,\theta^v\}} \tau\,dF(\theta)\right.$$

$$-\int_{min\{\theta^a,\theta^v\}}^{\bar{\theta}} c(\theta)\,dF(\theta)\bigg) + (1-P(\Delta))$$

$$\times\left(\begin{array}{c}\int_{\underline{\theta}}^{\bar{\theta}} \pi(\theta)\,dF(\theta)+\Phi\left(\theta^{-s},\theta^v\right)\int_{min\{\theta^a,\theta^v\}}^{\bar{\theta}}[s^*-c(\theta)]\,dF(\theta)\\-\Phi\left(\theta^v,\theta^{-s}\right)\int_{\theta^v}^{\bar{\theta}} c(\theta)\,dF(\theta)\end{array}\right). \tag{8.23}$$

From (8.23) we see that the functional form of expected industry profits changes as θ^v declines from $\bar{\theta}$. The following cases are possible: (1) $\theta^v >$

$\theta^{-s} > \theta^{a} > \theta^{-\tau}$, (2) $\theta^{-s} > \theta^{v} > \theta^{a} > \theta^{-\tau}$, (3) $\theta^{-s} > \theta^{a} > \theta^{v} > \theta^{-\tau}$. In each case we examine how $P(\Delta)$ changes as θ^{v} changes, and then we examine how profits under the tax policy and under the subsidy or no action policy change as θ^{v} changes. For the sake of brevity we present only case (3). In case (1) it is straightforward to show that neither $P(\Delta)$ nor any other component of industry profits changes with θ^{v}. In case (2), $P(\Delta)$ falls as θ^{v} rises, further industry profits under taxation are invariant and always lower than profits under a no action policy; thus profits are increasing in θ^{v}.

Case 3: $\theta^{-s} > \theta^{a} > \theta^{v} > \theta^{-\tau}$

In this case all firms that would adopt under the optimal tax have already adopted unilaterally. The impact of further unilateral adoption can be analyzed by examining

$$\Pi(\Delta) = P(\Delta)\left(\int_{\theta^{\tau*}}^{\bar{\theta}} \pi(\theta)\,dF(\theta) - \int_{\theta^{\tau*}}^{\theta^{v}} \tau^{*}dF(\theta) - \int_{\theta^{v}}^{\bar{\theta}} c(\theta)\,dF(\theta)\right)$$

$$+ (1 - P(\Delta))\left(\int_{\underline{\theta}}^{\bar{\theta}} \pi(\theta)\,dF(\theta) - \int_{\theta^{v}}^{\bar{\theta}} c(\theta)\,dF(\theta)\right). \quad (8.24)$$

Observe first that both

$$\int_{\theta^{\tau*}}^{\bar{\theta}} \pi(\theta)\,dF(\theta) - \int_{\theta^{\tau*}}^{\theta^{v}} \tau^{*}dF(\theta) - \int_{\theta^{v}}^{\bar{\theta}} c(\theta)\,dF(\theta) \quad (8.25)$$

and

$$\int_{\underline{\theta}}^{\bar{\theta}} \pi(\theta)\,dF(\theta) - \int_{\theta^{v}}^{\bar{\theta}} c(\theta)\,dF(\theta) \quad (8.26)$$

are increasing as θ^{v} rises. Next observe that (8.26) rises faster than (8.25) with an increase in θ^{v}. Thus, if $P(\Delta)$ also increases with an increase in θ^{v}, it will follow that industry profits rise as participation in the unilateral voluntary agreement declines (i.e. as θ^{v} rises). To see that this is so, observe from the definition of $\Delta(\tau)$ in (8.11) that $\Delta(\tau)$ is rising in θ^{v} and recall that $P'(\Delta) > 0$. ∎

Proposition 17: *If preemption is feasible, it is also profitable for large enough* K.

Proof: Industry profits under unilateral preemptive action are

$$E(\pi^{U}) = \int_{\underline{\theta}}^{\bar{\theta}} \pi(\theta)\,dF(\theta) - \int_{\theta^{-\tau}(K)}^{\bar{\theta}} c(\theta)\,dF(\theta). \quad (8.27)$$

For large enough K, the PVA will be not be offered because its benefits are less than its costs; let us define the value of K such that the regulator is just indifferent to offering the PVA as K^{-s}. Then for $K > K^{-s}$, the PVA is not offered and expected profits with no unilateral action are

$$
E(\pi^{NU}) = P(\Delta) \left[\int_{\theta^{\tau}}^{\bar{\theta}} \pi(\theta) \, dF(\theta) - \int_{\theta^{\tau}}^{\theta^{a}} \tau \, dF(\theta) - \int_{\theta^{a}}^{\bar{\theta}} c(\theta) \, dF(\theta) \right]
$$
$$
+ [1 - P(\Delta)] \int_{\underline{\theta}}^{\bar{\theta}} \pi(\theta) \, dF(\theta). \tag{8.28}
$$

The benefit of preemption is the difference between (8.28) and (8.27),

$$
E(\pi^{U}) - E(\pi^{NU})
$$
$$
= P(\Delta) \left[\int_{\underline{\theta}}^{\theta^{\tau}} \pi(\theta) \, dF(\theta) + \int_{\theta^{\tau}}^{\theta^{a}} \tau \, dF(\theta) + \int_{\theta^{a}}^{\tilde{\theta}} c(\theta) \, dF(\theta) \right]
$$
$$
- \int_{\theta^{-\tau}(K)}^{\tilde{\theta}} c(\theta) \, dF(\theta). \tag{8.29}
$$

The terms inside the square brackets represent savings to the industry if the tax is preempted. They consist of several parts: some firms are not forced to exit the industry, some do not have to pay the tax, and some are not forced to adopt the technology. The final term, which is not in brackets, reflects the difference between the level of adoption required to preempt, and the level that would be required under the voluntary agreement; this term may in principle be either positive or negative.

As K increases, so does $\theta^{-\tau}$, thereby reducing the direct cost of preemption by lowering the requisite level of unilateral adoption. Since the expression in (8.29) is continuous in K, there exists some K that makes preemption profitable. ∎

Proposition 18: *Expected social welfare is higher when unilateral industry action preempts government action, i.e. $W(\emptyset, \theta^{-\tau}) > \overline{W}(\tau^{*}, \bar{\theta}) - K$.*

Proof: By definition, preemption occurs when $W(\emptyset, \theta^{-\tau}) > W^{T}(\tau^{*}, \theta^{-\tau}) - K$. Differentiating expected welfare from the tax with respect to θ^{v}, we find that

$$
\frac{\partial \overline{W}(\tau^{*}, \theta^{v})}{\partial \theta^{v}} = P(\Delta) \frac{\partial W^{T}(\tau^{*}, \theta^{v})}{\partial \theta^{v}} + [1 - P(\Delta)] \frac{\partial W^{S}(s^{*}, \theta^{v})}{\partial \theta^{v}}
$$
$$
+ P'(\Delta) \frac{\partial \Delta}{\partial \theta^{v}} \left[W^{T}(\tau^{*}, \theta^{v}) - W^{S}(s^{*}, \theta^{v}) \right] < 0.
$$

The first two terms are less than or equal to zero for all $\theta^v > \theta^x$. The first term is zero for $\theta^v > \theta^a$ and negative for $\theta^v \in (\theta^x, \theta^a)$. The second term is zero for $\theta^v > \theta^{s^*}$ and negative for $\theta^v \in (\theta^x, \theta^{s^*})$. The third term is negative if $W^T(\tau^*, \theta^v) - W^S(s^*, \theta^v) > 0$, which must be the case if the government is choosing to propose the tax. Combining these terms, expected welfare always falls when θ^v rises, i.e. when industry undertakes less unilateral action. (Note that the foregoing logic also applies to the case where $s^* = 0$, i.e. where the regulator prefers not to offer a PVA.) As a result, $\overline{W}(\tau^*, \theta^{-\tau}) > \overline{W}(\tau^*, \overline{\theta})$. Combining this with the definition of preemption, we have $W(\emptyset, \theta^{-\tau}) > W^T(\tau^*, \theta^{-\tau}) - K > \overline{W}(\tau^*, \overline{\theta}) - K$. ∎

Proposition 19: *PVAs reduce the industry's incentives to engage in preemptive self-regulation, and consequently may reduce social welfare.*

Proof: Consider first a reference case in which the regulator commits not to offer a PVA. Then the preemptive level of unilateral adoption is $\theta^v = \theta^{-\tau}(K)$, where the latter is defined by $W(\emptyset, \theta^{-\tau}(K)) = \overline{W}(\tau^*, \overline{\theta}) - K$. Consider a K such that the industry is just indifferent between taking preemptive unilateral action and taking no action at all. Now compare this reference case to one in which the regulator makes available a PVA if the tax proposal fails. By Proposition 16, the presence of the PVA lowers social welfare if the tax elasticity of political resistance is high enough; let us assume this to be the case. Now note that the introduction of the PVA raises the expected profitability of taking no unilateral action by the amount $[1 - P(\Delta)] \int_{\theta^{s^*}}^{\overline{\theta}} [s - c(\theta)] dF(\theta) > 0$. Thus, the introduction of the PVA makes unilateral action unprofitable. But by assumption, it also reduces expected social welfare in the event that preemption does not occur. Thus, the availability of the PVA program reduces social welfare. ∎

9 | The design of public voluntary agreements

1 INTRODUCTION

Public voluntary agreements (PVAs) are primarily a US phenomenon.[1] In our view, the separation of power between the executive branch and the legislative branch that is characteristic of the US presidential system has contributed to the emergence of PVAs. In a parliamentary democracy, a single party controls both the executive and legislative functions, making it easier for the executive to issue credible legislative threats. Chapter 7's analysis of negotiated agreements (NAs) is applicable to such situations. In a presidential democracy like the USA, however, such threats are much less credible, as the legislative branch is often controlled by a different party from the executive. Even when a single party controls both branches, executive branch control is limited since legislators and the president are elected in separate elections. In this context, PVAs may play two different roles. In some cases, the executive branch wants to pursue stronger environmental policies but cannot get its proposals through the Congress, and falls back upon PVAs.[2] In other cases, the executive may have little interest in passing new environmental legislation, but may find PVAs a convenient way to reduce legislative pressure for environmental action.[3] In either case, however, PVAs tend to be relatively modest instruments useful in part due to splits between the goals of the executive and the legislative branches.

Chapter 8 presented a framework for comparing the performance of PVAs against that of mandatory emissions control programs such as emissions taxes or emissions permit trading schemes. The chapter characterized PVAs as providing modest subsidies – primarily technical assistance and public recognition – to firms that adopt environmentally beneficial

---

[1] These instruments are typically initiated by the Environmental Protection Agency (EPA) or the Department of Energy (DOE), two executive-branch agencies.

[2] Our analysis in chapter 8 deals with this case, which is broadly consistent with the Clinton Administration's experience with trying to pass an across-the-board energy tax.

[3] This case is similar to the role of NAs as analyzed in chapter 7, and is broadly consistent with the second Bush Administration's experience with proposed early reduction credits for greenhouse gas emission cuts.

technologies. Our broad conclusion was that voluntary programs are generally likely to produce weaker environmental results than mandatory programs unless there is strong industry political resistance to mandatory policies. The analysis presented an integrated perspective that was missing in previous work, much of which has tended to characterize voluntary programs as efficient low-cost alternatives to regulation. We argued that PVAs are better seen as modest tools that can be used when the political will for strong action is missing. Nevertheless, their ongoing popularity in the USA suggests the need for research that reveals more precisely the settings in which they are most valuable.

In the present chapter, we examine PVAs in more microanalytic detail. We begin in section 2 by characterizing the key elements of the various PVAs sponsored by the US EPA. In so doing, it becomes clear that most PVAs rely heavily upon a "suite" of informational strategies to accomplish their aims, although they often use other techniques as well. Given the centrality of information provision to PVAs, this chapter focuses on the informational aspects of these programs, seeking to bring to light insights that are not available when PVAs are simply considered a form of public subsidy. After a discussion of the main elements of the EPA's PVA programs, we develop in section 3 a simple model that captures important aspects of the information problems PVAs try to solve. We then use the model to help organize a brief review of the empirical literature on PVAs (section 4), focusing on the types of firms that participate and the environmental performance PVAs appear to have generated. We conclude in section 5 by discussing the industry settings in which different types of PVAs might be of greatest value.

2 AN OVERVIEW OF PUBLIC VOLUNTARY AGREEMENTS

In this section, we present a survey of the US EPA's PVAs, which the agency refers to as "partnership" programs.[4] The appendix to this chapter (p. 255) lists and gives a brief description of all PVAs on the EPA's web site as of this writing. PVAs have been developed to address a variety of application areas, including agriculture, air quality, energy efficiency and climate change, labeling, pollution prevention, regulatory innovation, waste management,

---

[4] Readers interested in further details can consult the EPA's very informative web site at www.epa.gov/partners/.

Table 9.1 EPA voluntary partnership program characteristics

Program	Information provision					Govt. R&D	P2P exchange	Certification	Public recognition	Regulatory benefits	Coordination	Grant funding	Info disclosure	Goal setting
	Software	Cases	Lists	Tech info	Tech. asst.									
AgSTAR		•					•		•					
Pesticide Environmental Stewardship Program		•							•			•		
Commuter Choice Leadership Initiative		•					•		•					
Green Vehicle Guide		•												
Indoor Air Quality		•												
Voluntary Diesel Retrofit Program		•												
Climate Leaders		•							•	•			•	•
Coalbed Methane Outreach Program		•					•							
Combined Heat and Power Partnership		•												
ENERGYSTAR	•	•					•	•	•					
Green Power Partnership			•						•				•	•
HFC-23 Emission Reduction Program			•											
Landfill Methane Outreach Program (LMOP)		•	•				•						•	
Mobile Air Conditioning Climate Protection Partnership							•				•			
Natural Gas STAR Program	•	•			•		•		•					•

Partnership for Electric Power Systems

Voluntary Aluminum Industrial Partnership

Consumer Labeling Initiative

Design for the Environment

Environmental Technology Verification Program

Green Chemistry

Green Engineering

National Waste Minimization Partnership Program

Sustainable Futures Initiative

National Environmental Performance Track

Project XL

Industry Sector Performance Programs

Environmental Technology Verification Program

Hospitals for a Healthy Environment

Waste Wise

Water Alliances for Voluntary Efficiency

and water. Among these, the application areas with the most PVA activity are energy efficiency and climate change, and pollution prevention.

A careful review of the EPA's partnership programs reveals certain common features found in many of these programs. In table 9.1 we identify these common features, and characterize each partnership program according to which features it includes. In the following paragraphs we discuss each of the main features used in PVA programs.

From a high-level perspective, the main emphasis of the programs is on disseminating information about emissions control techniques more broadly throughout the private sector, and on providing public recognition to those companies that go beyond compliance with existing regulations. Indeed, Skip Laitner and James Sullivan, two EPA officials involved in air-oriented voluntary programs, argue that "EPA's voluntary programs directly tackle the issue of a combined information and performance gap" in the marketplace for energy-efficient equipment and practices (Laitner and Sullivan 2001, p. 3). There are a number of different approaches to information provision, however, each of which is worth individual attention. For example, some programs provide third-party certification of the environmental effectiveness of certain technologies (Environmental Technology Verification Program), others provide a reliable compendium of information about the environmental attributes of competing products (Green Vehicle Guide), and still others work to improve labeling of consumer products (Consumer Labeling Initiative). In addition, there are several other techniques that are used in PVA programs. Some PVA programs provide regulatory benefits in the form of reduced regulatory delays for certifying new facilities (Project XL), reduced priority for inspection (Performance Track) or improved access to EPA officials (Climate Leaders).[5]

A few PVAs help industry solve coordination problems that can inhibit the adoption of environmentally friendly practices. For example, consumers might respond poorly if a single hotel chain unilaterally created a program to encourage hotel guests to re-use towels instead of washing them each day, which might seem to be just a cover for reducing the quality of the hotel's service. The EPA's Water Alliances for Voluntary Efficiency has helped hotels to coordinate on this simple but effective conservation program. Similarly, EPA's ENERGY STAR program helped the video cassette recorder (VCR) industry coordinate on the use of inexpensive circuitry that reduces power consumption during periods when the VCR is not in use.

---

[5] Chapter 5 presents a detailed analysis of programs like Performance Track that reward good corporate behavior with a reduced likelihood of inspection.

While adopting the use of this circuitry would provide negligible marketing benefits to any one manufacturer, a little bit of encouragement from EPA was enough to convince the industry to coordinate on this inexpensive energy-saving program.

While we do not wish to downplay the role that PVA programs can play in providing regulatory benefits, certifying the environmental performance of new technologies, or mitigating industry coordination problems, these approaches clearly play a secondary role in the larger picture of PVAs. Far and away the most common components of PVA programs are information provision and public recognition. Thus, in the remainder of this chapter, we focus on these components in detail.

2.1   Information provision and public recognition

As table 9.1 shows, there are several different types of information-oriented PVAs. First, some involve government-sponsored research aimed at creating new knowledge, which can then be diffused throughout an industry. Second, some programs codify the knowledge of certain leading firms, through case studies, for example, and make that information available to other firms in the industry. Third, still other programs place more emphasis on peer-to-peer sharing of information, rather than transmitting information through the regulator as intermediary. Each of these types of programs has certain special characteristics, which we now discuss.

2.1.1   Government-sponsored research

This is relatively unusual among PVAs. Design for the Environment and Green Chemistry are among the more prominent programs that utilize this approach. However, even Design for the Environment sponsored little original research. Its focus was instead on pulling together the existing body of knowledge on the environmental impacts of alternative technologies in particular industries, an approach we discuss in more depth below. Government-sponsored original research is unusual in the context of PVAs, and seems to be used primarily in industries where there are no or few large firms that can generate the knowledge themselves. For example, one of the first projects under the Design for the Environment program was aimed at the dry cleaning industry, whose firms are too small to undertake projects aimed at generating new knowledge (or even staying abreast of the existing knowledge base) on the environmental impacts of alternative dry cleaning technologies (box 9.1).

Box 9.1   Design for the Environment

Design for the Environment (DfE) is an EPA voluntary program that was begun in 1992 by the Office of Pollution Prevention. Its first project involved the use of perchlorethylene (PCE) by the dry cleaning industry. While the Clean Air Act Amendments of 1990 had regulated the use of PCE by dry cleaners, requiring them to employ late-generation technology, the large number of facilities involved (some 10,000) meant that enforcement had been costly and relatively ineffective. Some cleaners feared that the EPA would ban PCE altogether. At the same time, there was a growing interest at the EPA in developing alternative cleaning materials that would not involve the use of toxic chemicals. The water-based approach known as "wet cleaning" was promising for many cleaning applications, although dry cleaners were reluctant to use it because they would be held liable for any damage to "Dry Clean Only" clothing that occurred during wet cleaning, while they were protected from such liability if they used chemical solvents. A more exotic technological alternative was developed by Hughes Corporation, and involved the use of carbon dioxide, initially in supercritical form and later in liquid form.

Source: Personal Communication, Alice E. Tome, Abt Associates, Inc., October 22, 2002.

2.1.2   Programs that codify the existing knowledge of leading firms

These are the single most common tool used within the family of EPA partnership programs. For example, many PVAs provide case studies of successful projects undertaken by participating firms. Some types of knowledge, of course, are difficult for the EPA to generate directly. This is the case, for example, for learning-by-doing, that is, knowledge that accrues during the process of conducting business. Government-sponsored research is a poor means for attempting to create this knowledge. Even if the knowledge could be generated directly through government sponsorship, at least in principle, it is often more efficient for the regulator to collect data on the experience firms have already accumulated rather than to try and generate new knowledge on its own, assuming that firms can be persuaded to share their existing stock of information. Firms, in turn, are more likely to share such information if it is widely applicable across a variety of industries, rather than of use only to help out their rivals within the same industry. Sharing within an industry is also more likely if it involves information that reduces fixed costs rather than variable costs, since such cost reductions have no impact on market share within the industry.[6]

In cases where it is efficient for the EPA to obtain information from leading firms, the regulator must provide some form of inducement to these firms to compensate them for the knowledge they share. This is typically done through public recognition for the firm, recognition within the firm of its "environmental champions," providing access to regulatory officials, or offering regulatory flexibility of various sorts. This need to reward firms that share information helps to explain the structure of many PVA programs, which typically feature both information provision and public recognition. The information itself is of particular value to smaller firms, or privately held firms, which may have less of a knowledge base, while the public recognition benefits are attractive to larger firms with a more extensive knowledge base. Thus, the regulator can bring two specific sources of value to these interactions that are unlikely to be duplicated by the firms themselves. First, the regulator can help cover the cost of transmitting information from firm to firm, by undertaking the efforts needed to document successful case studies and make them available to others. Second, the regulator can provide public recognition with greater credibility than can individual firms or trade associations operating directly (box 9.2).

Box 9.2   Natural Gas STAR

"The US oil and gas industry has reduced emissions from unit operations and equipment leaks by 110 Bcf during the past 7 years by implementing management practices endorsed by the US Environmental Protection Agency's Natural Gas STAR program during the past 7 years."

The US EPA's Natural Gas STAR program encourages the oil and gas industry to reduce methane emissions through cost-effective actions. The program helps firms to identify management practices and technological improvements that meet these twin goals. Natural gas is a good target for such activity, since it is a potent greenhouse gas (22 times the greenhouse intensity of carbon dioxide) and also has a ready market value. According to EPA figures, over 110 Bcf of natural gas with market

---

[6] The standard result in competitive markets is that firms keep increasing output up to the point where marginal cost is equal to price. Thus, shifts in marginal cost will change output levels – and market shares – but shifts in fixed costs will not. For a review of the basic aspects of market equilibrium, see Baye (2003, chapter 8).

value of over $220 million was saved during the period 1993–2000. The STAR program has over 70 corporate partners – including Spirit Energy, Enron, and BP Amoco – each of whom agrees to study the "best management practices" (BMPs) identified by the program, implement those that would make economic sense in their operations, and report annually on their progress. The program focuses on a set of six core BMPs, two for gas production companies, three for transmission companies, and two for distribution companies. Replacing high-bleed pneumatic devices, for example, is recommended for both of the first two groups. Partners are also encouraged to identify additional practices and technologies, called "partner-report opportunities" (PROs), which account for over half of member firms' methane reductions.

Spirit Energy 76 provides an interesting case in point. In 1996, the company started a pilot project at its Fresh Water Bayou gas production facility in Louisiana. The idea was to avoid having the facility categorized as a major source of volatile organic compounds (VOCs), by switching from a natural-gas powered pneumatic instrument system to one powered by compressed air. Since pneumatic systems "bleed" or leak gas (along with VOCs) continuously, there was an opportunity to reduce pollution while conserving a valuable resource. The initial capital outlay for the project was $60,000, with annual maintenance costs of about $4,000. The compressed air system allowed the facility to save 62,415 Mcf of gas per year, worth $143,555 at 1996's average price of $2.30/Mcf, or $312,075 at a 2003 price of $5.00/Mcf. (According to the *Wall Street Journal*, April 8, 2003, p. C16, the May 2003 contract for natural gas on the New York Mercantile Exchange was $5.124/MMBtu, which is roughly equivalent to $5.00/Mcf.) The return on initial investment over a five-year period, even at the low estimate of gas prices, was well over 1000 percent.

Source: Frederick *et al.* (2000, pp. 75–80).

2.1.3   Peer-to-peer information sharing

This is an aspect of PVAs that is distinct from the transmission in written form of codified knowledge and case studies. Ongoing interactions with give and take are particularly useful when firms are engaged in long-term processes of continuous improvement in the environmental arena. One-time achievements can be documented and posted on the web, but web postings will always lag behind the ongoing creation of new knowledge. Face-to-face interactions are also helpful when it is difficult to replicate one firm's experience in another firm's operational setting. In such cases, the opportunity for immediate feedback helps firms to determine just how applicable other firms' experience is for their own idiosyncratic problems. This may have particular value when the technological processes involved are complex, and are difficult for EPA officials to convey accurately without having actual industry experience. For these types of information-sharing, one might expect that trade associations would provide sufficient forums to facilitate this type of exchange. However, firms may be reluctant to share industry-specific knowledge that can lower marginal costs, since such information represents a source of competitive advantage. What can regulators provide that trade associations cannot? Probably the most valuable thing they can offer is credibility in the form of public recognition for environmental performance. Thus, for PVAs that emphasize industry-specific information-sharing, especially through peer-to-peer programs, public recognition is a critical tool for inducing high-benefit firms to participate.

3   A MODEL OF PUBLIC INFORMATION PROVISION

As noted above, a common feature of many of the EPA's public voluntary programs is the provision of information. While this information is ostensibly aimed at program members, it is often freely made available to non-members. For example, case studies detailing the experiences of particular companies in installing and using particular green technologies are often posted as free downloads on the EPA's program web sites. In this section we develop a simple model aimed at illustrating the value of public information provision by the EPA. This model is similar in spirit to Kennedy, LaPlante, and Maxwell (1994) in which consumers face a decision of how much to invest in discovering the degree of environmental harm associated with their consumption of a product. In our model, firms are concerned with discovering the level of benefits they may derive from the installation of an environmentally friendly technology or process change. In both cases, there may be a role for publicly provided information if the action under consideration (i.e. a reduction in a consumer's consumption or a firm's adoption of a new technology) generates positive environmental externalities.

The installation of an environmentally friendly technology often involves an upfront cost that generates a stream of positive returns. These returns could arrive in a direct financial form (cost reductions) or in an indirect form, for example the action may improve relations with consumers, the local community, or employees. Due to the scarcity of capital, it is standard practice to set internal hurdle rates for new investments. To make rational decisions, firms must be able to calculate estimates of the returns on prospective investments before they are undertaken. In the case of environmental technologies, these returns may depend on technical and other characteristics of the investment that may not be known to the firm *ex ante*. In this case, a firm must decide whether to undertake its investment under conditions of uncertainty or to invest in resolving the uncertainty before undertaking the investment. If it is costly to gather the information that will resolve the uncertainty, then the firm may decide to either forgo investing or to undertake the investment under uncertainty. It is the provision of information aimed at resolving uncertainty that is our concern here.

To make things concrete, let us consider information provision in the EPA's Green Lights program.[7] Under this program firms were encouraged to replace their existing lighting systems with more energy efficient systems. Since the new lighting systems are more energy efficient, the investment is designed to "pay for itself" via reduced energy usage. In reality, however, the capital any firm invests in a new lighting system may be directed to alternative uses and therefore practical, rather than simply technical, information on the effectiveness of the systems is important. For example, rather than simple bulb replacement, additional lighting might have to be installed if employees complain that the new bulbs generate less light than desired. Such complaints may be negatively correlated with the amount of natural light entering a given building. Case studies of experiences with the installation of new lighting systems may provide this practical information, and allow firms to more accurately calculate the expected returns on their investment.

We consider a firm's decision regarding what level of environmental investment, e, to undertake. The firm may derive several benefits from this investment, including a reduction in energy usage; increased employee morale and productivity; and enhanced consumer, community, and regulatory relations. We summarize these benefits in the function $B(e)$, and assume that $B_e > 0$. It should be clear that these benefits may vary across firms, for several reasons. For example, if there are economies of scale in building employee morale, then larger firms may benefit more from an increase in morale than smaller firms.[8] Similarly, firms that deal with

---

[7] For more details on this program, see subsection 4.4 of this chapter.

[8] As we discuss in section 4, it is a common finding in empirical studies that large firms are more likely to participate in PVAs than are small firms.

regulatory authorities on a regular basis may benefit more from improved regulatory relations than firms that interact infrequently with these authorities. For these reasons, we allow for a variety of different types of firms, that we index with the parameter α. We will assume there is a continuum of firms with α distributed over the range $[0, A]$, according to some cumulative distribution $F(\alpha)$.

We model a type α firm's environmental investment decision as

$$\max_e N(e) = \alpha B(e) - e^2, \tag{9.1}$$

where $N(e)$ represents the net benefits of the firm's environmental investment. The term e^2 denotes the cost of the environmental investment, and exhibits the standard assumption of increasing marginal costs. The solution to this problem is given by

$$e^*(\alpha) = \frac{\alpha B'(e)}{2}. \tag{9.2}$$

Let us simplify by assuming $B(e) = \theta e$. The parameter θ captures the marginal benefit delivered by each unit of environmental investment, and is assumed to be unknown to the firm. For the sake of simplicity, we let θ take on one of two possible values, θ_L or θ_H ($\theta_H > \theta_L$) with equal probability. Then the expected value of θ is $\bar\theta = (\theta_L + \theta_H)/2$. Finally, we assume that at a cost $I > 0$ the firm can learn the true value of θ.

The question the firm must address is whether to incur the cost I to become informed. If it does so, then it makes its environmental investment under conditions of full information, and the investment is determined by (9.2), leading to $e^i(\alpha) = \alpha\theta/2$. If it does not accquire information, then its optimal investment choice under uncertainty is characterized by $e^u(\alpha) = \alpha\bar\theta/2$. The expected net benefits of the investment e^u are

$$EN(e^u) = \alpha\bar\theta e^u - (e^u)^2 = \alpha^2\bar\theta^2/4, \tag{9.3}$$

and substituting in for $\bar\theta$ we obtain

$$EN(e^u) = \frac{1}{16}\alpha^2(\theta_H + \theta_L)^2.$$

Is it worthwhile for the firm to spend I to learn θ in advance of its investment decision? If the firm knew $\theta = \theta_L$ it would choose $e^i(\alpha) = \alpha\theta_L/2$ and get net benefits of $(\alpha\theta_L)^2/4$, while if the firm knew $\theta = \theta_H$ it would choose $e^i(\alpha) = \alpha\theta_H/2$ and get net benefits of $(\alpha\theta_H)^2/4$. The firm's *expected* net benefits when making its decision after gathering information, are then

$$EN(e^i) = \alpha^2(\theta_L^2 + \theta_H^2)/8.$$

For a firm of type α, the value of gathering information about θ is simply the difference between $EN\left(e^i\right)$ and $EN\left(e^u\right)$, which we write as

$$V(\alpha) = \alpha^2(\theta_H - \theta_L)^2/8. \tag{9.4}$$

Clearly the value of information is rising in α, and also in the size of the "information gap" between θ_H and θ_L. For any given information acquisition cost, I, we can compute the set of firms that decide to invest in acquiring information. In particular, we can find a cutoff value α^I such that all firms with $\alpha \geq \alpha^I$ acquire information. This cutoff value is found by setting $V(\alpha^I) - I = 0$, which gives

$$\alpha^I = \frac{\sqrt{8I}}{(\theta_H - \theta_L)}. \tag{9.5}$$

It is easy to see that as the cost of information acquisition rises, so does the cutoff value of α, and fewer firms decide to acquire information. As the information gap $\theta_H - \theta_L$ grows, the cutoff value falls, and more firms decide to acquire information.

In equilibrium, firms will sort out into two groups, informed and uninformed, with the former group comprising firms with higher values of α. Informed firms undertake an investment of $e^i = \theta_L$ if the benefits are low, and $e^i = \theta_H$ if the benefits are high. Uninformed firms undertake an investment of $e^u = \bar{\theta}/2$ regardless of the true value of θ.

Faced with this investment equilibrium, the regulator is faced with two decisions. First, it must decide whether to invest in discovering the true value of θ, and, second, if it does so, it must decide the extent to which it will subsidize firms in acquiring the information. With regard to the first decision, the regulator has two options: it could undertake the cost I itself or it could attempt to obtain the information from firms that are already informed. In some cases, such as those in which firm-level experience with the environmental investment is necessary in discovering the value of θ, only the latter option will be open to the regulator. The latter option will be the most desirable option for the regulator to follow as long as the information being passed to the uninformed firms does not damage the competitive position of the informed firms. The Green Lights program provides such an example. The installation of an energy-efficient lighting system tends to lower a firm's overhead and should consequently have little impact on the firm's competitive position.[9] In this case, informed firms

---

[9] N. 6 pointed out that market shares are driven by the marginal costs of competing firms, not their fixed costs. Thus, if the installation of an environmentally friendly technology lowers a

need to be offered only minor inducements to provide the information to the regulator.[10]

Once the regulator learns the value of θ, she must then decide whether and how to transmit the information to uninformed firms. There are a variety of ways for sharing information, which subsidize information acquisition to different extents. For example, in many cases the regulator places case studies on its website, which provide at least partial information about θ to firms at a cost that is virtually zero. In other cases, such as the Climate Leaders program and the Green Power Partnership, the regulator offers direct technical assistance to participating firms. In still other cases, such as the Natural Gas STAR program, the regulator facilitates meetings at which firms can share information among themselves. Such meetings may allow for fuller information transmission, but it is costly for firms to travel to meetings and allocate employee time to attending them. Thus, there is a range of options for the regulator regarding the extent to which it subsidizes the information acquisition of uninformed firms. The regulator's primary concern in deciding what sort of program to create is the environmental externalities associated with the resulting investments made by uninformed firms. In particular, note that the regulator will wish to create an information program only if it learns that $\theta = \theta_H$, in which case $e^i > e^u$.[11] In other words, the regulator creates a program only if the benefits of the environmental investment appear to be high, since otherwise firms are unlikely to make the investment after they are informed about it.

In light of our simple information acquisition model, it is easy to see how information-oriented PVAs work. Typically, the regulator offers a group of informed firms some type of inducement that covers any cost to the firms of sharing information, which might include the costs of working with EPA officials to document the cost savings from a particular energy-efficiency application. Assuming the gains are found to be high, i.e. $\theta = \theta_H$, then

---

firm's marginal costs, informed firms will be reluctant to share information with their uninformed rivals.

[10] Minor inducements are likely to be necessary because informed firms likely incur positive costs in transmitting appropriate information to the regulator. For example, they may have to participate actively in the development of EPA case studies of their firm.

[11] The reader might argue that firms can interpret the non-existence of a PVA for a certain environmental issue as a signal from the regulator that $\theta = \theta_L$. While this is correct within the context of the model, reality is more complex and requires a more fully developed model. We have abstracted from such considerations as the regulator's cost of creating the PVA, as well as the environmental externalities from firms' operations. Were these effects modeled directly, the regulator would be unlikely to offer PVAs in settings where externalities are small or program costs are large. Therefore the ability of firms to make strong inferences based upon regulatory behavior is questionable in practice.

the regulator subsidizes the cost of that information for uninformed firms. The net benefits of the program obviously increase with the number of uninformed firms that participate. If the information is not competitively sensitive, then the regulator need offer only modest benefits to induce the informed firms to share information. For competitively valuable information, however, firms will be reluctant to share the information with rivals. In such cases, the regulator must provide more substantial benefits – e.g. access to the EPA Administrator, highly visible publicity, or perhaps a widely recognized logo that can be used on the firm's products – if it is to convince informed firms to participate.

The results we have just obtained are consistent with the work of Darnall (2003). She reports results from a small-scale survey that asked companies to identify their rationales for participation in the EPA's Environmental Management System Pilot Program, and the benefits actually obtained. Among the findings were a striking difference between privately held and publicly traded firms. For example, privately held firms were more likely to report learning valuable new information from participation than were publicly traded companies. In the context of our model, these firms are uninformed firms that did not invest in gathering information on their own. These results suggest that the design of PVAs ought to consider explicitly the different motives of private and public firms in participating in PVA programs.

4   PARTICIPATION IN AND IMPACT OF PUBLIC VOLUNTARY AGREEMENTS

There have been a number of empirical studies of public voluntary programs. The program that has received the most attention is the EPA's "33/50" program, which encouraged firms to reduce their emissions of seventeen key toxic chemicals, relative to a 1988 baseline, by 33 percent by 1992 and 50 percent by 1995. Other studies have examined the DOE's Climate Challenge program, EPA's WasteWise program, and the ENERGY STAR program sponsored jointly by the EPA and DOE. In light of the importance of information provision to PVAs, we also review empirical work on programs not generally considered under the rubric of PVAs, but which shed light on the impact of information provision on corporate behavior. In particular, we discuss empirical studies of utility-sponsored demand-side management (DSM) programs, energy-efficiency labels on home appliances, and the DOE's Industrial Assessment Centers program.

4.1   "33/50" program

The EPA's "33/50" program was initiated in 1988, and in some ways is the grandfather of all PVAs. Because the program builds upon the information reported through the EPA's Toxic Release Inventory (TRI), it is one of the most widely studied of voluntary programs. It is potentially misleading to treat "33/50" in the same category with other PVAs, however. The program emerged shortly after the deadly chemical release from Union Carbide's plant in Bhopal, India, which killed over 3,000 people. Chemical industry leaders became seriously concerned about the industry's "license to operate," especially after survey results found that the chemical industry's reputation among the public was in the same league with the tobacco and the nuclear industries, both of which had been saddled with intrusive and burdensome regulations. Indeed, the Chemical Manufacturers' Association (CMA) was concerned enough to create the Responsible Care® program to improve the public's trust of the industry.[12] It was in this context that William O'Reilly, EPA Administrator and former head of the World Wildlife Fund, called a small group of chemical industry leaders into his office and told them he expected substantial reductions in toxic emissions, which could be accomplished voluntarily or through regulations. The industry representatives preferred a voluntary approach, but there was clearly a regulatory threat looming behind the program.[13] The "33/50" program thus does not fit cleanly within the model of this chapter 9. It is in a sense a hybrid program, with some resemblance to the NAs discussed in chapter 8, but also including the provision of information to participating firms, which is why we discuss it here. In addition, it is worth discussing because it is widely considered as part of the EPA's public voluntary programs, and because it has been extensively studied. In particular, Arora and Cason (1995, 1996) and Khanna and Damon (1999) have explored the determinants of firms' decisions to join the EPA's "33/50" program (box 9.3).

Arora and Cason (1995) use firm-level data from 300 corporations, including financial data, advertising intensity, R&D intensity, firm size, and past toxic releases as explanatory variables. In Arora and Cason (1996) the dataset is expanded to more than 6,000 firms by using industry-level data, rather than firm-specific data, for some explanatory variables (e.g.

---

[12] See King and Lenox (2000) for a more complete discussion of the Responsible Care® program.

[13] Personal communication from David Buzzelli, Retired Vice President and Director, Dow Chemical, March 14, 2003.

industry means of advertising intensity and R&D expenditures are used). Khanna and Damon (1999) draw their data exclusively from corporations categorized under the SIC classification "Chemical and Allied Products." In addition to using many of the same firm and industry characteristics as Arora and Cason (1995, 1996), they include membership in industry associations (in this case the CMA) and a measure of "regulatory pressure" as explanatory variables.

All three papers find statistically significant evidence that larger firms were more likely to join the EPA's "33/50" program. This "large-firm" effect is perhaps the most consistent result in the empirical literature on PVAs, and is also consistent with our model, where α may be interpreted as a proxy for firm size. The model predicts that uninformed firms with high values of α are more likely to participate in PVAs. More detailed explanations for the large-firm result exist in both the formal literature and the popular

---

Box 9.3   The EPA's "33/50" program

Perhaps the best example of a negotiated agreement in the US context is the EPA's "33/50" program, which was initiated in 1988. Not all chemical firms participated in the agreement with the EPA. Khanna and Damon (1998) find evidence that members of the CMA were more likely to join the "33/50" program than their non-member counterparts, even though association members were larger emitters. This suggests that the trade association was a meaningful source of pressure on member firms to undertake corporate voluntary actions as a means to forestall threatened regulations. Khanna and Damon (1998) also find that "33/50" program participants reduced emissions significantly more than did other firms in the chemical industry, although they were by no means the only contributors.

This, too, is consistent with the view that negotiated agreements will not necessarily incorporate all industry members. A theory that can explain the observed participation patterns is an interesting area for future research.

Source: Personal communication from David Buzzelli, Retired Vice President and Director, Dow Chemical, March 14, 2003.

---

press. Because of their higher public profiles, larger firms may feel more pressure to act from environmental groups, politicians, regulators, and concerned citizens. It is often asserted that the fixed costs associated with environmental compliance are large enough to generate economies of scale that make it relatively cheaper for large firms to comply with regulations. It is reasonable to assume that the same is true for overcompliance. Finally, larger firms may have better access to capital markets and/or may engage in more R&D.

Some authors have argued that firms with larger R&D budgets find it easier to improve their environmental performance, and hence are more likely to participate in voluntary programs. In the context of our model, firms with larger R&D budgets might be expected to have higher values of α. Evidence on this point is mixed. Arora and Cason (1996) find that firms from industries with greater mean R&D spending intensities were more likely to join the "33/50" program. Khanna and Damon (1999), however, found that within the chemical industry R&D intensity was not a statistically significant factor motivating firms to join the "33/50" program.

All three papers find that firms with a history of high toxic emissions were more likely to participate in the EPA's "33/50" program. This may seem surprising, since poor performance in the past may signal unwilling-ness or inability to perform well in the future. However, if environmental performance is measured in percentage-reduction terms (as is often the case) poor past performance may imply lower costs of "performing well" today. In this case, a poor environmental record may actually encourage firms to undertake new voluntary actions, including joining voluntary pro-grams. Furthermore, firms found to be poor performers are likely to attract the attention of the media and of pressure groups, pushing them towards voluntary action.

Due to the fact that firms' facilities vary in size and type of production, many voluntary programs measure corporate environmental performance as percentage reductions in pollutants from a given base year. For exam-ple, the "33/50" program used 1988 as its base year, but firms were not invited to participate until 1991. Thus, firms knew at the time of their participation decision how successful they had been to date in reducing their emissions. A natural assumption, then, would be that a firm that had already been successful at reducing its emissions would be more likely to join the program (to enjoy the free publicity). However, both Arora and Cason (1996) and Khanna and Damon (1999) find that firms with larger percentage emission reductions, prior to making their participa-tion decisions, were not more likely to participate. One possible, but as yet untested, explanation for the result may have to do with the fact that, due to the public nature of the TRI, firms' progress in emissions reduction could be tracked by the public on an annual basis. Firms which undertook substantial emission reductions early may have feared bad publicity if they failed to maintain their outstanding performance, and may have felt that joining the program would only heighten the probability of such publicity.

Empirical evidence regarding the role of green consumers in driving corporate participation decisions is mixed. Arora and Cason (1996) find that firms in *industries* with higher advertising-to-sales ratios were more likely to join the "33/50" program, but Arora and Cason (1995) fail to find support for the hypothesis that *firms* with greater advertising-to-sales ratios were more likely to join the program. Khanna and Damon (1999) find, within the chemical industry, that final good producers were more likely to join the "33/50" program than were their intermediate good producing counterparts. Finally, when examining actual releases, Khanna and Damon (1999) find no support for the hypothesis that producers of final goods in the chemical industry exhibited significantly greater reductions in their emissions of TRI chemicals than firms not engaged in final good production.

Khanna and Damon (1999) – in addition to their aforementioned analysis of chemical manufacturers' decisions to join the "33/50" program – use a Heckman-style estimation procedure to examine whether "33/50" membership made a difference in the level of chemical reductions undertaken by firms over the period 1991–1993. To test this hypothesis, the authors do not simply include participation in the program as an independent variable, since it is an endogenous variable that results from choice on the part of the firm. Instead, the authors include as a right-hand side explanatory variable the *predicted* probability of participation in the "33/50" program, based on a first-stage estimation, the key independent variables for which were discussed above. This method provides a rigorous means for estimating the impact of program participation on actual emissions. The authors' overall conclusion was that "33/50" program participants reduced emissions significantly more than did other firms in the chemical industry.[14]

---

[14] It is interesting to compare the empirical findings about the impact of the "33/50" program with empirical assessment of the chemical industry's self-regulatory Responsible Care® program. King and Lenox (2000) study Responsible Care®, and conclude that participants in the program did not reduce emissions more rapidly than non-participants. If anything, they may have reduced less rapidly than non-participants.

4.2   Climate Challenge

Karamanos (1999) examines firms' decisions to join voluntarily the US Climate Challenge program. This program is a voluntary initiative by US electric utilities and the US DOE to reduce emissions of greenhouse gases. Participants can obtain support from the DOE for placing expenditures on emissions reductions into their ratebases, can count any reductions against future mandatory requirements, and may obtain positive publicity. The program was begun in December 1994, and by the end of 1996 had 114 participants. The DOE estimated that the program would lead to a reduction of about 47.6 million metric tons of carbon equivalent in the year 2000.[15]

Karamanos undertakes a probit analysis of participation in the program using data from all major investor-owned utilities in the USA (158 firms) and for a sample of publicly owned utilities (218 firms). His explanatory variables include ownership (public- or investor-owned), firm financial variables, firm size, and past environmental performance, and the environmental performance of the state in which the firm operates. He finds that larger investor-owned utilities were more likely to join the EPA's Climate Challenge program than were their smaller counterparts. In addition, investor-owned firms with a higher percentage of power from fossil fuels were more likely to join, as were firms with smaller boards of directors, and firms in states with poorer air quality. Companies with a greater percentage of retail sales, who might be expected to be more susceptible to pressure from green consumers, were no more likely to join the program. Nor did the presence of environmental group members in the firm's state have a significant effect on membership.[16]

It is interesting to note that the DOE's website for Climate Challenge lists a number of reasons for utilities to join, the first of which is "National and international officials are watching this program closely. Therefore, an effective voluntary effort may negate the need for legislation or regulations."[17] The Climate Challenge program was focused on achieving emissions goals by 2000, so is no longer accepting new members, although many preexisting

---

[15] The Climate Challenge website does not confirm whether this goal was actually met. For details, see http://www.eere.energy.gov/climatechallenge/.

[16] Karamanos (1999) supplemented his empirical analysis with a set of interviews with corporate executives, who reported a variety of benefits from participation, including reduced expected liability costs, reduced regulatory costs, and public recognition were all valued by firms.

[17] For more details, see http://www.eere.energy.gov/climatechallenge/.

members continue to act on their pledges to reduce greenhouse gas emissions.

4.3   WasteWise

This program was launched on January 1, 1994, and aimed to encourage participating companies to reduce their generation of solid waste, such as office paper, yard trimmings, packaging waste, and corrugated containers. Participants are expected to commit to a three-year period of activity. They are expected to set three waste-prevention goals, one recycling collection goal, and one goal for the buying or manufacturing of recyclables. The EPA provides free technical assistance to develop plans to achieve these goals, offers public recognition for outstanding achievements, and grants participants the right to use the WasteWise logo in advertising. Nearly 370 companies joined the program in 1994. Participating firms reported saving a total of 240,000 tons of waste through the reduction and reuse of packaging materials.

Videras and Alberini (2000) study participation in the EPA's WasteWise program, using Heckman-style techniques similar to those of Khanna and Damon (1999). They use data from the Investors Responsibility Research Center for the period 1992–1998, along with Compustat data; their sample includes 245 firms. They find that large companies, companies that do more R&D, and companies with a higher ratio of advertising expenditures/employee were more likely to join the program. Evidence was mixed on whether firms with poor environmental track records were more likely to join. Only the most serious offenders seemed to be significantly more likely to participate. In contrast, firms that have demonstrated commitment to environmental goals (through the adoption of environmental auditing and compensating managers based in part on environmental performance) were less likely to join the program. Firms that were members of the CMA were less likely to join, the opposite of what Khanna and Damon (1999) found for the "33/50" program. Finally, participation in WasteWise had no significant impact on firms' generation of hazardous or non-hazardous waste, nor did it have a significant impact on emissions of toxic chemicals.

4.4   ENERGY STAR

ENERGY STAR is a family of programs begun in 1994 by the EPA and the DOE that encourage the purchase of energy-efficient appliances and the use of energy-efficient processes within firms. Firms producing products that meet the program's requirements can use the ENERGY STAR logo on the product and in their advertising, sending a credible signal to purchasers that the product is efficient and environmentally beneficial. Participation in the program is widespread, and by 2000 the ENERGY STAR logo was recognized by over 40 percent of American consumers. According to Laitner and Sullivan (2001), over 600 million ENERGY STAR products were purchased through the year 2000. More than 1,600 manufacturers participate, labeling over 11,000 products in thirty different product categories. In addition, 1,600 builders participate in the ENERGY STAR Buildings program, and over 25,000 homes have been built with the ENERGY STAR seal. Over 330 office buildings and 215 schools are also ENERGY STAR partners. According to EPA estimates, in the year 2000 alone over 15 million tons of carbon equivalent were prevented from reaching the atmosphere, an amount equal to the emissions of 10 million automobiles. Nearly 10,000 megawatts was shaved from peak summer electricity demand.[18]

The precursor to this family of programs was Green Lights, launched in January 1991, and later folded into the ENERGY STAR family. Firms participate by signing a memorandum of understanding with EPA that promises that the firms will survey its facilities and make all investments that meet a clear profitability hurdle. For its part, the EPA provides technical expertise, a computerized expert system for analyzing lighting system upgrades, information about rebates and financing sources, information obtained from other participants in the program, and publicity for participating firms. Participants can drop out at any time, so there is really no binding commitment on their part. According to Howarth, Haddad, and Paton (2004), over 2,300 firms and non-profit organizations joined the program between 1991 and 1996, achieving savings of $440 million in reduced energy costs. The average participant managed a 40 percent reduction in energy used for lighting. DeCanio (1998) finds that the average real rate of return on energy-efficiency investments made through Green Lights was 45 percent.

DeCanio and Watkins (1998) study the participation decisions of firms that joined the Green Lights program. They find that large firms were more likely to join. Firms with higher earnings/share and higher price/earnings

---

[18] Laitner and Sullivan (2001) recognize the measurement challenges involved in assessing the performance of ENERGY STAR programs: "almost by definition, it is difficult to disentangle the influence of voluntary programs from the normal rate of progress expected in the marketplace" (p. 6). Moreover, they bemoan the fact that "making the data more readily available to researchers is proving to be more difficult than originally anticipated" (p. 7). No doubt further empirical work in this area will emerge over time.

ratios were also more likely to join. Greater insider control of the company was negatively associated with membership. Utilities were more likely to participate, while firms in the finance, insurance, real estate, and services sectors were less likely to participate.

Howarth, Haddad, and Paton (2003) discuss the ENERGY STAR Office Products program, which began in 1992. Aimed initially at computers, the program gradually expanded to encompass printers, copiers, and other devices as well. The program grants manfacturers the right to use the ENERGY STAR logo if their products meet certain technical requirements established by the EPA. For example, the first such requirement was that computers and monitors go into an energy-efficient "sleep state" when they are not in use. By the end of 1998, the number of participating companies had grown to over 600. By 2000, it was estimated that 80 percent of new computers were compliant with ENERGY STAR, as were 95 percent of new monitors, and 99 percent of printers. Part of the "bandwagon effect" observed in the market shift toward ENERGY STAR products is undoubtedly due to President Clinton's Executive Order 12845, which required government procurement offices to use ENERGY STAR products whenever possible. Howard, Haddad and Paton (2003, p. 13) acknowledge that "[m]easuring the performance of the Office Products program is problematic for several reasons," including the rapid turnover of office product models and the fact that many consumers deactivate the energy-saving features because they degrade equipment performance. Nevertheless, an EPA analysis found the program had reduced electricity demand by 2.3 billion kilowatt-hours for 1994 and 1995.

Although there are difficulties in measuring the effects of ENERGY STAR with precision, it is clear the label has become a strong "brand" that has penetrated deeply into the marketplace. In part the program appears to work because it has pocketbook appeal and works directly through the market mechanism. Unlike programs that create public goods alone, such as programs encouraging the purchase of green power, ENERGY STAR offers the potential for consumers to reduce energy bills while they reduce pollution. The opportunity for consumers to internalize a portion of the benefits from environmentally friendly actions undoubtedly fuels the program's vitality.

4.5   Other evidence on information and energy efficiency

ENERGY STAR was not the first government-sponsored program to provide information to energy consumers in the hopes of improving their energy efficiency. Given the measurement challenges involved in measuring the impact of ENERGY STAR, it is useful to examine evidence from other information-based programs as well.

Morgenstern and Al-Jurf (1999) study the question of whether utility demandside management (DSM) programs induced commercial building owners to invest in high-efficiency lighting. They make use of a random sample of commercial buildings collected by the DOE in 1992. They focus on which buildings made use of compact fluorescents, occupancy sensors, and/or specular reflectors. Overall, 64.3 percent of buildings had at least one of these technologies in place. The authors find that buildings whose managers received information from utility DSM programs were more likely to have installed two or three of the technologies. They conclude (p. 21) "it is clear the provision of technical information has a positive effect on the decision to adopt high-efficiency lighting technologies, particularly so when firms had prior experience with related technologies."

Anderson and Newell (2002) study the effects the DOE's Industrial Assessment Centers program, which has been making free energy audits available to small and medium-sized firms since 1976. The database covers over 10,000 audits, which recommended over 70,000 individual projects. Each audit estimates the cost and expected savings from each project recommended. The authors use these data to study which recommended projects were actually implemented, and what were the implicit hurdle rates used by firms in the study. They find that about half the recommended projects were adopted, and that the implicit hurdle rate used was between 65 percent and 80 percent, corresponding to required payback periods of 1.25–1.5 years. These are obviously high in comparison to standard economic assumptions about hurdle rates, though the authors claim they are consistent with what plant managers report in surveys. It is impossible to determine which projects would have been adopted in the absence of the energy audits, and hence hard to know what impacts the program had on technology adoption. The authors note that the main reason given for rejecting certain DOE recommendations was that the projects were not economically desirable.

Overall, the evidence on information programs for energy efficiency suggests that these programs do make a difference in the rate at which individuals and firms adopt new energy-efficient technologies. Measuring the effect empirically is difficult, however.

4.6   General findings

The literature on the participation in and the performance of public voluntary programs is still quite sparse. There are a few general results that appear to emerge, however, most of which can be captured in a general way within the simple model of section 3. Far and away the most robust finding is that larger firms are more likely to participate in PVAs; indeed, all of the studies discussed above find this. As mentioned above, there may be several reasons why large firms are more likely to participate. Large firms receive more public attention, and hence more public pressure, than their smaller counterparts. In addition, they may possess economies of scale in abatement efforts or total quality management (TQM) programs more generally. They may also spend more on R&D (which several studies find to enhance the likelihood of joining a PVA) and have better access to capital, both of which might make abatement easier. For all of these reasons, large firms are more likely to obtain high benefits from taking action (to have large α), as is suggested by our model.

Another fairly robust result is that "dirtier" firms are more likely to participate in PVAs. Such firms presumably have more "low hanging fruit" in terms of relatively low-cost abatement opportunities. In addition, firms found to be poor performers are likely to attract the attention of the media and of pressure groups, pushing them towards voluntary action. This is consistent with our simple model of information-sharing if the environmental benefits of taking a given amount of action are larger and "dirtier" firms.

Firms do not appear to free-ride on their own past cleanup efforts. That is, firms that have already undertaken more abatement do not appear more likely to join PVA programs just to "take credit" for things they have already done. This is just as our information-sharing model would predict. The EPA has incentives to encourage the participation of firms that have yet to undertake investments, rather than firms that have already done so. Even if the EPA obtains information from firms that have already successfully taken action, only a limited number of such firms is needed to create the case studies that will be shared with other participants in the program.

Somewhat more tenuous is the finding that members of trade associations also appear to be more likely to join government-sponsored PVA programs. It is unclear, however, whether this is because the trade association pushes members to participate, or simply because the kinds of firms likely to join a trade association (perhaps larger firms) are also more likely to join government programs in deciding to join voluntary programs.

Also weak is the support for the notion that pressure from green consumers is important in leading firms to participate in PVA programs. The empirical studies to date have come up with inconsistent findings on this topic, indicating that it is unlikely to be an important factor in corporate environmental decisions.

Evidence on the actual impact of PVA programs on environmental performance is scarce, and findings are inconsistent. The "33/50" program appears to have had a significant impact on firms within the chemical industry, while its impact on firms in other industries is still unclear. Furthermore, WasteWise appears not to have had a measurable effect on the waste disposal behavior of participants. Our sense is that these differences are best explained by the fact that the "33/50" program imposed a veiled threat of regulation on the chemical industry, while firms in other sectors may have felt less of a threat from the "33/50" program, and WasteWise did not to our knowledge come with any threat attached. In contrast, information-oriented energy-efficiency programs appear to have caused significant shifts in consumer purchasing behavior for energy-using durable goods, though the estimates of the strength of this effect are not terribly precise. Our sense is that these programs have succeeded in large part because they offer consumers direct benefits, i.e. a chance to save money through reduced energy bills, at the same time that they achieve environmental improvements. While the savings to an individual might not be large enough to justify substantial search costs, they may be large enough to motivate consumers to distinguish between a product with an ENERGY STAR label and one without. Thus, energy-efficiency programs appear to fit well into our simple information-sharing model. More research into PVAs is needed to determine what specific aspects of these programs led to greater or lesser effectiveness.

5   CONCLUSIONS AND POLICY IMPLICATIONS

Chapter 8 argued that PVAs can be seen as offering small subsidies to encourage environmental improvement, and that such programs are often adopted when the political will for more stringent policies is missing. In this chapter, we examined in more detail the exact nature of the subsidies involved. A detailed look at their structure shows that most programs operate through the subsidized provision of technical information to participating firms, along with favorable publicity. In addition, some facilitate the sharing of information between firms in an industry, provide government funding for research that is then disseminated to industry, or offer regulatory benefits such as flexibility or access to high-level administrators.

In this chapter we developed a simple model of information provision that illustrates how government programs can educate firms about opportunities for cost-effective reductions in emissions. While firms with large benefits from emission reduction will gather information on their own, firms with less to gain may forgo the search costs needed to learn the true benefits of particular environmentally friendly actions. As a result, government can, at least in principle, perform a useful service by subsidizing the provision of information to firms that are less motivated to obtain information on their own. In a related vein, government can facilitate information-sharing between firms in the industry by encouraging informed firms to share their knowledge with others. If the knowledge is not competitively sensitive, regulators may be able to induce such sharing with surprisingly inexpensive incentives, such as the provision of favorable publicity for participating firms. If the knowledge is competitively sensitive, then government may have to invest in knowledge creation directly, rather than relying on transfers between firms.

Overall, the empirical results that have been obtained to date provide limited guidance for the design of public voluntary programs. The most effective information-oriented programs appear to have been those promoting energy efficiency through the various ENERGY STAR programs. These programs make use of market forces, and offer consumers direct benefits in the form of energy savings, while producing indirect environmental benefits. Programs that attempt to encourage the provision of pure public goods directly appear to have been less successful, unless accompanied by a strong regulatory threat, as in the case of the EPA's "33/50" program.

APPENDIX: EPA PARTNERSHIP PROGRAMS IN 2003[19]

A.1   Agriculture

The AgStar program

Promotes cost-effective methods for reducing methane emissions at dairy and swine operations through improved manure management.

Pesticide environmental stewardship program

Promotes integrated pest management and reduces pesticide risk in agricultural and non-agricultural settings.

A.2   Air quality

Clean air transportation communities

The objective of the Clean Air Transportation Communities program is to spur community investment in projects demonstrating innovative methods and technologies to reduce transportation-related emissions of criteria pollutants and greenhouse gases.

Commuter choice leadership initiative (see also under energy efficiency and global climate)

Encourages employers to sign a voluntary agreement to offer their employees outstanding, traffic reducing commuter benefits (e.g. significant level of tax-free transit passes, vanpool benefits, telecommuting) as part of a comprehensive commuter benefits package; e-mail: commuterchoice@epa.gov.

Green vehicle guide

Reports both fuel economy and emissions of all newly manufactured vehicles. The guide is updated annually.

---

[19] The appendix lists programs alphabetically.

Improving air quality through land use activities

Encourages environmentally beneficial land use measures in a State Implementation Plan (SIP) or conformity determination and ongoing research exploring the interaction between land use and vehicular emissions in different urban designs such as transit-oriented or mixed-use development.

Indoor air quality

Promotes simple, low-cost methods for reducing indoor air quality risks.

Indoor air quality tools for schools

Demonstrates to schools how to carry out a practical plan of action to improve indoor air problems at little or no cost using straightforward activities and in-house staff.

It all adds up to cleaner air

Educates the public regarding the impact of travel choices on air quality, traffic congestion, and public health.

Voluntary diesel retrofit program

Works to build a market for clean diesel engines by working with state, local and industry partners to create demonstration projects around the country. This program results in substantial emission reductions on today's diesel truck fleet, providing immediate air quality benefits.

A.3   Energy efficiency and global climate change

Climate leaders

Businesses work with the EPA to inventory their greenhouse gas emissions, set an aggressive long-term reduction goal, and report their annual progress toward this goal.

Coalbed methane outreach program

Increases methane recovery at coal mines: OAR OAP Coalbed Methane Program. Report Dist.

Combined heat and power partnership

Works with industry, states and local governments, universities, and other institutional users to facilitate the development of efficient cogeneration (CHP) projects.

Commuter choice leadership initiative (see also under air quality)

Encourages employers to sign a voluntary agreement to offer their employees outstanding, traffic reducing commuter benefits (e.g. significant level of tax-free transit passes, vanpool benefits, and telecommuting as part of a comprehensive commuter benefits package.

Energy Star

Maximizes energy efficiency in commercial, industrial, and residential settings by promoting new building and product design and practices.

Green power partnership

Designed to increase demand for green power. In return for technical assistance and recognition, businesses, governments, and other organizations make a commitment to switch a specific percentage of their electricity to green power. Relies in large part on linking with NGOs providing certification and technical assistance.

HFC-23 emission reduction program

Reduces emissions of HFC-23, which is generated as a byproduct in the manufacture of the refrigerant HCFC-22.

Landfill methane outreach program (LMOP)

The Landfill Methane Outreach program (LMOP) is a voluntary assistance program that works with communities, landfills, states, utilities, power providers, and the landfill gas industry, to encourage the recovery and use of landfill gas. The LMOP provides technical and marketing assistance, and helps assess project feasibility, locate financing, and educate citizens about the environmental and economic benefits of utilizing landfill gas. The LMOP was created as part of the Climate Change Action Plan to reduce emissions of methane, a potent greenhouse gas, from landfills.

Mobile air conditioning climate protection partnership

Promotes improved vehicle air conditioning systems and service.

Natural Gas Star program

Encourages natural gas industry across all major sectors (production, processing, transmission, and distribution) to reduce leaks through cost-effective best management practices.

PFC emission reduction partnership for the semiconductor industry

Reduces emissions of perfluorocarbons from semiconductors manu-facturing.

SF6 emission reduction partnership for electric power systems

Reduces emissions of sulfur hexafluoride from the electric power industry.

SF6 emission reduction partnership for the magnesium industry

Reduces emissions of sulfur hexafluoride from magnesium production and casting operations.

SunWise school program

Increases educators' sun safety awareness. SunWise's dual focus on health and the environment helps children develop the skills necessary for sustained SunWise behavior and an appreciation for the environment around them.

Voluntary aluminum industrial partnership

Reduces perfluorocarbon gas emissions from aluminum smelting.

A.4   Labeling

Consumer labeling initiative

Promotes easier-to-read labels on household cleaners and pesticides to improve consumer safety.

A.5   Pollution prevention

Design for the environment

Helps businesses incorporate environmental considerations into the design of products, processes, and technical and management systems.

Environmental technology verification program

Verifies the performance characteristics of commercial-ready environmental technologies through the evaluation of objective and quality-assured data.

Green chemistry

Promotes the design of chemical products and processes that reduce or eliminate the use and generation of hazardous substances.

Green engineering

Promotes the design, commercialization, and use of processes and products that are technically and economically feasible while minimizing pollution at the source and risk to human health and the environment.

National waste minimization partnership program

Reduces persistent, bioaccumulative, and toxic chemicals in hazardous waste.

A.6   Regulatory innovation

National environmental performance track

Designed to motivate and reward top environmental performance by facilities of all sizes and types.

Project XL

Allows companies to test alternative approaches that achieve cleaner and cheaper environmental results than would be realized under existing requirements.

A.7   Sector programs

Industry sector performance program

The EPA works in voluntary partnership with industry trade associations, states, and other stakeholders to take actions that overcome regulatory and other barriers to performance improvement and to promote sector-wide EMS use.

A.8   Waste management

Hospitals for a healthy environment

Partnership between the American Hospital Association and the EPA. Provides American Hospital Association's institutional and professional members as well as other health care professionals with technical information, educational information, and practical strategies relating to pollution prevention opportunities that exist with respect to waste generated by hospitals and healthcare systems.

WasteWise

Encourages business, government, and institutional partners to reduce municipal solid waste through waste prevention, recycling, and buying/manufacturing products with recycled content, benefiting their bottom lines and the environment.

A.9   Water

Adopt your watershed

Challenges citizens and organizations to join EPA and others who are working to protect and restore rivers, streams, wetlands, lakes, groundwater, and estuaries.

Water alliances for voluntary efficiency (WAVE)

Promotes water efficiency in hotels, schools, universities, and office buildings.

10 | Conclusions

1 INTRODUCTION

The most notable trend in environmental policy since the 1990s has been the emergence of voluntary approaches to the control of pollution, including both industry self-regulation and non-coercive government programs. In this volume we have presented an integrated perspective in which these two trends can be understood. Indeed, we have argued that corporate environmentalism makes sense only against the backdrop of the public policy process, and that government voluntary programs can be understood only in a political–economic framework that explicitly accounts for corporate strategy. We have developed a set of economic models that captures important facets of the shift toward voluntarism, and have used these models for two purposes. First, we have demonstrated the various ways in which voluntary pollution abatement can be an effective part of a company's overall non-market strategy. Second, we have rigorously explored the circumstances in which voluntarism is likely to be socially beneficial.

In our view, corporate environmentalism is primarily a tool for influencing the behavior of environmental activists, legislators, and regulators, though it may have ancillary benefits such as attracting "green" consumers or reducing costs. Not long ago, business-led environmental initiatives were viewed by many executives as the naive pet projects of "tree-huggers" who had somehow infiltrated the corporate world and were taking advantage of managerial slack to indulge their own private preferences.[1] Today, however, there is growing recognition that corporate environmental initiatives can add substantially to the bottom line. Top executives of *Fortune* 100 giants such as Alcoa, Dow Chemical, DuPont, Ford, Home Depot, and Procter and Gamble, recognize the importance of corporate environmental strategy and actively use it to create competitive advantage. The advantage created

---

[1] Prakash (2000) argues that corporate environmental initiatives within Baxter International and Eli Lilly were highly dependent on the motivation of the individual managers who promoted them.

directly improves a firm's position in the non-market realm of public sentiment and public policy, and indirectly improves performance in the market realm of units sold and costs saved.

Government voluntary programs have also become more prominent in recent years, and include Dutch covenants with industry to reduce toxic emissions, French agreements on the disposal of automobiles, and US programs like ENERGY STAR that encourage firms to reduce releases of greenhouse gases. These programs reflect a growing awareness that traditional regulatory measures can be costly, ineffective, or politically infeasible tools for certain types of environmental problems. Environmental policy is difficult to formulate and implement when its benefits or costs are poorly understood, or when the sources of emissions are numerous and diverse. In the areas mentioned above, many nations have found voluntary programs preferable to mandatory ones. The performance of voluntary programs remains controversial, however, due to their recent emergence, the lack of good data, and a resulting shortage of solid empirical work. Nevertheless, our analytical frameworks suggest that negotiated agreements (NAs) between government and industry, increasingly common in Europe and Japan, can work well *if* their goals are clear, performance is monitored closely and there is a credible regulatory threat in the background. Public voluntary programs, the policy instrument of choice in the USA, typically focus on the provision of information and public recognition to participating firms. These programs generally emerge in the absence of a strong regulatory threat, and are likely to have less environmental impact than would environmental taxes or emissions caps.

We recapitulate our main conclusions below, and discuss remaining challenges for future research.

2 BUSINESS-LED INITIATIVES

As business-led environmental initiatives have proliferated, managers and analysts have offered a variety of rationales to explain their strategic purpose. Among these are increasing sales to "green" consumers willing to pay a premium for environmentally friendly products; reducing production costs by eliminating waste; improving employee morale, retention, and performance; and creating competitive advantage in the regulatory arena. All of these factors undoubtedly play a role in the emergence of corporate environmentalism, though there is little empirical evidence regarding their relative importance.

Our sense is that the evidence to date suggests that green consumers are a relatively weak force unless there are private consumption benefits from environmentally friendly products, as there may be with organic produce (lower health risks) or energy efficiency (lower energy bills). Products that offer strictly public environmental benefits, such as green electricity, struggle in the marketplace unless they receive government subsidies. Similarly, we believe the opportunities to cut costs by cutting emissions are inherently limited. For example, Dow Chemical agreed to work with the Natural Resources Defense Council (NRDC) to reduce toxic chemical emissions at its Midland, Michigan, plant complex. Although the company reported that the $3.1 million of process changes generated an annual cost savings of $5.4 million, its efforts to persuade other firms to take similar measures fell upon deaf ears. The small but positive net present value (NPV) of making the changes was apparently not enough to motivate most companies to act.[2] In any event, strategic analysis is not needed to justify profitable cost-cutting projects. With regard to employee morale, we suspect this is indeed an important element in many corporate environmental programs. Surely most workers want to feel good about the work they do, and this concern probably encompasses the environmental impacts of the company for which they work. Many companies display environmental awards prominently inside their own facilities. Unfortunately, there is no empirical work of which we are aware that attempts to measure the importance of this motive, which might be expected to manifest through improved retention, improved productivity, or reduced hiring costs. For all of these reasons, we focus on corporate environmentalism as a non-market strategy designed to influence public policy.

Corporate environmentalism can influence policy in a variety of different ways, some of which involve coordination between firms in an industry and some of which involve unilateral action:

(1) Industry self-regulation can preempt the imposition of mandatory regulations. Preemption avoids the costs of mobilizing to influence the political process and allows industry flexibility in the means of accomplishing goals. Since environmental advocates also gain by conserving

---

[2] The non-market strategic benefits of the project to Dow may have overshadowed the cost savings. As quoted in Baron (2003, p. 373), Samuel Smolnik, Dow's vice president for global environment, health and safety, argues that "When you reduce waste and emissions, a community is a lot more willing to issue permits for other operations down the road." See Decker (2003) for an empirical analysis of the effects of voluntary action on the length of time required for a company to receive a permit for new plant construction.

political capital when a political battle is avoided, they may be willing to accept a lower level of abatement under self-regulation than would be required under mandatory regulations. This makes preemptive self-regulation even more attractive for industry (see chapter 3).

(2) Even when legislation cannot be preempted, it can still be influenced through corporate environmental actions. After legislation has required regulation, but before the details have been hammered out, voluntary environmental improvement by a leading firm can influence the stringency of the policy that is ultimately set. By sinking an investment in pollution abatement, and locking in a specific abatement technology, a quality leader can make it very costly for it to change its own abatement trajectory. Regulators, in turn, become less likely to impose a change that might be exceedingly costly and produce relatively modest environmental benefits. Hence a quality leader may be able to effectively commit itself to a modest improvement rather than the more substantial improvement that the regulator would impose if it were unconstrained by the firm's prior investment (see chapter 4).

(3) Voluntary abatement by a leading firm can send a signal to regulators or legislators, indicating the feasibility of taking stronger measures than had been previously considered. Doing so can serve to impose regulation on industry, which can be profitable for firms that have developed a competitive advantage in complying with regulation. This strategy is a variant of the familiar predatory technique of "raising rivals' costs"[3] (see chapter 4).

(4) Voluntary abatement can induce regulatory officials to redeploy monitoring and enforcement effort towards firms they believe are less likely to comply with the law (see chapter 5).

Whether corporate environmentalism is good for society at large depends on the particular context and which of the foregoing strategic purposes it is intended to address. Preemption is typically beneficial, since it conserves on political transaction costs.[4] In contrast, quality leadership that influences the level of forthcoming standards can induce standards that are set too low from the overall perspective of society. Voluntary abatement that signals politicians to impose new regulations will produce positive outcomes for society if regulators maximize social welfare, but may be harmful if

---

[3] See Salop and Scheffman (1983) for more on this general category of strategies.

[4] As discussed in chapter 3, preemption could be harmful if interest groups vary in the efficiency (not just the level of resources) with which they can influence policy, or if Congress is motivated by the desire to avoid *ex post* criticism.

regulators deviate from this objective. Finally, voluntary actions designed to influence monitoring and enforcement can induce either too much or too little abatement, depending on the structure of the penalties built into the existing enforcement regime. Overall, then, the cup is half full – self-regulation is socially beneficial in some, but not all, situations. Concerned citizens and regulators should not blindly celebrate self-regulation, but should learn to discriminate between its positive and negative effects.

3   GOVERNMENT-LED INITIATIVES

Corporations are not the only institutions that have embraced the idea of voluntary environmental improvement. In recent years governments around the world have shifted towards non-coercive means of pursuing environmental objectives. While bureaucrats might be expected to welcome new regulations that expand the scope of agency authority, agency resources are limited, and monitoring and enforcement are costly. Indeed, government interest in voluntary programs appears to have grown with the cost of implementing and enforcing mandatory regulations. Voluntary programs are especially appealing when the costs or benefits of action are poorly understood, or emissions sources are so numerous that monitoring them is prohibitively costly. Voluntary programs also benefit regulators because they limit opportunities for lawsuits from intervenor groups. Intervention by non-governmental organizations (NGOs) can dictate agency priorities, and limit regulators' flexibility to pursue the issues they consider to be of greatest importance. Thus, in some cases, both regulators and industry may prefer to avoid the imposition of new regulations, and to use voluntary programs instead, which are less vulnerable to intervention by activists.

To the extent that voluntary programs are designed to lessen the influence of intervenor groups, they are more likely to be useful for preempting the imposition of new regulations than for enhancing the effectiveness of existing regulations. Once regulations are on the books, activists always have the option to sue for strict enforcement of the original legislative language, and for the allocation of enforcement resources to programs the groups care most about. Attempts to add flexibility to existing regulations, such as Project XL and the Common Sense Initiative, must earn the approval of local community and stakeholder groups, who have the option of demanding enforcement of existing statutes. It is much more costly for such groups to mobilize the grassroots campaigns needed to enact new legislation; hence voluntary programs have a better chance of dissuading groups from pushing for new legislation than of creating flexibility within existing programs.

One area where regulatory flexibility does seem to be increasing is in the allocation of monitoring and enforcement resources across firms. Regulators face chronic shortfalls in inspection budgets, and must allocate resources to monitor firms that present the greatest threat of non-compliance. Firms that build strong records for compliance, and that undertake voluntary overcompliance, are less likely to be inspected for violations. Indeed, the EPA's "Performance Track" program makes this reward explicit. But obtaining optimal environmental improvement through enforcement flexibility is easier said than done, unfortunately. The shift to flexible enforcement requires adjusting penalties for non-compliance, and makes it more complicated to set optimal fines, which must vary depending on the cost parameters, and likelihood of violation, of each particular firm. If such precise adjustment of penalties is impossible, it is not clear that enforcement flexibility will generate welfare improvements. Perversely, firms may actually overinvest in voluntary action to avoid fines if the fines are not adjusted appropriately.

In Europe and Japan, governments tend to rely upon NAs with industry that preempt potential regulatory threats. In the USA, however, such negotiations are unusual. Instead, the most common voluntary programs (referred to as "public voluntary agreements" or PVAs) involve the government subsidizing the provision of technical information and positive publicity to firms that agree to undertake voluntary environmental improvements. These PVAs tend to emerge in the absence of strong regulatory threats, rather than in response to such threats. In brief, they tend to be weak measures used when the political will for more stringent mandatory measures is lacking. Furthermore, there may be unintended negative consequences to the emergence of PVA programs. They may encourage industry to oppose new regulations more fiercely, in the hopes of receiving modest subsidies rather than regulatory obligations. In similar fashion, the possibility that a PVA will be developed may discourage firms from attempting to preempt new regulations through socially beneficial self-regulation.

Despite the fact that PVAs tend to be weak tools, they still have a place in the regulator's tool kit, and may be useful in circumstances where political resistance makes strong action impossible. In the USA, for example, political opposition to an energy tax and to the Kyoto Protocol have made strong action on global warming virtually impossible. The various voluntary programs created by the Department of Energy (DOE) and the Environmental Protection Agency (EPA) have facilitated incremental progress in reducing greenhouse gas emissions. They may have also reduced industry opposition to stronger policies, by reducing the cost of taking early reduction measures.

In light of their inherent limitations and of agency budget constraints, it is important to design PVAs to maximize their potential effectiveness. For the most part, the types of environmental activities that are amenable to treatment through a PVA are those in which the net cost of taking action is small, e.g. energy efficiency or waste reduction, where there are potential savings from taking action. Programs designed simply to produce public goods, without producing ancillary benefits in terms of cost reduction, are less likely to succeed. Green electricity programs, for example, have had very limited success to date. When just a small "boost" is needed to make abatement cost effective, a PVA may be able to spur environmental improvement. In many cases, this may be best done by gathering information about best practices from a relatively small number of leading firms, and then supporting the dissemination of this technical information to other firms. The attractiveness of such programs is understandable given the sizable scale economies inherent in the production and diffusion of information.

4 FUTURE RESEARCH ON VOLUNTARY APPROACHES

Our decision to write this book signifies our belief that the first wave of academic research on voluntary approaches has achieved substantial results. Researchers in this area now know much more about the causes and consequences of voluntary programs than we did at the end of the 1990s. The EU's support through the Concerted Action on Voluntary Approaches (CAVA) program helped greatly to build an international community of scholars working in this area.[5] Nevertheless, despite the progress that has been achieved, there remain a number of aspects of voluntary approaches that are not well understood.

From the perspective of non-market strategy, corporate environmentalism often needs to be complemented with other activities such as lobbying, coalition-building, vote recruitment, campaign contributions, etc. While some existing research incorporates aspects of these activities, a comprehensive theory of environmental strategy has yet to emerge. In a related vein, more work is needed on the role of activist groups in inducing corporate environmental action. Similarly, we need to learn more about the relative

---

[5] See OECD (1999) for a summary of early results.

importance of employee morale in motivating corporate environmental-ism. More broadly, there is a need for more complete study of integrated environmental strategy, that is, study of the interaction of market and non-market strategy with respect to the environment.

From the perspective of public policy, we need more empirical analysis of the actual impact of PVAs and NAs. Most work to date has studied which firms choose to participate in such agreements, but it is important to move to the next stage and identify the impact of the program on actual environmental performance. Further work is needed to understand the comparative political economy of Europe, Japan, the USA, and the developing world, and how these differences in political structure affect the type of voluntary approaches used, as well as their effectiveness. It would also be useful to study more thoroughly the optimal design of voluntary agreements (VAs). While there has been some work in this area, it is made difficult by the fact that our underlying models of industry collective action are simplistic and lacking in predictive power. Theoretical breakthroughs in the study of collective action will surely spill over into improved design of voluntary programs. There is also a need for theoretical work that studies the optimal mix of voluntary and mandatory mechanisms, or of combinations of voluntary approaches.[6] Global warming provides an excellent laboratory for the study of the optimal policy mix. At least for the near term, policy will likely involve a mix of taxes, tradable permits, voluntary programs, and technology standards. Different countries will experiment with different combinations of policies, creating a natural experiment highly worthy of detailed study.

[6] As an example of this type of work, see Glachant (2003b).

References

Abolafia, Mitchel Y., 1985. "Self-Regulation as Market Maintenance," in Roger G. Noll (ed.), *Regulatory Policy and the Social Sciences*, Berkeley, CA: University of California Press

Alberini, Anna and David Austin, 1999. "On and Off the Liability Bandwagon: Explaining State Adoptions of Strict Liability in Hazardous Waste Programs," *Journal of Regulatory Economics* 15: 41–63

Anderson, Soren T. and Richard G. Newell, 2002. "Information Programs for Technology Adoption: The Case of Energy-Efficiency Audits," Washington, DC, Resources for the Future Discussion Paper 02–58

Arora, Seema and Tim Cason, 1995. "An Experiment in Voluntary Environmental Regulation: Participation in EPA's 33/50 Program," *Journal of Environmental Economics and Management* 28: 271–286

1996. "Why Do Firms Volunteer to Exceed Environmental Regulations? Understanding Participation in the EPA's 33/50 Program," *Land Economics* 72: 413–432

Arora, Seema and Subhashis Gangopadhyay, 1995. "Toward a Theoretical Model of Emissions Control," *Journal of Economic Behavior and Organization* 28: 289–309

Ayres, Ian and John Braithwaite, 1992. *Responsive Regulation: Transcending the Deregulation Debate*, New York: Oxford University Press

Bagnoli, Mark and Susan G. Watts, 2003. "Selling to Socially Responsible Consumers: Competition and the Private Provision of Public Goods," *Journal of Economics and Management Strategy* 12: 419–445

Barnard, Jayne W., 1990. "Exxon Collides with the Valdez Principles," *Business and Society Review*: 32–35

Baron, David P., 1994. "Electoral Competition with Informed and Uninformed Voters," *American Political Science Review* 88: 33–47

2001. "Private Politics," *Journal of Economics and Management Strategy* 12: 31–66

2003. *Business and Its Environment*, 4th edn., Upper Saddle River, NJ: Prentice-Hall

Baron, David P. and John A. Ferejohn, 1989. "Bargaining in Legislatures," *American Political Science Review* 83: 1181–1206

Baye, Michael R., 2003. *Managerial Economics and Business Strategy*, 4th edn., New York: McGraw-Hill

Becker, Gary S., 1983. "A Theory of Competition Among Pressure Groups for Political Influence," *Quarterly Journal of Economics* 98: 371–400

Beierle, Thomas C. and Jerry Cayford, 2002. *Democracy in Practice: Public Participation in Environmental Decisions*, Washington, DC: RFF Press

Bernheim, B. Douglas and Michael Whinston, 1986. "Menu Auctions, Resource Allocation, and Economic Influence," *Quarterly Journal of Economics* 101: 1–31

Besanko, David, David Dranove, and Mark Shanley, 1996. *Economics of Strategy*, New York: John Wiley

Besley, Timothy and Stephen Coate, 1997. "An Economic Model of Representative Democracy," *Quarterly Journal of Economics* 112: 85–114

1998. "Sources of Inefficiency in a Representative Democracy: A Dynamic Analysis," *American Economic Review* 88: 139–156

Binmore, Ken, Ariel Rubinstein, and Asher Wolinsky, 1986. "The Nash Bargaining Solution in Economic Modelling," *RAND Journal of Economics* 17: 176–188

Bittlingmayer, George, 1987. "The Application of the Sherman Act to the Smog Agreement," *Antitrust Bulletin* 32: 371–400

Boom, A., 1995. "Asymmetric International Minimum Quality Standards and Vertical Differentiation," *Journal of Industrial Economics* 43: 101–119

Bose, Pinaki, 1995. "Regulatory Errors, Optimal Fines, and the Level of Compliance," *Journal of Public Economics* 56: 475–484

Boston, Gerald W. and M. Stuart Madden, 1994. *Law of Environmental and Toxic Torts: Cases, Materials, and Problems*, St. Paul, MN: West Publishing

Bovenberg, A. Lans and Lawrence H. Goulder, 1996. "Optimal Environmental Taxation in the Presence of Other Taxes: General-Equilibrium Analysis," *American Economic Review* 86: 985–1000

Boyd, James, 2001. "The Barriers to Corporate Pollution Prevention: An Analysis of Three Cases," in Scott Farrow and Paul Fischbeck (eds.), *Improving Regulation: Cases in Environment, Health, and Safety*, Washington, DC: RFF Press

Boyd, James, Alan J. Krupnick, and Jan Mazurek, 1998. "Intel's XL Permit: A Framework for Evaluation", Discussion Paper 98-11, Resources for the Future, Washington, DC, January

Braeutigam, Ronald R. and James P. Quirk, 1984. "Demand Uncertainty and the Regulated Firm," *International Economic Review* 25: 45–60

Brander, James A. and Barbara J. Spencer, 1983. "Strategic Commitment with R&D: The Symmetric Case," *The Bell Journal of Economics* 14: 225–235

Buchanan, James M. and Gordon Tullock, 1962. *The Calculus of Consent: Logical Foundations of Constitutional Democracy*, Ann Arbor, MI: University of Michigan Press

1975. "Polluters' Profits and Political Response: Direct Controls Versus Taxes," *American Economic Review* 65: 139–147

Buck, Susan J., 1996. *Understanding Environmental Administration and Law,* 2nd edn., Washington, DC: Island Press

Cairncross, Francis, 1992. *Costing the Earth,* Cambridge, MA: Harvard Business School Press

Carraro, Carlo and Domenico Siniscalco, 1993. "Strategies for the International Protection of the Environment," *Journal of Public Economics* 52: 309–328

    1996. "Voluntary Agreements in Environmental Policy: A Theoretical Appraisal," in A. Xepapadeas (ed.), *Economic Policy for the Environment and Natural Resources,* Cheltenham: Edward Elgar

Caulkins, P. and Sessions, S., 1997. 'Water Pollution and the Organic Chemicals Industry,' in R.D. Morgenstern (ed.), *Economic Analysis at EPA: Assessing Regulatory Impact,* Resources for the Future, Washington, DC

Caves, Richard E. and Marc J. Roberts (eds.), 1975. *Regulating the Product: Quality and Variety,* Cambridge, MA: Ballinger

Cawson, Alan., 1986. "Corporatism," in D. Miller and W. Connolly (eds.), *Blackwell Encyclopaedia of Political Thought,* Oxford: Basil Blackwell

Clark, Helen (ed.), 1996. *Developing the Next Generation of The US EPA's 33/50 Program: A Pollution Prevention Research Project,* Duke University, Durham, NC, July, mimeo

Coglianese, Cary, 2001. "Assessing the Advocacy of Negotiated Rulemaking: A Response to Philip Harter," *Environmental Law Journal* 9: 386–447

Cothran, Marie Christel, 1993. "Proactive Environmental Activity Eases Permitting Process," *Journal of Environmental Planning,* Summer: 293–300

Crampes, C. and Hollander, A., 1995. "Duopoly and Quality Standards," *European Economic Review* 39: 71–82

Crawford, Vincent and Joel Sobel, 1982. "Strategic Information Transmission," *Econometrica,* 50: 1431–1451

Darnall, Nicole, 2003. "Motivations for Participating in a US Voluntary Environmental Initiative: The Multi-State Working Group and EPA's EMS Pilot Program," in Sanjay Sharma and Mark Starik (eds.), *Research in Corporate Sustainability: The Evolving Theory and Practice of Organizations in the Natural Environment,* Northampton, VT: Edward Elgar

Dasgupta, S., H. Hettige, and D. Wheeler, 2000. "What Improves Environmental Compliance? Evidence from Mexican Industry," *Journal of Environmental Economics and Management* 39: 39–66

Davies, Terry and Jan Mazurek, 1996. "Industry Incentives for Environmental Improvement: Evaluation of US Federal Initiatives," Washington, DC: Global Environmental Management Initiative

Dawson, Na Li and Kathleen Segerson, 2002. "Voluntary Agreements with Industries: Participation Incentives with Industry-Wide Targets," University of Connecticut, Storrs, mimeo

Dean, T.J. and R.L. Brown, 1995. "Pollution Regulation as a Barrier to New Firm Entry: Initial Evidence and Implications for Future Research," *Academy of Management Journal* 38: 288–303

DeCanio, S.J., 1998. "The Efficiency Paradox: Bureaucratic and Organizational Barriers to Profitable Energy-Saving Investments," *Energy Policy* 26: 441–454

De Canio, S.J. and W.E. Watkins, 1998. "Investment in Energy Efficiency: Do the Characteristics of Firms Matter?," *Review of Economics and Statistics* 80: 95–107

Decker, Christopher S., 2000. *Corporate Environmentalism and Regulatory Responsiveness*, PhD dissertation, Kelley School of Business, Indiana University

2003. "Corporate Environmentalism and Environmental Statutory Permitting," *Journal of Law and Economics* 46: 103–130

Deily, Mary E. and Wayne B. Gray, 1991. "Enforcement of Pollution Regulations in a Declining Industry," *Journal of Environmental Economics and Management* 21: 260–274

Delmas, Magali, 2001. "Stakeholders and Competitive Advantage: the Case of ISO 14001," *Production and Operations Management* 10(3): 343–358

Delmas, Magali and Ann Terlaak, 2002. "Regulatory Commitment to Negotiated Agreements: Evidence from the United States, Germany, the Netherlands and France," *Journal of Comparative Policy Analysis* 4: 5–29

Denicolo, Vincenzo, 2000. "A Signalling Model of Environmental Overcompliance," University of Bologna, mimeo

DeSimone, Livio D. and Frank Popoff, 2000. *Eco-Efficiency: The Business Link to Sustainable Development*, Cambridge, MA: MIT Press

Dixit, Avinash K., 1996. *The Making of Economic Policy: A Transaction-Cost Politics Perspective*, Cambridge MA: MIT Press

Donnenfeld, Shabtai and Shlomo Weber, 1995. "Limit Qualities and Entry Deterrence," *RAND Journal of Economics* 26: 113–130

Downs, Anthony, 1957. *An Economic Theory of Democracy*, New York: Harper & Row

European Environment Agency, 1997a. *Environmental Agreements, Environmental Effectiveness*, Environmental Issues Series, vol. I, Copenhagen, Denmark

1997b. *Environmental Agreements, Environmental Effectiveness*, Environmental Issues Series, vol. II, Case Studies, Copenhagen, Denmark

Farber, Daniel A., 1992. "Politics and Procedure in Environmental Law," *Journal of Law, Economics, and Organization* 8: 59–81

Frederick, James, Marc Philipps, Gordon Reid Smith, and Carolyn Henderson, 2000. "STAR Partners Cutting Methane Emissions via Cost-Effective Management," *Oil & Gas Journal*, August 28: 75–80

Fudenberg, Drew and Jean Tirole, 1984. "The Fat Cat Effect, the Puppy-Dog Ploy and the Lean and Hungry Look," *American Economic Review* 74(2): 361–366

Gabszewicz, J. J. and J.-F. Thisse, 1979. "Price Competition, Quality and Income Disparities," *Journal of Economic Theory* 20: 340–359

General Accounting Office, 1983. *Waste Water Dischargers Are Not Complying with EPA Pollution Control Permits*, RECED-84-53, Washington, DC

Gilbert, Richard and Xavier Vives, 1986. "Entry Deterrence and the Free Rider Problem," *Review of Economic Studies* 53: 71–83

Glachant, Matthieu, 2003a. "Voluntary Agreements under Endogenous Legislative Threats," Working Paper, CERNA, Ecole des Mines de Paris

2003b. "Using Voluntary Measures to Improve Tax Compliance," Working Paper, CERNA, Ecole des Mines de Paris

Glazer, Amihai and Henry McMillan, 1992. "Pricing by the Firm under Regulatory Threat," *Quarterly Journal of Economics* 107: 1089–1099

Greison, R.E. and H. Singh, 1990. "Regulating Externalities Through Testing," *Journal of Public Economics*, 49: 333–349

Groseclose, Timothy and James M. Snyder, 1996. "Buying Supermajorities," *American Political Science Review* 90: 303–315

Grossman, Gene M. and Elhanan Helpman, 2001. *Special Interest Politics*, Cambridge, MA: MIT Press

Hackett, Steven C., 1995. "Pollution-Controlling Innovation in Oligopolistic Industries: Some Comparisons Between Patent Races and Research Joint Ventures," *Journal of Environmental Economics and Management* 29: 339–356

Hahn, Robert W., 1994. "United States Environmental Policy: Past, Present and Future," *Natural Resources Journal* 34(2): 305–348

Hall, Bob and Mary Lee Kerr, 1991. *1991–92 Green Index: A State-By-State Guide to the Nation's Environmental Health*, Washington, DC: Island Press

Hamilton, James T., 1995. "Pollution as News: Media and Stock Market Reactions to the Toxics Release Inventory Data," *Journal of Environmental Economics and Management* 28: 98–113

Hansen, L.G., 1999, "Environmental Regulation through Voluntary Agreements," in C. Carraro and F. Lévêque (eds.), *Voluntary Approaches in Environmental Policy*, Norwell, MA: Kluwer Academic

Hart, Stuart and Gautam Ahuja, 1996. "Does It Pay to be Green? An Empirical Examination of the Relationship Between Emission Reduction and Firm Performance," *Business Strategy and the Environment* 5: 30–37

Hemphill, Thomas A., 1993–1994. "Corporate Environmentalism and Self-Regulation: Keeping Enforcement Agencies at Bay," *Journal of Environmental Regulation*, Winter

Henriques, Irene and Perry Sadorsky, 1996. "The Determinants of an Environmentally Responsive Firm: An Empirical Approach," *Journal of Environmental Economics and Management* 30: 381–395

Heyes, Anthony G., 1996. "Cutting Environmental Penalties to Protect the Environment," *Journal of Public Economics* 60(2): 251–265

Holmes, Thomas J., 1998. "The Effect of State Policies on the Location of Manufacturing: Evidence from State Borders," *Journal of Political Economy* 106: 667–705

Howarth, Richard B., Brent Haddad, and Bruce Paton, 2004. "Energy Efficiency and Greenhouse Gas Emissions: Correcting Market Failures using

Voluntary Participation Programs," in Andrea Baranzini and Philippe Thalmann (eds.), *Voluntary Agreements in Climate Policies*, Cheltenham: Edward Elgar, forthcoming

Hunt, Michael S., 1975. "Trade Associations and Self-Regulation: Major Home Appliances," in Richard E. Caves and Marc J. Roberts (eds.), *Regulating the Product: Quality and Variety*, Cambridge, MA: Ballinger

International Academy of the Environment (IAE), 1998. *Climate Change in the Global Economy: Case Studies on Voluntary Industry Initiatives for Climate Change Mitigation*, Geneva

Kagan, Robert A., 2000. "Consequences of Adversarial Legalism," in Robert A. Kagan and Lee Axelrad (eds.), *Regulatory Encounters: Multinational Corporations and American Adversarial Legalism*, Berkeley: University of California Press

Karamanos, Panagiotis, 1999. "Voluntary Environmental Agreements for the Reduction of Greenhouse Gas Emissions: Incentives and Characteristics of Electric Utility Participants in the Climate Challenge Program," Working Paper, School of Public and Environmental Affairs, Indiana University, July

Kaserman, David L. and John W. Mayo, 1995. *Government and Business: The Economics of Antitrust and Regulation*, Fort Worth, TX: Dryden Press

Kennedy, Peter W., Benoit LaPlante, and John W. Maxwell, 1994. "Pollution Policy: The Role of Publicly Provided Information," *Journal of Environmental Economics and Management* 26(1): 31–43

Khanna, Madhu and W.R.Q. Anton, 2001. "Corporate Environmental Management: Regulatory and Market Based Pressures," Working Paper, Department of Agricultural and Consumer Economics, University of Illinois, Urbana-Champaign

Khanna, Madhu and L. Damon, 1999. "EPA's Voluntary 33/50 Program: Impact on Toxic Releases and Economic Performance of Firms," *Journal of Environmental Economics and Management* 37: 1–25

Khanna, Madhu, W. Quimio, and D. Bojilova, 1998. "Toxic Release Information: A Policy Tool for Environmental Protection," *Journal of Environmental Economics and Management* 36(3): 243–266

Kiedens, Jean-Pierre, 2002a. "'Good Wood Bill' Re-Examined by NY City Council," *Home Channel News*, July 9

2002b. "Forest Certification and Responsible Procurement," Talk given at Resources for the Future, October 25

King A. A. and M. J. Lenox, 2000. "Industry Self-Regulation without Sanctions: The Chemical Industry's Responsible Care® Program," *Academy of Management Journal* 43: 698–716

Kleit, Andrew N., Meredith A. Pierce, and R. Carter Hill, 1998. "Environmental Protection, Agency Motivations, and Rent Extraction: The Regulation of Water Pollution in Louisiana," *Journal of Regulatory Economics* 13: 121–137

Konar, Shameek and Mark A. Cohen, 1997a. "Information as Regulation: The Effect of Community Right-to-Know Laws on Toxic Emissions," *Journal of Environmental Economics and Management* 32: 109–124

1997b. "Why Do Firms Pollute (and Reduce) Toxic Emissions?," Working Paper, Owen Graduate School of Management, Vanderbilt University

1998. "Does the Market Value Environmental Performance?," Working Paper, Owen Graduate School of Management, Vanderbilt University

Krishna, Vijay and John Morgan, 2001. "A Model of Expertise," *Quarterly Journal of Economics* 116: 747–775

Kroszner, Randall and Thomas Stratmann, 1998. "Interest Group Competition and the Organization of Congress: Theory and Evidence from Financial Services' Political Action Committees," *American Economic Review* 88: 1163–1187

Laffont, J.-J. and J. Tirole, 1993. *A Theory of Incentives in Procurement and Regulation*, Cambridge, MA: MIT Press

Laitner, John A. and James T. Sullivan, 2001, "Exploring the Seemingly Unexpected Successes of EPA Voluntary Technology Programs," Washington, DC: EPA Office of Atmospheric Programs

Landy, Marc K., 1995. *The New Politics of Public Policy.* Baltimore, MD: Johns Hopkins University Press

Lehmann-Grube, U., 1997. "Strategic Choice of Quality When Quality is Costly: The Persistence of the High-Quality Advantage," *RAND Journal of Economics* 28: 372–384

Lévêque, F. and Nadaï, A., 1995. "A Firm's Involvement in the Policy-Making Process," in H. Folmer, H.L. Gabel, and H. Opschoor (eds.), *Principles of Environmental and Resource Economics*, Aldershot: Edward Elgar

Lewis, Tracy R., 1996. "Protecting the Environment When Costs and Benefits are Privately Known," *RAND Journal of Economics* 27: 819–847

Lewis, Tracy R. and David E.M. Sappington, 1997. "Information Management in Incentive Problems," *Journal of Political Economy* 105: 796–821

Linneman, P., 1980. "The Effects of Consumer Safety Standards: The 1973 Mattress Flammability Standard," *Journal of Law and Economics* 23: 461–479

Lizzeri, Alessandro and Nicola Persico, 2001. "The Provision of Public Goods under Alternative Electoral Incentives," *American Economic Review* 91: 225–245

Lohmann, Suzanne, 1993. "A Signaling Model of Informative and Manipulative Political Action," *American Political Science Review* 87: 319–333

Lutz, Stefan, Thomas P. Lyon, and John W. Maxwell, 2000. "Quality Leadership when Regulatory Standards are Forthcoming," *Journal of Industrial Economics* 48: 331–348

Lyon, Thomas P., 1991. "Regulation with 20–20 Hindsight: Heads I Win, Tails You Lose?," *RAND Journal of Economics* 22: 581–595

Lyon, Thomas P. and John W. Maxwell, 2002. "Voluntary Approaches to Environmental Regulation," in Maurizio Franzini and Antonio Nicita (eds.), *Economic Institutions and Environmental Policy*, Aldershot: Ashgate

2003. "Self-Regulation, Taxation, and Public Voluntary Environmental Agreements," *Journal of Public Economics* 87: 1453–1486

2004. "Astroturf. Interest-Group Lobbying and Corporate Strategy," *Journal of Economics and Management Strategy*, forthcoming

Maloney, Michael and Robert McCormick, 1982. "A Positive Theory of Environmental Quality Regulation," *Journal of Law and Economics* 35: 99–123

Manzini, Paola and Marco Mariotti, 2003. "A Bargaining Model of Voluntary Environmental Agreements," *Journal of Public Economics*, 87(12): 2725–2736

Mater, Catherine M., V. Alaric Sample, and Will Price, 2002. "Certification Assessments on Public and University Lands: A Field-Based Comparative Evaluation of the Forest Stewardship Council (FSC) and the Sustainable Forestry Initiative (SFI)," Washington, DC: Pinchot Institute for Conservation, May: 3–4

Maxwell, John W., 1998. "Minimum Quality Standards as a Barrier to Innovation," *Economics Letters* 58: 355–360

Maxwell, John W. and Thomas P. Lyon, 2001. "An Institutional Analysis of US Voluntary Environmental Agreements," in Eric Orts and Kurt Deketelaere (eds.), *Environmental Contracts: Comparative Approaches to Regulatory Innovation in Europe and the United States*, Dordrecht: Kluwer Law International

Maxwell, John W., Thomas P. Lyon, and Steven C. Hackett, 2000. "Self-Regulation and Social Welfare: The Political Economy of Corporate Environmentalism," *Journal of Law and Economics* 43: 583–618

McCubbins, Mathew, Roger Noll, and Barry Weingast, 1987. "Administrative Procedures as Instruments of Political Control," *Journal of Law, Economics and Organization* 3: 243–277

McCubbins, Mathew and Thomas Schwartz, 1984. "Congressional Oversight Overlooked: Police Patrols versus Fire Alarms," *American Journal of Political Science* 28: 165–179

McKinney, Michael L. and Robert M. Schoch, 1998. *Environmental Science: Systems and Solutions: A Web Based Approach*, Boston: Jones and Bartlett Publishers

Moe, Terry, 1989. "The Politics of Bureaucratic Structure," in J. Chubb and P. Petersen (eds.), *Can the Government Govern?*, Washington, DC: Brookings Institution

Morgenstern, Richard D. and Saadeh Al-Jurf, 1999. "Can Free Information Really Accelerate Technology Diffusion?," *Technological Forecasting and Social Change* 61: 13–24

Nash, Jennifer, 2002. "Industry Codes of Practice: Emergence and Evolution," in Thomas Dietz and Paul C. Stern (eds.), *New Tools for Environmental Protection*, Washington, DC: National Academy Press. 235–252

Nash, John, 1953. "Two-Person Cooperative Games," *Econometrica* 21: 128–140

Newell, Richard G., Adam B. Jaffe, and Robert N. Stavins, 1999. "The Induced Innovation Hypothesis and Energy-Saving Technological Change," *Quarterly Journal of Economics* 114(3): 941–975

Niskanen, William A., 1971. *Bureaucracy and Representative Government.* Chicago: Aldine-Atherton

Noll, Roger G., 1985. "Government Regulatory Behavior: A Multidisciplinary Survey and Synthesis," in Roger G. Noll, (ed.) *Regulatory Policy and the Social Sciences,* Berkeley: University of California Press

Noll, Roger G. and Bruce Owen, 1983. *The Political Economy of Deregulation: Interest Groups in the Regulatory Process,* Washington, DC: American Enterprise Institute

North, Douglass C., 1990. *Institutions, Institutional Change and Economic Performance,* New York: Cambridge University Press

OECD (Organization for Economic Cooperation and Development), 1999. *Voluntary Approaches for Environmental Policy,* Paris: OECD

Olson, Mancur, 1971. *The Logic of Collective Action: Public Goods and the Theory of Groups,* Cambridge, MA: Harvard University Press

Pagonis, Wendy, 2002. "Merck to Va.: Raise the Bar," *Daily News-Record,* Harrisonburg, Virginia, September 19: 9–10

Palmer, Karen, Wallace E. Oates, and Paul R. Portney, 1995. "Tightening Environmental Standards: The Benefit-Cost or the No-Cost Paradigm?," *Journal of Economic Perspectives* 9: 119–132

Palmer, Karen and Margaret Walls, 2002. "Economic Analysis of the Product Stewardship Movement: Understanding Costs, Effectiveness, and the Role for Policy, RRF, August

Pargal, Sheoli and David Wheeler, 1996. "Informal Regulation of Industrial Pollution in Developing Countries: Evidence from Indonesia," *Journal of Political Economy* 104: 1314–1327

Pashigian, B. Peter, 1985. "Environmental Regulation: Whose Self Interests Are Being Protected?," *Economic Inquiry* 23: 551–584

Peltzman, Sam, 1976. "Toward a More General Theory of Regulation," *Journal of Law and Economics* 19: 211–248

Persson, Torsten and Guido Tabellini, 2000. *Political Economics: Explaining Economic Policy,* Cambridge, MA: MIT Press

Piasecki, Bruce, 1992. "Good Deeds and Good Numbers," *Los Angeles Times,* September 20

Pirrong, Stephen Craig, 1995. "The Self-Regulation of Commodity Exchanges: The Case of Market Manipulation," *Journal of Law and Economics* 38: 141–206

Polski, Margaret M. and Elinor Ostrom, 1998. "An Institutional Framework for Policy Analysis and Design," Workshop in Political Theory and Policy Analysis, Indiana University W98-27

Porter, Michael E. and Claus van der Linde, 1995. "Toward a New Conception of the Environment Competitiveness Relationship," *Journal of Economic Perspectives* 9(4): 97–118

Portney, Paul (ed.), 1990. *Public Policies for Environmental Protection*, Washington, DC: Resources for the Future

Prakash, Aseem, 2000. *Greening the Firm: The Politics of Corporate Environmentalism*, Cambridge: Cambridge University Press

Rabe, Barry G., 1994. *Beyond NIMBY: Hazardous Waste Siting in Canada and the United States*, Washington, DC: Brookings Institution

Reinhardt, Forest, 1989. "DuPont Freon Products Division (A)," Harvard Business Case 9-389-111, Harvard Business School

Rogerson, William P., 1990. "Quality vs. Quantity in Military Procurement," *American Economic Review* 80: 83–92

Ronnen, U., 1991. "Minimum Quality Standards, Fixed Costs, and Competition," *Rand Journal of Economics* 22: 490–504

Rugman, Alan, John Kirton, and Julie Soloway, 1999. *Environmental Regulations and Corporate Strategy: A NAFTA Perspective*, Oxford: Oxford University Press

Russell, Clifford S., 1990. "Monitoring and Enforcement," in Paul Portney (ed.), *Public Policies for Environmental Protection*, Washington, DC: Resources for the Future

2001. *Applying Economics to the Environment*, Oxford: Oxford University Press

Russell, Clifford S., Winston Harrington, and William J. Vaughan, 1986. *Enforcing Pollution Control Laws*, Washington, DC: Resources for the Future

Salanié, Bernard, 2002. *The Economics of Contracts*, Cambridge, MA: MIT Press

Salop, Steven C. and David T. Scheffman, 1983. "Raising Rivals' Costs," *American Economic Association Papers and Proceedings* 73: 267–271

Schaefer, S., 1993. "Cleaner Fuels for Competitive Advantage: ARCO and EC-1," Stanford Graduate School of Business, Case BE-10

Sedjo, Roger A., forthcoming. "Forest Sustainability Issues and Certification Activities since UNCED," in Michael, A. Toman (ed.), Rio Plus 10, Washington, DC: RFF

Sedjo, Roger A., Alberto Goetzl, and Steverson O. Moffat, 1998. "Sustainability of Temperate Forests," Washington, DC: RFF: 48–51

Sedjo, Roger A. and Stephen K. Swallow, 2002. "Voluntary Eco-Labeling and the Price Premium," *Land Economics* May: 272–284

Segerson, Kathleen and Na Li Dawson, 2000. "Voluntary Approaches to Environmental Regulation," in Hank Folmer and Tom Tietenberg (eds.), *The International Yearbook of Environmental and Resource Economics*, Boston: Kluwer Academic

Segerson, Kathleen and Thomas Miceli, 1998. "Voluntary Environmental Agreements: Good or Bad News for Environmental Protection?," *Journal of Environmental Economics and Management* 36: 109–130

Shaked, A. and J. Sutton, 1982. "Relaxing Price Competition Through Product Differentiation," *Review of Economic Studies* 49: 3–13

Shapiro, Carl, 1992. "Theories of Oligopoly Behavior," in Richard Schmalensee and Robert D. Willig, (eds.), *Handbook of Industrial Organization*, vol. 1, Amsterdam: North-Holland

Simmons, Peter and Brian Wynne, 1993. "Responsible Care®: Trust, Credibility, and Environmental Management," in Kurt Fischer and Johan Schot (eds.), *Environmental Strategies for Industry*, Washington, DC: Island Press

Smart, Bruce, 1992. *Beyond Compliance: A New Industry View of the Environment*, Washington, DC: World Resources Institute

Stauber, John and Sheldon Rampton, 1995. *Toxic Sludge is Good for You: Lies, Damn Lies and the Public Relations Industry*, Monroe, Maine: Common Courage Press

Stevens, William K., 1993. "US Prepares to Unveil Blueprint for Reducing Heat-Trapping Gases," *New York Times*, October 12: C4

Stigler, George, 1971. "The Theory of Economic Regulation," *Bell Journal of Economics and Management Science* 2: 3–21

(ed.), 1988. *Chicago Studies in Political Economy*, Chicago: University of Chicago Press

Sugiyama, Rie, 1998. "Voluntary Approaches in Japan," CAVA Working Paper 98/11/9

Sullivan, Thomas F.P. (ed.), 1995. *Environmental Law Handbook*, 13th edn., Rockville, MD: Government Institutes, Inc.

Tirole, Jean, 1989. *The Theory of Industrial Organization*. Cambridge, MA: MIT Press

Tullock, Gordon, 1967. "The Welfare Cost of Tariffs, Monopolies, and Theft," *Western Economic Journal* 5: 224–232

US EPA (Environmental Protection Agency), 1994. "EPA's Voluntary Programs: A Summary List Prepared by The 33/50 Program," Washington, DC, June

1998a. *US EPA – NEW England StarTrack Program Guidance Documents*, Office of Environmental Stewardship, United States Environmental Protection Agency – Region 1, New England, August

1998b. Office of Enforcement and Compliance Assurance, *Audit Policy: Incentives for Self-Policing*, wysiwng://78/http://es.epa.gov/oeca/auditpol.html, March 5

1998c. Office of Enforcement and Compliance Assurance, *Audit Policy Update*, March

1998d. Office of Enforcement and Compliance Assurance, *Enforcement and Compliance Assurance Accomplishments Report, FY 1997*, EPA 300-R-98-003, July

2001. *The United States Experience with Economic Incentives for Protecting the Environment*, EPA-240-R-01-001, US EPA, Washington DC

2003. *Inside EPA Weekly Report*, January 20

US Office of Global Change, 1997. *US Climate Action Report – 1997*, US Department of State Publication 10496, Washington, DC, July

Videras, J. and A. Alberini, 2000. "The Appeal of Voluntary Environmental Programs: Which Firms Participate and Why?," *Contemporary Economic Policy* 18: 449–461

Viscusi, W.K., John M. Vernon, and Joseph E. Harrington, Jr., 1995. *Economics of Regulation and Antitrust.* Cambridge, MA: MIT Press

Walley, Noah and Bradley Whitehead, 1994. "It's Not Easy Being Green," *Harvard Business Review*, May–June

Weingast, Barry and Mark Moran, 1983. "Bureaucratic Discretion or Congressional Control? Regulatory Policymaking by the Federal Trade Commission," *Journal of Political Economy* 91: 765–800

Welch, Eric W., Allen Mazur, and Stewart Bretschneider, 2000. "Voluntary Behavior by Electric Utilities: Levels of Adoption and Contribution of the Climate Challenge Program to the Reduction of Carbon Dioxide," *Journal of Policy Analysis and Management* 19: 407–425

Williamson, O. E., 1985. *The Economic Institutions of Capitalism*, New York: Free Press

Winer, Michael, 1993. "Energy Plan's Foes Poured on the Coal Starting Last Year," *International Herald Tribune*, June 15

Zywicki, Todd J., 1999. "Environmental Externalities and Political Externalities: The Political Economy of Environmental Regulation and Reform," 73 *Tulane Law Review* 845

Index